D1339684

THE OXFORD UNION

THE OXFORD UNION

Playground of Power

David Walter

Macdonald

A Macdonald Book

First published in Great Britain in 1984
by Macdonald & Co (Publishers) Ltd
London & Sydney

British Library Cataloguing in Publication Data
Walter, David
The Oxford Union.
1. Oxford Union – History
I. Title
808.53'06042574 PN4009.093

ISBN 0-356-09502-9

Printed in Great Britain by
Purnell & Sons (Book Production) Ltd
Paulton, Bristol

Macdonald & Co (Publishers) Ltd
Maxwell House
74 Worship Street
London EC2A 2EN

A BPCC Plc Company

For Natalie and Peter

CONTENTS

LIST OF PLATES

ACKNOWLEDGEMENTS

I would like to thank a great many people for their help with this book. Mr Malcolm Acheson's painstaking research in the Union's records was invaluable. Mr Raymond Walters of the Union's Library provided constant help and advice. The Union's Steward Mr Walter Perry and his staff have been equally helpful, as have been the successive Presidents of the Union while this book has been in preparation, Mr Christopher Wortley, Mr Hilali Nordeen, Mr Andrew Sullivan, Mr Neale Stevenson and Mr Malcolm Bull.

Mr Harold Macmillan, now Earl of Stockton, Lord Hailsham, Mr Edward Heath, Mr Michael Heseltine and General Sir John Hackett all gave very generously of their time for the Oxford Union film and have kindly agreed to my quoting extensively from what they said in this book.

Mr Michael Crick, Sir Robin Day, Mr Patric Dickinson, Mr William Hague, Mr Howard Shuman and Mr Godfrey Smith have all given me access to material which has enhanced the book, as well as providing a great deal of detail about their respective Union eras. Mr Crick, Mr Acheson and Mr James Naughtie all made helpful suggestions about the manuscript.

Many others have been very generous with their memories, their time and their hospitality. My thanks are due to Mr Tariq Ali, Mr Michael Barsley, Lord Beloff, Mr Jeremy Beloff, Lord Boyd-Carpenter, Dr Martin Ceadel, Mr Leslie Crawte, Mr Julian Critchley MP, Mrs Edwina Currie MP, Mr Mervyn Evans, Mr Roger Gray QC, Mr Damian Green, Frau Geraldine Greineder, Mr Kenneth Harris, Mr Alan Haselhurst MP, Sir Nicholas Henderson, Mr Douglas Hogg MP, Dr Leofranc Holford-Strevens, Mr Anthony Howard, Sir David Hunt, Mrs Caroline Jackson, Mr Robert Jackson MP, Mr Roy Jenkins MP, Mr Gerald Kaufman MP, Mr Warwick Lightfoot, Lord Longford, Dr Steven Lukes, Lord Mayhew, Dr Janet Morgan, Mr Daniel Moylan,

Acknowledgements

Mr Colin Moynihan MP, Hon Gerald Noel, Miss Libby Purves, Sir William Rees-Mogg, Herr Adolf Schlepegrell, Miss Victoria Schofield, Mr Madron Seligman MEP, Lord Stewart, Mr Jeremy Thorpe, Mr Brian Walden, Mr David Warren, Mr Rudi Weisweiller, Dr Philip Williams and Mrs Shirley Williams.

Mr Anthony Condue and Mr Perry Richardson agreed to the use of material prepared for their film.

I owe a great debt of gratitude to my wife Pamela for suggesting the idea of the book and for living with its consequences.

All errors and misjudgements remain, of course, my own.

I am very grateful to the following authors and publishers for the use of quotations in the book.

The Oxford Union by Herbert Morrah (Cassell Ltd)
The Life of G.D.H. Cole by Dame Margaret Cole (Macmillan Ltd)
Harold Laski by Kingsley Martin (Victor Gollancz Ltd)
My Dear Timothy by Victor Gollancz (Victor Gollancz Ltd)
The Life of Ronald Knox by Evelyn Waugh (Methuen London)
A Spiritual Aeneid by Ronald Knox (Burns and Oates Ltd)
A.P.H., His Life and Times by A. P. Herbert (William Heinemann Ltd) (by kind permission of Lady Gwendoline Herbert)
Speeches and Writings by S. W. R. D. Bandaranaike (privately published)
My Oxford ed. Ann Thwaite (Robson Books Ltd) for quotations from Angus Wilson, Jo Grimond and Nina Bawden
Evelyn Waugh's Diaries ed. Michael Davie (Weidenfeld and Nicolson)
Letters of Evelyn Waugh ed. Mark Amory (Weidenfeld and Nicolson)
Evelyn Waugh by Christopher Sykes (Collins Ltd)
The King and Country Debate 1933: Student Politics, Pacifism and the Dictators by Martin Ceadel (Historical Journal 1979)
Life and Labour by Michael Stewart (Sidgwick and Jackson Ltd)
A Chapter of Accidents by Goronwy Rees (Chatto and Windus Ltd)
Beyond the Tingle Quotient by Godfrey Smith (Weidenfeld and Nicolson)
Stand Up Nigel Barton in *The Nigel Barton Plays* by Dennis Potter (Penguin Books Ltd)
The poem *Annus Mirabilis* in *High Windows* by Philip Larkin (Faber and Faber Ltd)
The Crossman Diaries by Richard Crossman (Hamish Hamilton and Jonathan Cape Ltd)
A Short Walk on the Campus by Jonathan Aitken and Michael Beloff (Secker and Warburg Ltd)
The Castle Diaries by Barbara Castle (Weidenfeld and Nicolson)
The Unforgiving Minute by Beverley Nichols (W. H. Allen Ltd)

FOREWORD

The Oxford Union is unique in that it has provided an unrivalled training ground for debates in the Parliamentary style which no other debating society in any democratic country can equal. The Oxford Union occupies a special place in the history of our nation, as a glance at the list of those who have held office and have distinguished themselves later in life will show.

Harold Macmillan
Earl of Stockton

INTRODUCTION

When the Oxford Union heard that Gladstone was dead, the debate on the order paper was set aside and the guest speaker F. E. Smith delivered a tribute to the late Prime Minister. 'In one sense,' he said, 'we shall not even yield up our claim to the House of Commons. We cannot forget that, if the splendid maturity of his life was theirs, ours, and ours only, was its brilliant dawn, and our claim to mourn over its pathetic end is not less.'

Brilliant dawns constitute the Oxford Union's claim to fame. Again and again in its history, the young speakers who catch the President's eye have gone on to catch the eye of the country, occasionally even the eye of the world. Within a university for the élite, the Union caters for an inner élite, ambitious to shine in politics, the law, the church, diplomacy, the media and the arts.

Of course by no means everyone who succeeds in the Union goes on to bigger and better things afterwards. Many careers which have dawned brilliantly at Oxford have turned out no better than a succession of wet Wednesday afternoons. Conversely, many people have gone on to dazzle the world, but have passed through Oxford almost unnoticed. The catalogue of Union successes is formidable all the same. There are five Prime Ministers, Gladstone, Salisbury, Asquith, Macmillan and Heath. During the last decade each of the four main political parties has been led by a former Union officer. The Conservatives have had Edward Heath, Labour Michael Foot, the Liberals Jeremy Thorpe and the SDP Roy Jenkins. The Union has had Ministers in most twentieth-century cabinets, including Lord Birkenhead, Sir John Simon, Lord Curzon, Lord Milner, Sir Walter Monckton, Leslie Hore-Belisha, Lord Gardiner, Lord Hailsham, Michael Stewart, John Boyd-Carpenter, Anthony Greenwood,

Anthony Crosland, Tony Benn, Sir Edward Boyle, Geoffrey Rippon, Norman St John Stevas and Michael Heseltine.

Commonwealth leaders have started their careers in the Union too. David Lewis went home to found the New Democratic Party in Canada. S. W. R. D. Bandaranaike returned to Sri Lanka eventually to become its Prime Minister. Lalithe Athulathmudali is Minister of Trade there now. Eric Abrahams is Minister of Tourism in Jamaica.

Then there are the lawyers. Apart from the Union's clutch of Lord Chancellors, Lord du Parcq, Sir Vincent Lloyd-Jones, Lord Diplock, Sir James Comyn, Sir Ralph Gibson and Sir Raymond Walton are among those who have made the transition from officers' chairs in the Union to the Bench. Many others are barristers.

Among the diplomats are two recent Ambassadors to the United States, Peter Jay and Sir Nicholas Henderson. The Union boasts its literary names as well; Hilaire Belloc, John Buchan, A. P. Herbert, Beverley Nichols, Evelyn Waugh, Philip Toynbee, Kenneth Tynan and Dennis Potter all took part in its debates. It has spawned journalists and media men in profusion: Robert Barrington-Ward and Sir William Rees-Mogg to give double-barrelled authority to the editorship of *The Times*, Sir Robin Day, Jeremy Isaacs and Brian Walden to make their marks on the world of television. Only the Union's supply of bishops has been dwindling in recent years, compared with the periods which produced Archbishop Temple and Archbishop Lang. An ex-Secretary, Rt. Rev. Stanley Booth-Clibborn, is however installed in the See of Manchester.

So the Union is undoubtedly a prolific contributor to *Who's Who*. The qualities which it admires in its leading performers are powers of persuasion, panache and wit. Knowledge is of much less consequence. Few people have become President of the Union without being able to tell a joke well; many have done so without a great command of economics or history.

For good or ill, it would be very surprising if the Society did not affect those who pass through it, even though, in Lord Hailsham's phrase, they may have been ground through a great many mills after their Union days. Several have changed their views, some quite radically; many have altered their speaking style; but most admit the Union has influenced them, if only through friendships made there which have carried on into adult and public life.

There is, in any case, a great fascination in glimpses of successful men on their first stage up the greasy pole. Moreover, although the Union does value humour, it is far from entirely frivolous. It does debate the great issues of the day, sometimes passionately; and the views which the undergraduates express in the debating hall do mirror the preoccupations of successive generations of articulate young people, even if they are sometimes rather eccentrically refracted. The debates even, from time to time, make an impact on the outside world. They did so in 1933 when the undergraduates voted not to fight for King and Country, and again in 1975 when, on the eve of the EEC Referendum and in front of the television cameras, they were persuaded that Britain should stay in Europe.

Then again there is the flood of visiting speakers who have taken the five o'clock train from Paddington to go down and speak as the Society's guests. Some go for old time's sake, some because it is a platform from which what they say will be noticed, some because they are only too happy to hear the sound of their own voices whenever they can, others simply because they enjoy it. Occasionally a foreign visitor, Jawaharlal Nehru, Robert Kennedy or Richard Nixon, is invited to give an address. Normally, however, guests are asked to debate with the Society's members. It is a challenge which has been taken up by such diverse figures as Edouard Benes, Horatio Bottomley, James Callaghan, Sir Edward Carson, Sir Winston Churchill, Bernadette Devlin, Hugh Gaitskell, Neil Kinnock, George Lansbury, David Lloyd-George, Malcolm X, Sir Oswald Mosley, Enoch Powell, Diana Rigg and W. B. Yeats.

The Union, it is often said, is overrated outside Oxford and underrated within the university. Certainly, it has always had strong critics. It is accused of being pompous, mannered and outdated, or alternatively infantile. Some say it is an institution which is irrelevant to Oxford and should not be considered relevant as a qualification for the best careers. The really brilliant minds at Oxford, it is alleged, do not bother with the Union and never have. Even the best of the vintage periods of the past were subjected to these criticisms.

The Union has numbered some prominent people amongst its critics. In 1975, Mrs Barbara Castle attacked it as 'the cadet class of the establishment'. Most students, she said, were 'at a level of income that left no room for luxuries like entrance fees to exclusive clubs'. Mrs Shirley Williams, who has visited the Union frequently, once said that it was excellent training for Parliament because both institutions were dotty out-of-date gentlemen's clubs. She is sceptical, though not completely dismissive of the Union's value.

'I think it is a useful training and grounding,' she says, 'but perhaps too much emphasises parliamentary traditions. In my view some of those traditions maybe do need to be changed now, and I think the difficulty about the Union is that in some ways it encourages the most traditional of the traditions, including a particular style of speech which depends very much on wit and style rather than on the substance of what is being said. Nevertheless I think it would be excessively pompous and gloomy to suggest that the Union has to be terribly sombre all the time, and I do believe that it has done much to encourage excellence of speaking. I would simply plead that it should not be taken so seriously that all its support for parliamentary tradition becomes a sort of endorsement for those traditions which I think many people from rather different backgrounds at Oxford found quite hard to stand, or indeed to accept.'

The cabinet ministers, judges and bishops who have come from the Union were only nineteen, twenty and twenty-one-year-olds when they spoke there. They had barely emerged from adolescence and had little experience of the world on which to base their pronouncements in the debating hall. For every pearl of political wisdom, it must have resounded to a hundred clichés. For every brilliant epigram, there must have been fifty jokes which fell flat. The nursery of statesmen has seen its share of childish behaviour.

Yet the Union does have its merits. Above all, it places a high premium on debating skill; its members are all connoisseurs of the art of debate. Parliament is far more concerned with the content than the style of a speech. The majority of contributions are made there to a chamber which is three-quarters empty. The ability to speak effectively in the Commons or on a public platform is becoming less important than the ability to perform well on television. So the Union is preserving a type of formal debate which may be going out of fashion, but which many nevertheless believe is very much worth preserving.

Certainly, the Union has its ardent defenders. For Harold Macmillan, it provides the means of preserving the liberty of government by discussion. 'I have heard in this room,' he said in the debating hall in 1975, 'great speakers, witty speakers, brilliant speakers. But I have always felt that behind the extraordinary versatility and technique that you and I have heard here, there is something deeper: Oxford, Britain, everything we believe in.'

Michael Heseltine identifies the Union with what he sees as the virtues of the parliamentary tradition: 'It has managed to absorb the wildest firebrands, the most outspoken and non-conformist people who have emerged in British public life in a hundred years. They have come to understand the immense civilization of that process, of dehumanizing if you like, of getting the personal bitterness out of the argument, of conforming to a set of rules which mean that everyone gets a chance to say what they do. It is part of a very sophisticated democratic process. Of course, anyone who has come through this particular place has been brought up on it.'

Brian Walden says simply that the Oxford Union is 'the best debating institution in the world.' The standard is, he believes, definitely higher than the House of Commons.

This book is not intended as a continuous history of the Union. That has already been written by Christopher Hollis in 1965 and by Herbert Morrah before him in 1923. My purpose is more limited. It is to chronicle the dawns, brilliant or otherwise, of the careers of some of those who have gone on from the Union to make their mark in the world. At the same time, I have tried to recapture the atmosphere of Oxford and the Union as they have evolved through, and tried to come to terms with, the twentieth century.

My starting point was a series of interviews for a film about the Union, extracts of which are reproduced in the book. It was striking to find how much detail very eminent people could recall of their efforts in the Union, and how much it obviously meant to them. Since then, I have had many conversations with former officers and members, most of whom look back on it with great nostalgia and affection, and as a significant influence on their lives.

The written sources are uneven. Before and just after the First World War, the *Morning Post* gave an account of Union debates in the manner of a parliamentary report. When these reports ceased, the city newspaper, the *Oxford Mail*, continued to provide a reasonably full account of the proceedings for many years. There was also the dons' weekly, the *Oxford Magazine*, where the Union report was generally written by the President of the day. Less reliable, but sometimes more entertaining, were the descriptions in the undergraduate publications *Isis* and *Cherwell*. Their correspondents saw themselves as parliamentary sketch writers, and they concentrated more on the foibles of the speakers than on the content of the debates. In the 1960s, coverage of the Union began to become more skimpy. At the same time, however, the Society started tape-recording its debates. Many of these tapes have gone missing, but I have made use of the ones which remain extant.

Nothing that is said and done in the Union needs to be treated with deadly seriousness. No one should bear responsibility for life for a view expressed at the age of nineteen. Behaviour branded as skulduggery at the time can be excused in retrospect as harmless youthful indiscretion. The activities of the Union's young meteors have to be chronicled with due allowance made for youth. The Union acts as an imperfect crystal ball in whose depths the future of some performers can be seen with great clarity while the future of others is clouded and distorted. It is intriguing, nonetheless, to peer into the glass.

CHAPTER ONE

GLADSTONE'S LEGACY

1823–1910

Today's Oxford Union would seem quite familiar to a member from a hundred years ago. The gaunt Victorian debating hall, the officers in their formal evening dress, the parliamentary language would all make him feel at home. This is primarily a book about the Union in the twentieth century, but some account of its origins is essential in order fully to appreciate such a nineteenth-century institution.

The Union, eight years younger than its Cambridge counterpart, dates from 1823, when it was founded as the United Debating Society. Originally, it did not have a fixed meeting place; the members would hire rooms in one or other of the colleges. In 1829, they began renting a permanent base in Wyatt's Rooms in the High Street. They found the wherewithal to start building their own premises between Frewin Court and St Michael's Street in 1853. The Union has remained there ever since.

When the new debating hall was nearly finished the architect Benjamin Woodward was visited by his artist friend Dante Gabriel Rossetti. Looking round the building, Rossetti noticed that the walls were bare, and offered to decorate them. A few years previously he had founded the Pre-Raphaelite Brotherhood, dedicated to realism, and a revolt against materialism. For the Union project Rossetti gathered around him a group of sympathetic and talented artists, William Morris, Edward Burne-Jones, Val Prinsep, John Hungerford Pollen, Rodham Spencer Stanhope and Arthur Hughes. Most of them were young men at the beginning of their careers.

The theme was to be the Arthurian legend. According to Morrah, the Brotherhood's intention was that 'the orators below, if they lifted their eyes, would perpetually be reminded that their own aim must be truth, and truth in beauty: a thing which adhesion to political or other parties tended to obscure.' At all events, the artists tackled their task with great exuberance, working fast, but also giving themselves plenty of time for joking and drinking. On one occasion, the nineteen-year-old Prinsep, who was six feet one and weighed fifteen stone, picked up Burne-Jones under one arm and carried him up to the gallery where they were working. Morris even had a suit of chainmail made for himself to stimulate his imagination about the period which he was depicting.

The only trouble was that, in their enthusiasm, the artists had not prepared the surfaces properly for painting. The murals displayed brilliant colours when they were first completed, but within a year they had faded very badly. Rossetti's own final judgement was: 'the one remedy for all is whitewash, and I shall be happy to hear of its application.' The fate of the murals, potentially a great asset to a Society often accused of philistinism, has been the subject of much deliberation by the Union's Committees ever since their execution. An attempt to restore them was made in 1930, but they have again lost all brilliance of colour. Plans are currently afoot to try a second restoration.

The Union outgrew Woodward's debating hall in twenty years. The membership had increased to such an extent that a larger one had to be built across the garden. The foundation stone was laid in 1878. The old debating hall became an extension of the library, which was rapidly turning into the best lending library in Oxford. The future Labour Prime Minister Clement Attlee, a strong Tory at Oxford, was one of many undergraduates to use the library extensively without ever setting foot in the debating hall. Alongside the library, the Union began to develop other facilities to attract those who were not interested in debating, as well as to provide for the comforts of those who did perform regularly across the garden. The Union acquired all the accoutrements of the perfect Victorian gentlemen's club; reading rooms, a smoking room, a billiard room, a bar, later a dining room and a gentlemen's lavatory of monumental proportions.

It is inconceivable now to think of undergraduates raising the money to build facilities for themselves on this sort of scale, even with the help that they had at the time from senior members.

Relatively, undergraduates were of course much richer then than they are today. An equally important factor was the very considerable demand for the club-like facilities the Union offered.

Nineteenth-century college life could be very restricting. A man was sent down from St John's for not shaving. At another college, undergraduates had to attend the University Sermon every Sunday and produce notes on it afterwards to prove that they had been listening. The formal pictures of Victorian undergraduates attending the Union in their top hats give a misleading impression, because in fact the Union was a refuge from the restrictions imposed on them in their colleges.

The most important escape was for their minds. In the early days of the Union, the notion of the free exchange of ideas was foreign to Oxford. A University was a place where the young went to imbibe wisdom from their elders and betters. No argument or discussion was permitted in their formal education, and it was frowned upon in their extra-curricular activities as well. The authorities disliked the idea of debates, which might prove subversive and would, at best, distract undergraduates from their studies. So the Union had some difficulty in establishing itself.

Still, as Lord Salisbury commented later, the Society thrives on 'that gentle stimulus which is always given to any English institution by the disapproval of those in authority'. At first, the Union was supposed to avoid anything too controversial, especially politics. Its remit was to debate 'the historical previous to the present century, and the philosophical exclusive of religion'. Speakers in the first debate discussed 'Was the revolution under Cromwell to be attributed to the tyrannical conduct of Charles, or to the democratic spirit of the times?'

Soon, however, political topics began to intrude. The first decade of the Union's life was a period of enormous political excitement and disturbance in the country, dominated by the great issue of parliamentary reform, to which the Union and Oxford in general were passionately opposed. There was even a move to contribute the Union's entire funds to the anti-reform cause. One undergraduate in particular, W. E. Gladstone, became the first of many illustrious products of the Union to make his name championing a cause which he was later bitterly to oppose. During the debates in Parliament on the 1866 Reform Bill, Disraeli taunted Gladstone with his views as an undergraduate. Gladstone's riposte could still prove useful to politicians wishing to live down their pasts. 'I grant,' he said, 'my youthful mind and imagination were impressed with some idle and futile fears which still bewilder and distract the mature mind of the Right Honourable Gentleman.'

Gladstone made a great *tour de force* with a speech in the Union against reform in 1831. He spoke for three-quarters of an hour, quite a modest length by his later standards, but three times as long as any undergraduate could get away with today. His amendment to the motion stated 'that the Ministry has unwisely introduced and most unscrupulously forwarded, a measure which threatens not only to change the form of our Government, but ultimately to break up the very foundations of social order, as well as materially to forward the views of those who are pursuing this project throughout the civilized world.' His theme was that reform would inevitably lead to revolution, and he carried the day by 94 votes to 38.

Later in life Gladstone claimed, 'I do not think that the general tendencies of my mind were, in the time of my youth, illiberal,' but 'there was to my eyes an element of the anti-Christ in the Reform Act.' In a society dominated by noblemen who still had the power to blackball unwanted members, it was perhaps natural that Gladstone's conservative instincts were nurtured. Yet his illiberal tendencies at that stage do not seem to have been confined to the Reform Bill. He voted against the removal of measures which discriminated against Jews. He spoke against a motion favouring the establishment in London of colleges for the higher middle classes. On slavery he was ambivalent, perhaps not surprisingly since his father owned slaves.

As Secretary of the Union, Gladstone was so carried away by the success, by a majority of one, of a motion which he had moved himself, criticizing the Duke of Wellington's administration for deviating from Tory orthodoxy, that he wrote in the minute book 'tremendous cheering from the majority of one'. Partisan comments of this kind were not allowed, and the words 'from the majority of one' were later erased. Even the great Mr Gladstone was not immune from making youthful errors in the Union. On one occasion, he spoke at great length against a motion, then voted for it.

Gladstone and the Oxford Union did one another a great deal of good. The future Prime Minister learnt his speaking technique there. Indeed the Union probably persuaded Gladstone against a career in the Church and swayed him in favour of politics instead.

The Society even, indirectly, provided him with his first seat in Parliament. Lord Lincoln, a friend from his days at Eton, was so impressed with his anti-reform speech that he persuaded his father, the Duke of Newcastle, to offer him one of the seats in Parliament which he controlled. As a result, Gladstone was able to enter Parliament before his twenty-third birthday.

More than anyone else, Gladstone put the Union on the map. His career kindled the idea of the Union as a nursery of statesmen. Even today, many aspiring Union Presidents hope to find modern equivalents of Lord Lincoln and his father, who may not any more be able to give them seats in Parliament but who can at least smooth their paths towards the Conservative Research Department or the BBC. The nineteenth-century Union was obsessed with Gladstone throughout his career, and Gladstone reciprocated by retaining throughout his life a strong affection for the Society.

Because the hottest controversies in nineteenth-century Oxford were religious as much as political, the Union became an episcopal as well as a political nursery. Henry Manning, later Cardinal Manning, was President in 1829. Although he was an Anglican at the time, his dominating personality earned him the prescient nickname of 'the Pope'. Manning actually resigned the Presidency after he had been elected but before he had taken the chair for any debates; he seems to have believed that his preoccupation with worldly matters was placing him in danger of ending up in hell. Archibald Tait, later to become Archbishop of Canterbury, was President in 1833.

Not everyone in the Union's early days was destined to carry off glittering prizes. A Mr Mozley from Oriel College rose one night to speak in a debate about the seizure of the Danish fleet. He very soon dried up completely, collapsed and had to be led from the room. Speaking in the Union has always been a daunting experience; it may not be a great test of intellect or knowledge, but it is certainly a good test of nerves. Monckton Milnes, a Cambridge undergraduate who took part in the first visit from the Cambridge Union to the Oxford Union, described how he entered 'a neat little square room, with eighty or ninety young gentlemen sprucely dressed, sitting on chairs or lounging about the fireplace.' It was enough, he added 'to unnerve a more confident person than myself.'

The good Union speaker has always needed the hide of a rhinoceros. Few, however, have had the panache of Frederick

Lygon, who in his early Union days developed a reputation as a spectacularly bad speaker. He generally rose to his feet to a chorus of groans, accompanied by a 'scraping down', which was the noise of boots scraped on the boards of the floor of the chamber in such a way as to drown out anything an unpopular speaker said. On one occasion the members greeted Lygon with a prolonged disturbance, which ended in them stamping out a version of a popular tune called the *Rum Polka* on the floor. When he could make himself heard Lygon said, 'I intend to speak on this question, Sir, and as I am in no hurry it is a matter of perfect indifference to me how long I have to wait for the conclusion of the musical prelude with which honourable members have been so good as to welcome my remarks.'

In his undergraduate days the Union's second Prime Minister Lord Robert Cecil managed the difficult feat of positioning himself politically to the right of the young Gladstone. Cecil was deadly earnest about his politics, and single-minded about his ambitions for a political career; he was not at the time in line to succeed his father Lord Salisbury. As Gladstone had attacked the Duke of Wellington, so the young Robert Cecil attacked the Conservatives of his day for conceding too much to their opponents. The Conservatives' policy, he told the Union, 'is always to stand on the defensive. They will struggle when power is attempted to be taken from them, but once gone, they never attempt to regain it. Thus it is that Radicalism is permitted to gain the ascendant; everything that can be wrested from the Conservative classes becomes the object of attack, and they who are deprived of the power and the influence which properly belongs to them feel precluded by their principles from endeavouring to get it back.'

Later in the century Cecil's children were true to the family political tradition in the Union. Though he later became President of the Society, his son Lord Robert was not at all sure if he should be slumming it in the place at all. 'This is about the first letter I ever wrote from here and I think it'll be the last,' he wrote to his brother from the Society's rooms. 'People may say what they like, but I hate the lower middle classes and they infest the Union.'

Another son, Hugh Cecil, was also active, though he did not stand for office on the grounds that people would vote for him because of his name rather than because of his qualities. His attitude in the Union can be adduced from a speech which he made in the High Tory Canning Club. 'It is irritating,' he said, 'to hear of the wrongs of the labourer. Never have wages been higher; never the price of bread so small a part of the workman's daily expense. How can he say that he is badly off? His own improvident marriage is the cause of most of his misery.' At the time the average agricultural wage was under fifteen shillings a week.

For most of the nineteenth century Conservatism dominated the Union. It was not, however, all-pervasive. As early as 1833, the Liberal Massie of Wadham was elected President, and by 1850 there was even a Socialist, C. H. Pearson, active in the Society's debates. Gladstone's decision to join the Liberal Party brought over many Union members to his new cause. Then, following reforms in the University, reforms in the Union swept away the old system of blackballing and opened the Society's ranks to anyone in the University who wanted to join. By the 1870s, although the majority of members were still Conservative, the most prominent figures included more Liberals.

It was not surprising therefore that a Liberal non-conformist from a family of modest means could capture the President's chair in 1874. By all accounts, H. H. Asquith took the Union very seriously. He had taken a great interest in oratory as a schoolboy, attending Parliament and the law courts and, without being outstandingly religious, becoming a great aficionado of sermons, so that he was already a mature public speaker when he came up to Oxford.

Asquith was, perhaps, a little too serious for his contemporaries. Unlike the Union's first Liberal Prime Minister, his political views as an undergraduate did not change greatly as he grew older. In the Union, he consistently espoused progressive views; he made a notable speech on disestablishing the Church. True to his principles, he was a reformist Treasurer, introducing smoking and afternoon tea for the first time into the Society's rooms claiming that these reforms would encourage undergraduates to come to the Union and improve themselves by reading outside their subjects.

Asquith was defeated in his first attempt at the Presidency. His Conservative opponent Ashmead-Bartlett seems to have bribed the electors by giving lavish breakfast parties. Asquith, who was short of money, could not compete – in those days, there were no rules against canvassing as there are now. However, Asquith was very determined to become President, and was prepared to stand for office even for the term in which he was due to take his final exams. In the event, he won both the Presidency and a first-class degree.

By Asquith's time, the Union's *cursus honorum* through the offices of Secretary, Treasurer and Librarian to the Presidency was seen as an obvious first step on the political ladder. There was no Duke of Newcastle any more to offer young men a rotten borough, but a network of old members of the Union could be used in other helpful ways. When he was reading for the bar, Asquith himself became the pupil of a distinguished former Union President, Charles Bowen.

Six years after Asquith, George Nathaniel Curzon became President of the Union during what one contemporary described as 'the brief interval which must intervene between Eton and the Cabinet'. Tall and handsome, Curzon already had the enamelled self-assurance which he was to carry through life as Viceroy of India, Foreign Secretary and Chancellor of Oxford University.

> 'My name is George Nathaniel Curzon.
> I am a most superior person.
> My cheek is pink, my hair is sleek.
> I dine at Blenheim once a week',

went the stanza about him in the contemporary Masque of Balliol.

At the Union he spoke tirelessly, taking a Disraelian Tory paternalistic line. His fluency and self-confidence inspired admiration rather than affection amongst his fellow-members. He tended to speak for too long. He was described once as 'lengthy and discursive though eloquent'; another time, 'he spoke for about fifty minutes and would have gone on for fifty minutes more had the President not interposed.' He crammed his speeches with classical quotations, metaphors and literary allusions. His Balliol scholarship was, it was said, painfully conspicuous.

The 1880s were in general regarded as a rather thin patch for the Union. The Society revived again in the 1890s under the influence of a series of famous names. In 1894 F. E. Smith was President; he was to become Attorney-General, Lord Chancellor and Secretary of State for India as Lord Birkenhead. The next year, the chair was taken by the writer Hilaire Belloc. A year later again, the future Foreign Secretary Sir John Simon was elected to the Presidency. Then in 1899, another writer, John Buchan, took the office. The decade set a style and a tone for the Union which was to persist well into the twentieth century. Smith in particular was a constant visitor in his later life. Lord Hailsham, who was President as late as 1929, recalls that even then speakers in the Union were trying to imitate him. 'He was a very bad influence on the young from the point of view of doing it well,' he says, 'because he had a style which was peculiar to himself, and insofar as he represented a period, he represented the pre-First World War period. By the time the First World War was over, I think it was already dated.'

Nevertheless, Smith's style worked well enough for himself. His contemporaries were quick to appreciate his talent for argument. The famous sportsman C. B. Fry drafted Smith into the Wadham soccer team, on the grounds that his forensic skills would be invaluable for arguing with the referee and drafting protests.

Smith took the Union very seriously. Simon, who was on the same staircase in Wadham, recalled that he used to march up and down in his rooms in elaborate rehearsal. His first speech in the Union made a great impact. The subject was local option, the proposal that there should be local referendums to decide whether licensed premises should be allowed in particular areas. A well-known teetotaller of the time, Sir Wilfred Lawson, came down to the Union to champion his cause. Lawson was famous for the gesture which he had made against the demon drink in pouring the very substantial contents of his family's cellars down the drain. Smith's attack on him became a legend, though one probably embellished with the passage of time. 'The honourable gentleman,' he said, "inherited a noble cellar, in which the piety of his ancestors had laid to rest noble clarets, sustaining ports, stimulating champagnes, and warm and ancient brandies. What did the honourable gentleman do with his cellar? He destroyed that priceless heritage of the ages, in which was stored the bottled sunshine of the south – he destroyed it under circumstances of such barbarity that even the thirstiest throat in Carlisle was denied participation! I tell you, sir, that if in years to come, the honourable gentleman comes to me when I am lounging in Abraham's bosom, and asks me for a drop of water, I shall say to him: "No, not a drop! You dissipated greater liquor."'

Smith was nineteen at the time. The image of this callow youth lounging like Lazarus in Abraham's bosom appealed to the House more than anything they had heard for a long while. They applauded him for five solid minutes, and the speech played a major part in launching him on his career. It became so celebrated in fact that thirty years later an account of it turned up in of all places the *Licensed Victuallers' Gazette.*

Smith became very adept at a time-honoured Oxford variant of the English disease, pretending to do hardly any academic work while actually working quite hard. It has seldom been fashionable at Oxford, particularly in the Union, to admit to great diligence. It has not only been important to do things well; it has been considered equally vital to appear to do them without effort. Just as Smith worked hard at his speeches in order to make them sound effortless in the Union, so he put in time at his books when everyone thought he was in bed. He had considerable powers of concentration and, so it was claimed, trained himself to make do with very little sleep so that he could work far into the night.

Smith's great Liberal opponent in the Union was Hilaire Belloc, the son of a French lawyer. He used to make great play in his speeches about the insularity of the English and the superiority of Continental and particularly French institutions. He was, by all accounts, a dazzling speaker. Smith admitted that at the Union he was an immense and unparalleled success. 'I can bear testimony to this,' he added, 'because I opposed Mr Belloc on nearly all his great occasions.'

Like Smith's, Belloc's style at this distance of time seems rather too flowery for modern tastes. The two young orators once debated the motion 'that this house would approve of any measure which would give undergraduates a share in the government of this university.' This has been a regular subject for debate down the generations at the Union; it is curious to find the demand for student power as far back as the nineteenth century, but at this stage it seems to have been intended as little more than a joke.

Belloc proposed the motion. The University, he said, was like 'a lofty and well-proportioned cathedral, in which the representation of undergraduates would be a conduit and drain for the buoyancy of youth.'

'When I contemplate the scheme of the honourable gentleman from Balliol,' replied Smith, 'I see it as a high, vast, lofty, well-proportioned drain.' Smith's flair for making fun of his opponents once again won over his audience.

By this time, Union debates had settled down to much the same pattern they have today. Officers, main or 'paper' speakers and their guests would attend a dinner beforehand, at which those who were due to perform would pretend that their nerves were not spoiling their appetites. Then the President would lead his party over to make a grand entrance into the debating hall, where he and the officers would take up their exalted positions on the dais at the end of the chamber. The rules of debate are modelled closely on those of the House of Commons.

Guest speakers were rare at this time. Until 1888, there were none; the members preferred to debate among themselves. That year, however, Lord Randolph Churchill was invited down to speak on Home Rule, and thereafter, until the First World War, one or two outside speakers a term would visit. Guests would hardly ever be pitted against each other, and, in accordance with its gentlemanly traditions, the Union would normally see to it that a majority of those present voted for the side on which the guest had spoken. In the 1980s, the President has to find at least two guests for every debate. Big outside names are considered the only way to fill up the debating hall. The undergraduate 'paper' speakers generally speak before the guests.

We have seen Gladstone putting the skills he learnt in the Union to immediate use in Parliament. F. E. Smith had an urgent need to employ his oratorical powers to rather more mundane ends. When he went down from Oxford he was £400 in debt, and his creditors were pressing him. He called a meeting of them, and, in a speech which must have tested his abilities to the limit, he managed to persuade them to give him longer to pay up.

Like Asquith before him, Sir John Simon was an uncompromising defender of Liberalism, and the party of which he was later to become a leading member, when he was an undergraduate. Simon took on the Conservatives, defending a miners' strike and supporting reform of the House of Lords and disestablishment of the Church. Later in life, he remained a great champion of the Union. 'There is a great deal to be learnt in trying to persuade that fastidious audience,' he wrote, 'and there are friendships to be made with the fiercest of your opponents which will last through life.'

If the Union has not changed a great deal in a hundred years, the University itself is unrecognizable. In 1900 it had only two thousand undergraduates, a small proportion of today's student population. Very few of those were women, kept ruthlessly segregated from the men. 'The great point of Oxford,' wrote Compton Mackenzie, 'in fact the whole point of Oxford, is that there are no girls.' The University was the lifeblood of the town. William Morris was in business, but only with a bicycle shop from which undergraduates could hire machines for sixpence a day to pedal off into the countryside. The bicycle ride had replaced the long intellectual walks of Gladstone's time, but otherwise the University was keeping modern technology safely at bay.

John Buchan, President of the Union in 1899, was well-placed to give an outsider's view of Oxford at the turn of the century. A graduate of Glasgow University before he went up to Brasenose College, he knew the Scottish university system well as a yardstick for comparisons. When he first arrived, he found Oxford somewhat soft after Glasgow. 'There are no cheerless walks on sharp winter mornings,' he wrote, 'no shivering on bare benches in windy classrooms, no scribbling in dark lecture halls at rickety desks. Nor is there the pinching, the scraping for an education, the battling against want and ill-health, which make a Scots college such a noble nursery of the heroic. Again, there are not so many gentlemen with designs on the reformation of the world. Things are quieter, easier, more contented. It is like some comfortable latter-day monastery. The harsh struggle for existence goes on without its knowledge.'

Nevertheless Buchan was soon at ease with the undergraduates of Oxford, exotic though he found them. Despite his shyness he made his mark at the Union, and was elected first Librarian, then President. It is a curious psychological phenomenon that many of the Union's great successes have been men who are shy in private, people who find it easier to communicate with an audience of a thousand than with an audience of one. Buchan's first book was published while he was at Oxford, and he was considered an important enough figure to be listed in *Who's Who*, providing the only entry where the profession listed was 'undergraduate'.

Buchan felt afterwards that he had been a horrid young prig at Oxford. In fact, for all his Scottish uprightness, he was capable of unbending. When he was elected President, his two closest friends sent him a message at two o'clock in the morning. It read, 'We are both drunk, but that does not prevent us from tendering to you our very heartiest congratulations on our own behalf and on that of all right-thinking men in this University and the world upon your election. I wonder if you are as drunk as we are? We all hope so.'

The nineteenth-century Oxford Union aimed very high, even if it did not always live up to its ambitions. At an anniversary dinner, Cardinal Manning talked about the young men before him who 'are to form the material of future legislators, not prompted by the low ambition of calculating minds, but by the high aspiration of men who desire to do good service to the Commonwealth, and who are now training themselves in all the fire of youth, the vigour of their fresh intellect, and the energy of their will, set upon our great public service, in the Oxford Union.'

CHAPTER TWO

HAROLD MACMILLAN AND HIS FRIENDS 1910–1914

Vintage periods at the Union have usually coincided with particularly turbulent times in national or international affairs. As politics are the mainstay of the debates, it is not surprising that a time of intense political interest and activity should draw the most able to the debating hall.

The period just before the First World War was an era which fostered exceptional talent in the Union. A single generation included the future Prime Minister Harold Macmillan, the future Cabinet Minister Walter Monckton, the author and independent MP A. P. Herbert, and three leaders of left-wing thought, Harold Laski, G. D. H. Cole and the publisher and founder of the Left Book Club, Victor Gollancz. The quality of this generation seems all the more remarkable when so many of their contemporaries, no doubt of equal ability, died in the First World War.

For the most part these men have looked back on Oxford, and particularly on the Union, with great affection. Harold Macmillan has written about the intoxicating feeling, after the severe discipline of an Edwardian home, of being on one's own in a society of countless friends. Seventy years after he first went up to Oxford, his memory of his time there is still fresh and vivid, as I found when I went to talk to him in the Carlton Club in London.

'I went to Oxford in 1912,' he told me, 'and I had two years there, two years in which it never occurred to anybody, I think, whether undergraduate or graduate or professor, and indeed to very few politicans, that they would be the last two years of what one might call civilized society; that there would suddenly descend upon us, like a bolt from the blue, this terrible First World War. For the First War was not like the Second War, which many of us could see coming – the rise of Hitler, the gradual aggression. Those of us who had eyes could see it coming. But the First War – nobody ever thought about it.

'So we had two wonderful years, which I look back on as the years of happiness. There was a lack of any kind of shadow hanging over the world. Ever since then, the sky has been overcast and still is. So they are to me the halcyon years. I think it was Talleyrand who said anyone who had not known France before the revolution had never known the beauty of life. To some extend it is true of England, the simplicity, the quiet, the calm. Of course there were political disputes and battles, even the beginning of some industrial problems, but they were nothing compared with what now hangs over the world.'

The undergraduate Harold Macmillan plunged himself into every available activity in Oxford. 'We all took part in everything. I was a scholar and I worked hard. I never, of course, did the final degree, because instead of going off having two years more, we all went off to war. At the end of July, instead of going off on a reading party to start reading for Greats, I found myself on a barrack square. We were full of activities, not, I think, so regularized or formalized as now. For instance, in the politics, I was a member of the Liberal Club and of the Conservative Club and of the Fabian Society. We were much more seeking about. I rather regret the tendency now to form up young people into fixed political party views. They are too young for that. What they should be is looking and searching and listening and hearing and talking. The Union was fun because it was an opportunity to learn something of the parliamentary system, to which I always had ambitions. It was organized like the House of Commons. The President, like the Speaker, was in the chair. You addressed the chair. There were front benches and back benches and so forth, and it was the drill of the House of Commons, as it had been since it was founded by Mr Gladstone and his friends.

'I remember I spoke extremely badly at first. I was first what was called "put on the paper" in my first or second term through the kindness of Walter Monckton, who was President. I took broadly then the support of the Liberal Government of Mr Asquith, but not always. I remember that the tone had been set, of course, by the people immediately before, the great speakers like Raymond Asquith and Ronald Knox and Philip Guedalla. So there was a sort of style. We all affected the epigram and wit of that kind. Very second rate stuff it was, a lot of it.'

Harold Macmillan has outlived most of his generation, but others have left written records of their Oxford days. To A. P. Herbert, it was 'a delight, a dream, merely to walk about the streets of Oxford'. He shared digs with Walter Monckton and other leading undergraduates, where they talked politics even at breakfast. He too joined all the clubs, and enjoyed particularly sitting on the floor at the Canning or Chatham Club drinking mulled claret and settling the future of the world. In the Union, Herbert confessed to being terrified whenever he had to speak, and indeed his mannerisms made him an unlikely debater. As a child, he had been dropped on his head by an overexuberant friend of his father's who was playing with him and as a result had a tendency to stoop, from time to time involuntarily jerking his head upwards. He blinked very noticeably and came close to stuttering. The undergraduate magazine *Isis* however proclaimed him unequalled. His notices are consistently good: 'one of the most brilliant debating speeches that has been made in the Union for a long time'; 'the union's finest debater'; 'he woke us all up with a typical Herbertian speech, debating, with his jerky fluency, with most of the previous speakers'.

The truth is that a speaker without any mannerisms would be extremely dull. The secret is to harness them positively, to make an asset out of a potential disadvantage like a slight stutter or an inability to pronounce the letter 'r'. A. P. Herbert evidently triumphed over his shortcomings.

Herbert made a choice which few of the Union's best performers have subsequently followed. After a term as Secretary, he abandoned the Union to concentrate on obtaining a first class degree. When he succeeded in his ambition, he walked about, he said, like Hector or Ulysses.

Walter Monckton like Harold Macmillan, was at Balliol, a college where most undergraduates had radical sympathies. Monckton was a Tory, but he seems at this stage to have possessed an ability to get on with people of all types which earned him his 'oil- can' nickname when he was Churchill's Minister of Labour. A cricket fanatic, he would go almost straight from the wicket to the Union. He worked hard on his speeches all the same, and modelled his style on F. E. Smith, so closely, in fact, that he is said to have taken pains to brush his hair the same way as the great orator.

Monckton became President of the Union. Victor Gollancz never climbed higher than the Library Committee, the lowest rung on the ladder to the Presidency, although not from want of trying. Looking back, he considered himself an outsider socially and too serious as a speaker. Nonetheless he had fond memories of the Union. He was there constantly. He particularly relished the facility to members of free postage; the system of initialling envelopes made him feel so important that he used to think up recipients and subjects for his letters just for fun. Upstairs in the reading room he liked the armchairs, deeper than any in the world, and the fires like the fires of a railway engine. In the debating hall itself, he remembered the members of the Standing Committee, lolling on the green leather benches beside the President's chair, imitating the front bench at Westminster.

Harold Laski was an extremely untypical undergraduate, particularly for his period. He had married, secretly, at the age of eighteen, and he and his wife had to live apart until he went down from Oxford. Unlike most other active members of the Union, Laski read science, though he did later change to history. He was extremely clever. According to a contemporary, he was 'a devastating critic of almost everything and very nearly everybody, the prototype of all the wonderful fictional undergraduates one had read of or heard of but had never met. He seemed to be a well of knowledge and sparkled with statistics.'

Laski never attained office in the Union. His socialist politics, his earnest self-importance, may have told against him. Nevertheless, he had good write-ups for his Union speeches in *Isis*. 'I only fear that his vigorous and sincere eloquence will one day bring him within the prison gates,' its critic once commented.

According to his wife Dame Margaret, G. D. H. Cole would have regarded the Union as part of the Establishment, if the word had been invented then, 'that is, associated with authority and social advancement and so anathema to a good Morrisite socialist'. Cole did not, however, eschew the Union altogether. He was even coopted onto the Library Committee. On one occasion, he went along to move the adjournment of the House in the private business session before the main motion of the evening was debated. He wanted to call the members' attention to the Oxford Tram Strike, arguing that wages for those who operated the city's trams were grossly inadequate. His speech was judged brilliant and, although he withdrew the motion, he was said to have swayed most opinion in his favour. A year later, there is a rather more snide reference to a speech which he made in a debate on South Africa. 'Oxford Socialism,' wrote the *Isis* critic, 'is nothing if not immaculate in attire, and G. D. H. Cole, feeling that another faultless dress-suit might prove one straw too many for the camel's back, sought to disguise his outward and visible respectability under an overcoat.'

As a city Oxford had changed little since John Buchan's day, except for the fact that William Morris now hired out motorbicycles as well as bicycles. Public transport was by the horsedrawn trams whose drivers were the subject of Cole's adjournment motion. The cabs were also horsedrawn. They could be picked up outside the Mitre Hotel, where the horses waited patiently munching their nosebags. The Oxford which A. P. Herbert was later to describe as a 'city of screaming tyres' lay far in the future.

Though undergraduates lacked modern conveniences like baths with running water they lived a very comfortable life all the same. College servants were in plentiful supply, and were loyal, industrious and deferential. A radical like Gollancz was to admit later that the spaciousness and leisure which he valued so much had been gained at the expense of those less privileged than himself. Meals were immense. Breakfast alone could consist of porridge with brown sugar and cream followed by steak with fried onions. The Cadena Café advertised in *Isis* a six-course dinner including coffee for two shillings and sixpence. The really frugal could have five courses for one and ninepence. A good bottle of champagne could be bought for five shillings; a great many were.

Undergraduates did of course dress more formally than they do now, though *Isis* once devoted a whole leader to criticizing current vogues in fashion. 'The spat has been overdone,' fulminated its leader for 19 October 1912. 'It has leaked out. With a tweed cap, however, it is impossible. The gross realism of the tweed cap cannot consort with the merely suggestive spat.'

For the aristocracy and upper middle classes, it was comparatively cheap to send their children to Oxford, about £160 a year, and most of them enabled their offspring to live extremely well when they were up. Undergraduates did not even have to work particularly hard if they did not want to do so. Many simply did not bother to take a degree. Of those who did have academic ambitions, many would reserve their serious work for the vacations, leaving the term for social activities and societies like the Union.

In any case, the Oxford system then as now put all the emphasis on success or failure at the end of the three or four year course with in some cases a minor hurdle half way through. It was perfectly possible for an undergraduate to neglect his studies for three-quarters of his time at Oxford, and still to achieve a respectable result by working feverishly in the remaining quarter. Victor Gollancz was hauled in to explain to the Warden of his college, the famous Warden Spooner, why he had not been turning in essays to his tutor. The excuse was that Gollancz had been busy at his clubs and societies. 'I shan't interfere,' said Spooner. 'If you pull off a First, I shall congratulate you. If not, I shall take away your scholarship and send you down.'

Academic work was done very much for its own sake. There were no economists who came to dazzle the Union with statistics about the velocity of money; engineers did not queue up to lend their technical expertise to their discussions. The élite academic discipline was Classics, properly known as Honour Moderations and Literae Humaniores. The undergraduates could exchange quips in Greek or Latin with graceful ease; the world a few miles down the road in which William Morris was shortly to build his first mass-produced motor car was much more foreign to them than the Athens of the fifth century BC. Literae Humaniores, or Greats, was considered the finest discipline for the mind, the most apposite training for those who were going on to run the British Government and the Empire. Greats does have considerable strengths. Command of language, clarity of thought, an understanding of logic, a feeling for history and literature are all qualities which a narrow technical education would not develop in the same way. The dominance of Greats did, however, undoubtedly increase the remoteness of undergraduates from the real world.

The Union was the place where the Greats men and the others could descend to the real world to talk about the issues of the day. Style, though, was as important as content there, with the tone, as Mr Macmillan remembers, being set very much by two Presidents of the recent past, Ronald Knox, who held the office in 1909, and Philip Guedalla, who was in the Chair in 1911.

Knox was particularly close to Harold Macmillan. He had acted as his tutor for a short time before he went up to Oxford. 'He was the wittiest,' Mr Macmillan recalls. 'It is inevitably difficult to describe the extraordinary quiet, simple epigram after epigram, paradox after paradox, and all at the same time covered by the sweetness of character. He became an institution.' One of Macmillan's contemporaries, like him a freshman in 1912, wrote to his mother about a vintage Knox performance in the Union: 'An ascetic-looking pale-faced hollow-chested shrivelled up young man', he described him, 'with a hideous face, dull eyes, sensual lips and a weak chin – a figure whose sole significance lay in its frailty and its ugliness. This puny figure, supporting itself carelessly against a table, without any apparent effort, without seeming to arouse itself for an instant from a sort of habitual lethargic condition, held the large house composed of the most varied elements spellbound as long as the unbroken flow of words poured forth from the unfaltering, but scarcely moving, lips.'

Later, as Monsignor Ronald Knox, this spellbinder was to produce a notable translation of the Bible. As a debater, he scarcely minded what cause he was championing. He recorded himself that he could be relied upon to support any view in any debating society. He once, not in the Union itself, proposed and opposed the same motion because of a shortage of speakers.

'The honourable gentlemen have turned their backs on their country and now have the effrontery to say they have their country behind them,' was a typical Knox line. When he was an undergraduate, he had called himself a Tory-socialist and had belonged to a nominally socialist institution called the Orthodox Club. It is doubtful that its members took the proceedings too seriously. To show how radical they were, they had a red voting urn and red balls, so that they could redball instead of blackball members they did not want.

The other *éminence grise* of this generation was Philip Guedalla. Compared with some, he made relatively little impact on the world after his Oxford days, although he did become a respected writer and historian. As President of the Union, however, he was considered among the all time greats. He was so well-known and admired as an undergraduate that people stared at him as he walked down the High Street. His epigrams are said to have rivalled Oscar Wilde's. He was the ultimate champion of style over content.

All the same, for all the admiration of verbal gymnastics, the nature of the events taking place in the period immediately before the First World War was such that arguments did begin to become more impassioned. There were a whole host of issues forcing themselves upon the attention of politically active young men – only excluding the approach of the war itself. Victor Gollancz confirms Harold Macmillan's impression of war coming as a bolt from the blue. After forty years of peace, he says, and with so many preoccupations in domestic politics, the threat of a European war was without actuality. Ronald Knox, by then a Fellow of Trinity, imagined the staid portraits of Trinity men long dead looking down scandalized on the frivolity of a later generation at dinner. 'Or did they know,' he asks, 'the ordeal that lay before that generation, and rejoice that from us the shadow was still hidden?'

Very few people at Oxford realized what was going to happen. When the historian Lewis Namier, a Fellow of Balliol who was Austrian by birth, returned from the Continent and told a group of undergraduates in the front quad of the college that a European war was round the corner, they all burst out laughing. As late as the beautiful summer of 1914, A. P. Herbert and his friends could 'strut the world, boasting about our degrees or explaining them away, and in either case considering ourselves the lords of life.' For Gollancz, there was 'a breathless quality of incommunicable magic' about that summer.

What the active members of the Union were expecting during this period was not a European war but a civil war in Ireland. The Society debated Home Rule again and again and had as its guests many of the most prominent participants in the struggle.

The Union voted mainly against the Liberal Government and Home Rule, although the votes were quite close and depended to some extent on who the guest was; it was considered discourteous in those days to vote against a visiting speaker. In 1912, Sir Edward Carson came down to the Union. The champion of the Ulster loyalists spoke alongside the undergraduate Walter Monckton against the Government's plans. 'Home Rule,' he thundered at the Union, 'was brought forward for no other reason than to keep the present Government in power. England would lose a great deal if she passed this bill; she would lose her honour.' The House applauded loudly.

The next term they were applauding the Irish Nationalist leader John Redmond. 'We began by admiring the loudness of Mr Redmond's voice,' said *Isis*, 'which, it is said, was distinctly heard in North Oxford. Towards the end, we realized the enthusiasm which real Irish oratory can evoke.' Redmond, however, was not, for once, the only visitor. The President had also invited J. H. M. Campbell, a former Attorney-General who had previously been responsible for prosecuting the Nationalist leader for his part in land agitation in Ireland. The exchanges between them were acrimonious. At one point, when Campbell was trying to intervene in Redmond's speech, Redmond retorted, 'This is not the House of Commons, so let us have order.'

The next time Home Rule came up in the Union, Harold Macmillan emerged as its champion against A. P. Herbert. Macmillan appealed for greater sympathy and understanding of the Nationalist cause. The account of his speech preserves some of the flavour of his style as a nineteen-year-old. 'If, with the strange fatality of Irish history, there must be a war, he appealed to the House to throw its weight, strong in the hopes of the future, and not poisoned with the bitterness of the past, on the side of toleration not bigotry, on the side of unity and not of discord, for the healing of old sores, not for the infliction of fresh wounds, for the equality of all, not for the fanatical ascendancy of a small and privileged minority.' The House applauded, but Macmillan's side lost narrowly.

The next year Macmillan, now Treasurer of the Union, took on another visitor, Austen Chamberlain, on the same subject. Chamberlain was down for the debate in Eights Week, the week of the summer term devoted to rowing, parties and entertaining lady visitors. Fairy lights twinkled in the Union gardens. Mothers, sisters, cousins and aunts crowded into the gallery; but the debate was rather more serious than the normal Eights Week fare.

According to *Isis*, Macmillan was in first-rate form. It was better to overlook the flaws of the Home Rule Bill, he said, than to plunge Ireland whose hopes had again been roused, into an agony of despair. 'By what right,' Chamberlain answered, 'do you refuse to Ulstermen the liberty of choice of the government under which they shall live, which you are so ready to accord their countrymen in the South and West of Ireland?'

The other issue which preoccupied the Union at this time was votes for women. In the University, a Men's Political Union for Women's Enfranchisement and an Anti-Suffrage Society competed for attention. Harold Laski and Victor Gollancz were heavily involved in the campaign for women's suffrage. In 1914, they hit upon a form of protest which they thought was particularly suited to Oxford. During Eights Week, they chartered a launch on the river and steamed up and down shouting 'votes for women' through a megaphone. Gollancz, fearing retribution from the oarsmen, deemed it prudent to go into hiding at the end of this subversive voyage. He retired to the Classical Reading Room and hid under a low table until he decided it was safe to come out.

In the Union, Laski claimed that 'women could infuse into the political discussion at the present time an attitude of mind, more serious perhaps, and certainly nonetheless valuable, than that given to political problems by men at the present day.' His delivery was reported to be too monotonous to hold the House, but Harold Macmillan was acclaimed as 'highly amusing' on the same side. He claimed that 'if women could not be soldiers, they were the mothers of soldiers, and in motherhood there had been more danger and more loss of life in the past few centuries than there had been in all the wars Europe had taken part in during the same period.'

The votes in the Union on women's suffrage were close. In November 1912 they rejected 'women should have the vote' by 200 to 179, but in May 1913 they carried 'this House approves of women's suffrage' by 199 to 190.

Among the opponents of the idea was Walter Monckton, who suggested that women Cabinet Ministers would be an anomaly. It would be giving women more than their fair share of the burden. Militant suffragettes, according to A. P. Herbert, were 'intolerable harpies preying on the country'. A speaker in the same debate, P. R. S. Nichols, suggested that women did not need the vote because there were always chivalrous men ready to come forward, like the proposers of the motion, and champion women's interests. Ronald Knox turned the whole question into a joke. 'The debatable point,' he said, 'was whether women would be more of service to the nation in the House of Commons than in pouring vitriol in letter-boxes and destroying a lot of abominable Christmas cards, or whether it would be best to enlarge Holloway or the House of Commons.'

His role in the suffragette question was one of the reasons that the Chancellor of the Exchequer David Lloyd George had such a noisy reception when he came down in 1913 to dazzle the undergraduates with oratory the like of which they had never heard before. Harold Macmillan remembers the occasion vividly. 'It was the height of his pre-war fame, when he was regarded as a radical demagogue by many and looked up to as a prophet by others. There was great doubt about his coming to Oxford. There was a fear there would be a row and demonstrations, and the police and the dons were a bit worried.

'He arrived with huge crowds, the Union packed with people who did not normally attend. I can remember the extraordinary effect of this man. For the first time I saw, or heard, a man who really knew how to speak. First of all, when he came in, if he were to come into a room, a hall, anywhere, he was the man. He filled it. He had that extraordinary power, like a great actor. He held the stage without speaking. Then he charmed everybody. They expected there to be rows and boos, but he charmed them all, with a mixture of quick bits, short bits, amusing bits, serious bits. There was a continual play of light and shade in his speech. When I got to know him afterwards, he taught me how to speak. I remember what he said to me, 'When you get up, say to yourself: "vary the pitch and vary the pace"'. Nearly all of us young speakers made speeches all on the same note. You must have continued variation, and at this he was the master. This was the great occasion, and one realized that our little efforts to imitate Demosthenes or to speak like Mr Gladstone or to make jokes like Father Knox were very small beer. Here was a master.'

The police had assembled in large numbers to cope with the demonstration against Lloyd George. He had to be taken by a back route from Christ Church to the Society's premise to avoid protestors. When he arrived, he was attacked with a volley of mangel-wurzels, one of which broke the windscreen of the Chancellor's car. Then a demonstrator struck him in the face with a pheasant. Finally, as Lloyd George was being hustled to safety inside the Union buildings, an undergraduate threw a turnip at him, and was arrested for his pains.

The debate, about the Government's land policy, provided Lloyd George with the occasion for a wide-ranging defence of himself and the Liberal Government's policies. 'No man,' he said, 'can obtain any prominence in public life in this country without going through years of strife and contention, which raise personal partisan fury and prejudice against himself, and do you think I am not conscious of that? Every politician is, and I am not alone in that respect. All I ask you tonight is to judge these proposals if you will on their merits, forgetting if you like that obnoxious Chancellor of the Exchequer, forgetting that they come from a Radical.'

He went on to make a devastating attack on the Unionists for equivocating over protection. 'That baby has been abandoned by its nurses, and the last I heard of it was Mr Bonar Law trying to croon it to sleep.' The members laughed and cheered at that. 'There are only just a few in this great assembly,' Lloyd George went on, 'who will do that policy reverence by a faint cheer. It has been left high and dry on Mount Ararat, and the waters have receded and all the animals have gone down to the more fertile valleys.'

Then Lloyd George came to the case for the land policy. 'No man can defend the wages paid to agricultural labourers. I have a list here of the wages of agricultural labourers in the parishes around Oxford – 12 shillings, 13 shillings, 14 shillings and I think the highest is 15 shillings a week. You cannot maintain a family in any comfort and you cannot keep it above semi-starvation on wages of that kind.' He ended on a note calculated to flatter his young audience. 'I appeal to you, do not underrate your influence as students of this great university. It will be known tomorrow that you have, without distinction of party, swept aside partial and partisan prejudices and declared that you will do your share to remove the degradation of the labourers' conditions of living, and thrill them with a new hope for the morrow.' The cheers were loud and prolonged.

The debating hall had been crammed to capacity. When the votes were counted it emerged that the Chancellor's side had won the day, with 654 votes to 586. Lloyd George, said *Isis*, had surprised the majority of his critics by arguing with them instead of denouncing them. It was obvious that many people did not know the right answer to his contentions. 'They knew that there was one, but they could not see where the fallacy lay.'

A fortnight later, the Union invited down F. E. Smith to put the case for the other side, which he did with great gusto. 'Mr Lloyd George says that agricultural wages are a pressing evil today. He told you so a fortnight ago. I reply to him by saying, if this is a pressing evil today, why don't you deal with it today? The Liberal Party do not intend to do away with slums. They cannot afford to do away with slums. They need them for their perorations.' Smith carried the House against the motion that 'this House has complete confidence in His Majesty's Government' by 500 votes to 290, a rather greater margin than Lloyd George had secured for the Liberals before.

The President Gilbert Talbot had had a spectacularly successful term, with debates of great quality and record attendances. Of this talented generation, he was the one tipped most often as a future political leader. Instead, he died two years later in the first battle of Ypres.

The Union mostly supported the Conservative cause at this time, partly because the Society, like the University, *was* on the whole Conservative, partly because the Union tends to be against the government of the day, whatever its political colour. Some students, however, opposed the Government because they were socialists. 'This House approves the basic principles of socialism' was regularly debated. Some who supported socialism in these debates were liberals who felt only a vague sympathy for socialist ideas. Harold Macmillan spoke more than once in favour of a motion of this kind. 'Socialism,' he is on record as saying, 'is coming either piecemeal or all at once.' *Isis* called his speech very ingenious. He was opposed by A. P. Herbert, who said that socialism meant the nationalization of everything, and the municipalization of the electric railway in London proved that public ownership did not work.

Laski, who had a rather deeper commitment to socialism, was in the meantime becoming incensed about the activities of Labour MPs in the House of Commons. Ever since there have been Labour MPs, it would appear, radical students have accused them of betraying their principles. The Labour Party in the House of Commons, according to Laski, was completely futile. It was there to alter industrial conditions, but had failed to do anything of the kind. It had become an adjunct, and a not very handsome adjunct, to the Liberal Party. As for Ramsay Macdonald, he was the most efficient angler after office he had ever come across.

Much of the comment about the debates of the time concentrates on the style of the speakers. 'Mr V. Gollancz has yet to master himself. He bubbles over with excitement and enthusiasm. One is always made strikingly aware of the opposite view by reason of his obvious inability to realize that there is one. Still, he can be quite eloquent'. Of Harold Macmillan there are many assessments. He is listed in a review of the term's debates in 1913 as a good exponent of the Oxford manner, 'the most polished of the mere epigrammists'. But, 'just as a hint for the future,' says the critic on another occasion, 'we may require a little more originality of thought.'

One speaker who never seemed to have any bad notices was

Walter Monckton. 'He came to Oxford with a reputation for torrential eloquence and catholic energy,' said the *Isis Idol* devoted to him. 'His maiden speech was acclaimed as the next best thing in its line to Lord Randolph Churchill's; the fact that we had heard neither that nor any of the intervening virgin efforts did not spoil our conviction that this was true.'

The writer had hit upon the great problem in comparing one Union era with another. Hardly anyone remains a regular attender for more than four years. Those revisiting the Society after a lapse of time cannot tell whether today's immature gaucheries are really any worse than what appeared the height of wit and polish years ago.

Certainly, even in this richly talented period, the Union still had its detractors. In June 1913 *Isis* likened the Society to a lunatic asylum, whose inmates were only concerned with fighting one another over a series of worthless positions of authority. 'What do they aim at? At a position which no longer counts for anything in our present world of fast-changing values; at the very shady shadow of a joke. They do not see it: that is why so few of them are men of first-rate intelligence.'

C. E. M. Joad, later to play an important role in the controversy over the 'King and Country' debate, wrote a lengthy attack on the Union in which he objected to the separation of humorous and serious debates into watertight compartments. 'Seriousness,' he said, 'is not so much a virtue as indolence. One takes oneself seriously because one finds by experience that it is the easiest thing to do. This explains the heaviness of old men. It is easy to be heavy, hard to be light. It is much easier to talk sense about Home Rule than to make a good joke about it. The fact that one tells the truth in a funny way does not invalidate the fact that one is telling the truth.'

Joad went on to attack the Union for being conventional and predictable. 'The same sort of questions are always asked, the same sort of speeches are always made. One must not say anything really new, and one must not talk about any of the old things in a new way.' Once the Union knows the sort of speeches you make and the sort of things you say, it gives you every facility for repeating them. The Union was started as an organ for the expression of undergraduate thought. It is now restricted to playing three or four notes.'

Next week, the organ blasted back at Joad, known as a bit of a buffoon in the Union. He was acting, said the reply, out of sour grapes at his own lack of success. 'What remedy does our critic suggest as a cure for this dullness which jars his aesthetic sensibilities so acutely? Perhaps he himself will appear one evening to speak on the paper in the garb of a Bashi Bazouk, or in the disguise of the wild man of the woods.'

Throughout the century, undergraduates have had a clear vision of what the Union ought to be. They have expected oratory of sparkling brilliance, spellbinding logic, stirring appeals to the emotions, devastating denunciations, masterly interventions, above all superlative wit. Against this ideal the real Union is often a disappointment. Young people under twenty-one could never be expected to sound like crosses between Demosthenes and Oscar Wilde all the time. Occasionally, though, the real Union does provide a glimpse of the ideal. There may have been more glimpses than usual in the years 1912 to 1914.

With the trenches only just over the horizon, a piece called 'In the Shadow of Big Ben', ostensibly the London column in *Isis*, written in June 1914, reads ironically, 'We are soon to see them here,' it says, 'every one doing their shopping at the outfitters preparatory to nailing down the Empire in some distant parts, or finding a place on some office stool in a Government department or business house.' Others, like Harold Macmillan, who had just been elected Librarian of the Union by a margin of two votes, still had a year or two to go at Oxford.

Instead, they all went off to war.

CHAPTER THREE

HEARTIES AND AESTHETES

1918–1931

The years immediately after the First World War were untypical of what was to follow. Briefly, the University filled with men slightly older and vastly more mature than the normal run of undergraduates. The first President after the war, typical of this generation, was Leslie Hore-Belisha, afterwards a Cabinet Minister and begetter of the eponymous beacons. In 1919 he was a veteran of the campaign in Salonika. He had been up at Oxford before the war and served on the Union's Library Committee. Now, according to *Isis*, he brought to the Society an air of courtly solemnity.

As befitted their maturity, the first post-war undergraduates were rather more serious than those who followed and who were too young to have fought in the war. They debated worthy subjects like post-war reconstruction, attitudes to India, Turkey and Russia, and the industrial problems of the day. They were greatly preoccupied with making the land one fit for heroes like themselves to live in; the urgent priority being to develop the new League of Nations and thus ensure that the war which they had fought really would not be repeated.

'Pre-war Oxford realized its culture,' claimed an *Isis* leader in 1921, 'but post-war Oxford its purpose – its purpose to follow the path of practical Idealism which would render war impossible – its purpose to wipe out for all time the traditional prejudices which continue to canker the life of the University and the nation.'

In 1921 eighty young men representing thirty-four different nations met in the Union Debating Hall to reproduce the Assembly of the League of Nations. Among those who took part was Anthony Eden, the future Prime Minister, who never took an interest in debates in the Union itself. Another future Prime Minister attended, S. W. R. D. Bandaranaike from Ceylon, unlike Eden an active member of the Oxford Union. Gerald Gardiner, the future Labour Lord Chancellor, also combined speaking in the International Assembly with speaking in the Union.

The Assembly was chaired by Professor Gilbert Murray who, according to *British Weekly*, inspired the delegates to discard their set speeches and enshrine 'in broken English, but with heart-fervour, their longings to see a fair world rise from the dust and ashes of war.'

Bandaranaike, who represented India in the Assembly, at one time had rooms in Christ Church next to Anthony Eden. Eden would drop in on him to pay diplomatic visits to discuss the affairs of the Assembly. Bandaranaike afterwards exempted Eden from the mental insularity and racial arrogance which he believed were the common characteristics of the Englishmen he met. 'He possessed a tact and a charm of manner that always struck me as very un-English.' With so many other English undergraduates 'one was always being shown, politely but unmistakably, that one simply was not wanted.'

Later, when the earnestness of the immediate post-war years gave way to the frivolous twenties in Oxford, the League remained the main talking point among politically minded undergraduates. It was at the League of Nations Union that the fictional Paul Pennyfeather of Evelyn Waugh's novel *Decline and Fall* listened to a paper about plebiscites in Poland, while the young bloods of the Bollinger Club were drinking themselves into the right mood for debagging him.

Alongside the serious-minded idealists, a sybaritic generation was developing which was to dominate the image of the University during the decade. The undergraduates were every bit as affluent as their pre-war predecessors had been, and even more disposed towards enjoying themselves. Descriptions of breakfasts, that most accurate gastronomic indicator to the state of the University, rival the most sumptuous pre-war recollections. Even Bandaranaike would expect his scout to wake him with porridge, followed by fish, an omelette, liver and bacon or devilled kidneys, then toast with Oxford marmalade and coffee.

For those who wished to avoid them, the pressures of life could be almost non-existent. The novelist Henry Green, for instance, would start the day at eleven in the morning with an orange juice and a glass of brandy; then he would shave, bath and dress for lunch, which would normally consist of steak and a bottle of claret at the Carlton Club. In the afternoon, he would go to the cinema. Between five and six, he would play billiards with the professional at the University billiards club. He would spend the evening dining and drinking.

'*Nur eine Luststadt*' commented the forbidding German Classical scholar Ulrich von Wilamowitz-Moellendorff at the time; Oxford is a mere pleasure resort. Many socialists took the same view. For a critic of the system like Goronwy Rees, who was up at New College in the late twenties, the decade was the last time the English ruling classes and their children could exploit their privileges and their prosperity wholeheartedly. They made the most of it.

The undergraduate world divided itself into hearties and aesthetes. The hearties spent their time playing games and drinking. They wore sports coats, college pullovers, college ties and grey flannels. Although their contacts with girls were rather limited, they were theoretically heterosexual. The aesthetes affected homosexuality for the most part, declaimed poems through megaphones and lavished infinite care on the decoration of their rooms. They wore silk ties, and the more outrageous went in for strawberry pink trousers. Aesthetes were always in danger of being assaulted by the hearties. Sir John Betjeman tells the story of a Balliol aesthete called Michael Dugdale who used to walk into the hearty-dominated Brasenose College with a stick and limping, in the hope that the hearties would be too sporting to attack him.

The aesthetes frequented a society known as the Hypocrites Club in rooms above a bicycle shop. Its ambiance was dissolute, aristocratic and, in part at least, flagrantly homosexual. The man whose personality penetrated the Turkish cigarette fumes in the club most notably was Sir Harold Acton, who at the time was trying to bring a kind of Gothic revival to Oxford, to which end he wore a grey bowler hat, black silk stocks, a Benedictine coloured waistcoat and sidewhiskers.

Evelyn Waugh, briefly the club's secretary, found there the models for some of the characters in his books. 'The Hypocrites,' he wrote once, 'like Gatsby's swimming pool, saw the passage, as members or guests, of the best and the worst of the year 1923. It was the stamping ground of half my life and the source of friendships still warm today.'

By comparison with the Hypocrites Club, the political clubs and the Oxford Union must have seemed far less exotic. They still, however, had their adherents. The largest political grouping at Oxford for most of the twenties was the Liberal Club. Liberalism has usually been stronger at Oxford than in the country as a whole, at least since the demise of the last Liberal Government; Oxford Liberals have grown used to the taunt of their opponents that they are sustaining the University's reputation as the home of lost causes. Throughout the splits and disappointments of the 1920s, a large proportion of undergraduates remained loyal to the party. In 1924, after the Liberals had lost a hundred seats in the General Election including Asquith's own, their supporters in the Union were largely responsible for defeating a motion approving of the election result. The Liberal Club doubled its membership and had to look for larger premises on which to hold its meetings.

Union speeches of the time give the impression that most members took themselves much more seriously than the political issues which they were debating. Not for the first time, the acquisition of office in the Union became a burning ambition for its most active members. Elections, though always interesting, became an obsession which has often since then distorted the Union's proper function and made it an object of ridicule and derision for non-members. Endless intriguing and gossiping about personalities and their position on the slippery pole is endemic to politics. When, however, it becomes an exclusive concern and all-consuming object of interest, it betrays a depressing narrowness of mind and lack of imagination which can only stunt the development of the budding politicians at the Union.

Writing of a slightly later period, the novelist Angus Wilson says, 'I was not an ambitious young man, using the university and its contacts for worldly advancement. When I meet such young men occasionally – presidents or secretaries of this or that – I am repelled and saddened, for they seem to be wasting their youth in exploiting it for their adult years.' He has a point.

More sensitive souls in the Society know that, for all the Union's glamour, it can at times appear rather unattractive. In 1924 there was a debate on the motion 'that this House deserves its doubtful reputation'. One undergraduate claimed that members came to debates not for profitable discussion, but guided by ambition. Another produced the definition that the Union was a school of oratory where everyone agreed to be bored provided that they might have a chance of boring other people in their turn. The motion, which was not take entirely seriously, was defeated by fourteen votes.

Some people maintain there is nothing wrong with healthy ambition in a bright young man. Certainly, the dedication which many have shown to the pursuit of success in the Union is remarkable. Beverley Nichols, who became President in 1920, is a good example. He was an aesthete before the aesthetic movement in Oxford really got going, an accomplished musician who published his first novel while he was at Oxford and also edited *Isis*. In politics, he was a Liberal and a pacifist, but he saw himself primarily as an orator. For his first paper speech in the Union he learnt three versions all by heart, so that he could adapt to the mood of the House and use the most suitable one. He would take them with him on walks along the towpath of the Oxford Canal. One day, he was so absorbed in practising his speech that he strayed off the towpath and fell in.

A similar fate nearly befell S. W. R. D. Bandaranaike. The son of a wealthy Christian in Ceylon, he was put down for Christ Church ten years before he went up. Long before he actually set sail for England, he conceived the ambition of becoming President of the Oxford Union. He used to compose perorations for Union speeches while out riding. 'In the moment of inspiration,' he writes, 'I dropped the reins to gesticulate, and as a result very nearly dropped off my seat. Many years after, I used this same peroration in one of my best Union speeches, and, as a storm of applause greeted me, could scarcely refrain from bursting into laughter at the comic recollection of my ride.'

Bandaranaike needed to be more ambitious than most, to fight the undoubted colour prejudice he encountered. His tenacity, as he himself claimed, was due to his conceit. Not content to believe he was the equal of the English undergraduates, he set about proving that he was their superior.

For him, the Union was not just a place in which to enjoy oneself. He claimed that it profoundly influence his entire career and outlook. Certainly he went up as the loyal son of a father who believed strongly in the Empire, but came down a convinced nationalist.

India was frequently on the Union's order papers throughout the interwar years. Bandaranaike supported a motion saying that the present unrest in India was due to the Government's policies, which was lost narrowly. Later the same year, his speech helped to carry the motion that the indefinite continuance of British sovereignty in India was a violation of British political ideals.

He was eloquent about the racial issue too. The *Morning Post* called him 'rare and persuasive' when he successfully opposed 'that the maintenance of colour barriers is consistent with the progress of civilization'. Bandaranaike became the third Asian in the Society's history to be elected to office. He served first as Secretary, then as Treasurer, though he was defeated for the Presidency. There has been some suggestion that life members who were no longer undergraduates came down to vote against him to stop an Asian becoming President. However, the poll was lower that term than it was in either the preceding or the succeeding one, so the allegation seems unlikely to be true.

When Bandaranaike was Treasurer, the President was the future Lord Chancellor Gerald Gardiner. At the time he was rather hostile to the Labour Party which he was later to serve in such a distinguished capacity. Instead, he supported the National Government, although his real desire as an undergraduate was for a centre party. 'The present unemployment,' he said in 1921, 'is largely due to the insidious propaganda of the Labour Party and the present high wages.' The case for a centre party, he claimed in 1923, was that many important and urgent questions, such as birth control and divorce reform, had never seriously been taken up because no party had included them in their programme.

Gerald Gardiner also took part in a debate on a subject which came up regularly during the twenties, Britain's attitude towards Russia. He spoke in favour of trade with the infant Soviet Union. It might help Lenin, he conceded, but what really mattered was that it would be the salvation of the Russian people.

As President, Gerald Gardiner eschewed hackneyed political motions for more exotic subjects. 'This House attributes to supernatural causes what are commonly known as psychic phenomena,' was one of his efforts. Interest and involvement in politics was not particularly strong at the time, and several Presidents attempted to attract undergraduates to the Union by going for fresh themes. 'Shakespeare did not intend Hamlet to be mad' was another proposition which they debated around the same time. Such topics introduced the Union members to the talents of people outside their regular circle. Even Harold Acton spoke in a debate once.

Perhaps the name from this period which will be remembered longest is that of the candidate who came sixth and last when Bandaranaike was elected Secretary of the Union. Evelyn Waugh failed to attract votes, but he often spoke in the Union, and wrote about it for both *Isis* and *Cherwell* as debate critic.

Bandaranaike recalls Waugh as an undersized, red-faced, rather irresponsible youth, while another and more flattering description comes from his friend Harold Acton. 'Short, slim, alert with wavy hair and wide-apart eyes that often sparkled with mischief, he seemed a faun, alternately wild and shy.' Harman Grisewood, later of the BBC, knew him too. 'Very pink in the cheeks,' he called him, 'small, witty and fierce, quite alarming.'

The shy streak in Waugh's character seemed to predominate when he attempted to speak in the Union. He had been President of the school debating society at Lancing, but like many others he found speaking at Oxford a far more daunting experience. At first, he felt that his chances of making a success of it were reasonable. 'I spoke at the Union, not over well, the other week,' he wrote to his friend Dudley Carew. 'Still, it seems to have made a fairly good impression.' The debate in question seems to have been about private enterprise in industry. According to *Isis*, Evelyn Waugh went back as far as he could and referred to several episodes in Greek history, all of which signified that socialism was undesirable. 'They made me tell at the last debate,' the letter continues. 'A job which necessitates sitting until half past eleven in tails, a white waistcoat and a draught, to be followed by second-rate port, whiskey and sandwiches with the officers. The other teller was an Earl of Something. He seemed quite a pleasant soul – self-assured but one can't help that with a coronet.'

Somehow, triumph eluded Waugh. When he spoke on the subject of the League of Nations, *Isis* commented that he was not conscious of the presence of his audience, so that his argument lost much of its effectiveness. He described that debate in another letter, admitting that he had been a flop. 'I just can't go down in that House. I get very nervous.'

All the same he was asked to speak on the paper in a debate on the attitude towards the Central Powers who had fought against Britain in the First World War. The question, he claimed, could only be settled by the man in the street, and he represented the man in the street. In fact, he was the only man in the street present. He had a better write-up this time. *Isis* said, 'Mr Waugh was both amusing and attractive, and will do better upon a subject which provides more scope.'

The *Oxford Magazine* was encouraging too. 'Mr Evelyn Waugh is a distinctly promising speaker. He frankly based his case on sentiment, and in an exceedingly agreeable way he unfolded a strong doctrine of patriotic hate.' Other speeches of this period, however, tend to be damned with faint praise. 'Commendably brief,' a critic wrote of one. Of another, Gerald Gardiner wrote, 'Mr Waugh was sorry that all the speeches had so far been so bad. His was no better.'

Waugh really found his *métier*, however, when he became Union correspondent for both *Isis* and *Cherwell*. The union reporters for these undergraduate journals do not always aspire to the highest standards of accuracy and objectivity. Not infrequently, they are active members of the Union who seek in their columns to do down their opponents and boost their friends, even sometimes to boost themselves. An important object of the column is to entertain its readers, and in this Waugh was outstandingly successful.

Instead of praising his own speeches, Waugh took the much better course of either ignoring them or knocking them as hard as he could. After he had spoken in the debate about Hamlet being mad, he wrote, 'Mr Evelyn Waugh attempted to justify prejudice with pedantry.' On his contribution to a debate about the public school system, he commented, 'Mr Evelyn Waugh was guilty of a breach of good manners for which he is sorry.'

Usually, Waugh was scathing about the quality of debates and participants alike. The fate of the Liberal Party, he wrote in *Isis*, had been overdebated. 'The chief arguments upon each side could without much dexterity be written upon a postcard, and when that was done there would be little material for elaboration or wit.'

Kenneth Lindsay, the first Labour President of the Union and at the time Labour candidate for Oxford, comes in for more of the Waugh treatment. 'The thing I most disliked about his speech was the continual lapsing into vote-catching almost as obvious as music-hall parody. What I stand for is better homes and happier homes, and better beer and beer of better quality, and wholesome, decent, English homely beer. They are not actually his words, but they are the sort of thing he said.'

Compared with other victims, Gerald Gardiner is let off quite lightly. On a debate on foreign policy, Waugh writes, 'He had the real Union manner and can honestly be said to have come off best from the debate. He told two stories, one of which was fairly new and the other fairly funny. He was competent, but uninspired.'

Waugh's friends liked to think of themselves as heavy drinkers. He himself wrote to Tom Driberg in 1922, 'Do let me seriously advise you to take to drink. There is nothing like the aesthetic pleasure of being drunk.' One night in the Union his friend John Sutro made a speech in a state of considerable inebriation. He became so incoherent that the President sent him a note suggesting that he should sit down. Later, when another speaker made a reference to him, Sutro applauded loudly, then staggered out to collapse in the garden. Waugh recorded the whole episode in his column in *Cherwell*. It emerged, however, that Sutro's parents were regular subscribers to the journal, and a special copy had to be printed for them with Waugh's description of their son's performance judiciously cut out.

Jokes and epigrams were at a particular premium in the Union at this time. The most effective way to quash an opponent was to make a joke at his expense. Lord Haddo, a member who was very talkative, complained once that there were no sponges for moistening stamps in the Writing Room. The Secretary replied that it was the first time he had ever known the honourable member unwilling to use his tongue.

In the age of the hearties and the aesthetes, great attention was paid to dress in the Union. Bandaranaike recalls Lord Robert Cecil coming to speak without sock suspenders. 'I defy any man to be eloquent with his socks hanging down,' he writes.

During the twenties, the Society still stuck to the pre-war habit of only inviting two or three guest speakers each term. Most of the debates were occasions for undergraduates to attempt to dazzle each other with their brilliance without outside interference. Debates with visiting speakers were still treated as special occasions. The poet W. B. Yeats was invited to speak on Ireland in 1921, at the height of the conflict between the IRA and the Black and Tans. Yeats is reported to have made a moving speech about the horrible tragedies which had taken place in his native County Galway. The cause, he said, was lack of discipline amongst the Black and Tans. He went on to prophesy the downfall and disgrace of the British Empire. He was not a Sinn Feiner himself, he said, but he believed the time would come when

Ireland would emerge finally triumphant and ennobled by the struggle.

The next month, Asquith was the guest. The motion was that 'the Government has failed to secure a peace worthy of the sacrifices or adequate to the purposes of the war.' The former Prime Minister spoke strongly against demands for reparations from Germany. 'It should be borne in mind,' he said, 'that excessive demands would inevitably defeat their own purposes. Our statesmen, instead of cherishing punitive schemes, should have encouraged the restarting of productive industries.'

Ramsay Macdonald visited the Union the same year, for the motion 'the Labour Party is capable of forming an effective Government', which was carried by 251 votes to 194. 'In stentorian tones,' said *Isis*, 'he assured us that a Labour Party Government would bring about the millennium.'

Macdonald was often in Oxford at this time because his son Malcolm was an undergraduate. Malcolm proved a faithful champion of his father's policies in the Union, as well as in later life. He complained that Oxford was still largely the resort only of the sons of the rich 'who did not have the opportunities to meet men and women of different social status.' There must be complete intermingling of all classes, he suggested. Greater economy should be practised in order to enable the poor man to participate in University life equally with the rich.

Lloyd George came back to the Union in 1923, ten years after his previous visit. He was not Chancellor of the Exchequer or Prime Minister any more, but he still cast the same spell over the Union's members. A thousand undergraduates in the debating hall watched him do battle with a leading Asquithian Liberal, W. M. R. Pringle, over the Treaty of Versailles.

Bandaranaike was there. 'He started quietly with an almost unnatural calm. Gradually the tempo quickened. He defended his actions with a growing passion; with a toss of his leonine locks he turned to the unfortunate Mr Pringle, and pointing a shaking finger at him, poured on him a torrent of withering scorn. It was like a storm at sea; the dead calm amid the gathering cloud, the low, preliminary rumble and the rustle of the wind, and then the full blast of the storm. We were raised high on the crest of a wave, then dashed down into the trough of the sea. We were knocked sideways, rolled over and over, and whelmed in the boiling waters; till at last we emerged, battered, bruised and breathless, while poor

Mr Pringle sat on his bench, bedraggled and forlorn. The House voted for Mr Lloyd George by a large majority. His zest for life, his exuberant vitality, vividness, his entire lack of self-consciousness and unpatronizing cameraderie won the hearts of all of us.'

The notorious Horatio Bottomley, soon to be convicted of fraudulent conversion and expelled from the House of Commons, also came to the Union in Bandaranaike's time. 'In appearance,' he wrote, 'he was terribly disappointing, short, with almost the shortness of a dwarf, thick-set with a large head covered with straggly grey hair, set on square shoulders.' There were titters when Bottomley rose to speak. 'Gentlemen,' he began, 'I have not had your advantages. Such poor education as I have received has been acquired in the University of Life.'

Another visitor was the famous Dean Inge of St Paul's. He was pitted against the young Beverley Nichols in a debate on the motion 'that this House would welcome a return to Victorian ideals'. It is the sort of motion that the Union often sees as an excuse for a string of jokes and witticisms. In among the badinage, however, the debate reveals something of the flavour of the battle of the generations, which was perhaps more acute in the 1920s than at most times; fathers had been brought up during the height of the Victorian Age, while sons were turning against conventional morality, and even attending the Hypocrites Club.

The age of Victoria was a great age, the Dean told the Union. No nation had been less corrupted by a long period of unbroken prosperity, achieved by Victorian ideals, inspired by prudence, loyal family life, reverence for law and order and a steady patriotism. The romantic idea of love before and after marriage had inspired some of the world's greatest literature, and this was Victorian. There had lately grown up a vicious and untrue theory about personal love, the Dean warned the undergraduates; that it had no connection with the will, but that it was at the mercy of the passions.

Beverley Nichols spoke for the majority, who were against the Dean. The political grandeur and honour of the Victorians, he said, concealed superficially conditions in this country which were unbelievably terrible. The Victorians had built a prison and thus created a revolution. The whole legend of Victorian morality was composed to frighten an alarming generation by parents who could not understand them. Victorian ideals were rejected by 417 to 333.

Despite the large turnout for occasions like the Dean's visit, the

Union was not to everyone's taste at this time, any more than before or afterwards. An American undergraduate wrote in the *Daily Herald*, 'I came to this University expecting to find it the centre of all that was good and all that was noble in European culture, but I found a very different proposition. The famous Union Society is a haunt of political lobby lizards, who try to hide their lack of sincerity by decorative flippancy and dyspeptic sneers.'

The Union was in no mood to countenance such *lèse majesté* when the good and the great from its ranks gathered to celebrate its hundredth anniversary in 1924. First, there was a centenary debate. The debating hall, once again, was crowded. 'For sheer physical discomfort,' wrote Evelyn Waugh, 'I have never known such a successful debate.' The motion was 'that civilization has advanced since this House first met'. Professor Gilbert Murray and Philip Guedalla were in favour; John Buchan and Ronald Knox were against. Murray suggested that the large increase in the use of soap in the past hundred years proved his case; it was even, apparently, being used in the manufacture of beer. Guedalla pointed out that there was one thing with which Oxford had never been charged, and that was modesty; for this reason the motion was bound to be carried.

Buchan struck a rather more serious note. 'Youth should have an adventurous spirit,' he said, 'a wide world to travel in, and security of soul. These have gone; science lays bare the secret places of speculation, the world is almsot all mapped out, and where is the unconquerable dogmatism and assurance of the founders of the society? They have disappeared, and we are none the better for it.' Knox was his usual epigrammatic self. 'One hundred years ago,' he quipped, 'England was the nursery of art and now we have nothing left but the art of the nursery.'

The Centenary Dinner was an orgy of self-congratulation for the Union. 'Everyone felt that it was only some extraordinary accident that had prevented all of us becoming archbishops, premiers and Lord Chancellors,' wrote one person who was there. 'The only thing which tempered my belief that the presidency of the Oxford Union was the high road to success was the fact that none of these eminent gentlemen, except the bishops, had succeeded in holding his job.' Birkenhead made an inevitable appearance among the after-dinner speakers, along with Sir John Simon. He replied to the toast to the Law, one of a very long series of speeches which must have threatened to keep the diners there until breakfast time. 'The law is an arid science,' said the former Lord Chancellor. 'It is also a remunerative one. If you seek an example of its aridity you may look to me. If you prefer to be entertained by its remunerative aspect, consider Sir John Simon.'

Other former Presidents dwelt on their memories of the Union, and were extravagant in retrospect in the qualities which they ascribed to it. Lord Curzon, who had nearly become Prime Minister instead of Baldwin the year before, said he used to think that the Union was like the House of Lords, 'that Chamber in which I spend the evening of my days in the company of many other ex-Presidents. I do not know whether I ought to carry the resemblance as far as that, but, at any rate, it was infinitely superior in all respects to that temple of bourgeois mediocrity, the House of Commons.'

Asquith, standing up for the temple of bourgeois mediocrity, took it as read that the current generation of undergraduates in the Union would be running the country before long. 'Bring to the new problems, as you have brought in the past from this great University and its great training ground in the Union, the same spirit of hope, faith and trained intelligence, and I am perfectly certain the future of this country is assured.'

One lesson which the great training ground did not appear to have taught the Union's officers was how to treat the Press. The President refused to make any arrangements for the reporters who wanted to cover the eighteen speeches to attend the dinner. Most journalists, as a result, refused to report the occasion. The London District of the Institute of Journalists passed a resolution which 'cordially approved' of the action of the greater part of the Press in refusing to report the proceedings, 'the usual courtesies to the Press not having been extended'.

When the Union chose to be serious in the early 1920s, it usually debated foreign affairs. The question of disarmament was debated again and again; the King and Country motion of 1933 was only one of a long series of debates on the issue. In 1924 the Union carried a motion which said that disarmament was the best security for peace. The movers struck an idealistic note. The whole weight of the Empire, they argued, should be used to steer the world towards disarmament. It was a question not merely of reducing the materials of war but of abolishing the spirit in which war became not only possible, but inevitable. Lord Birkenhead's formidable presence on the other side, arguing that peace was not secured by disarming in the face of an aggressive enemy who desired Britain's destruction, was not enough to stop the motion being approved. At the same time, politically minded undergraduates were watching developments in Europe. In 1923, the Union carried overwhelmingly a motion which said that Mussolini's government was a menace to its well-being.

Debates about Britain's domestic problems were rather less popular. In 1921 the members expressed the view that unemployment was the unavoidable result of the Great War. In general, however, they favoured all-embracing motions expressing no confidence in the Government or applauding or condemning the achievements of the political parties. A few days after Ramsay Macdonald came to power for the first time, the Union voted in favour of the advent of a Labour Government by 248 votes to 161.

Passion did creep in to debates sometimes, but the mood was one which put style and eloquence first, until the General Strike of 1926 initiated a change in Union attitudes. Michael Stewart, later Foreign Secretary but an undergraduate at St John's College at the time, believes that the strike precipitated a change in Oxford politics. In his view, a great many young men who had previously taken the existing distribution of wealth for granted began during the Strike to think afresh and consider the conditions in which many of their fellow citizens had to live.

If the General Strike generated a new interest in politics, not all undergraduates drew the same conclusions about it. The members of the Labour Club threw themselves into activities on behalf of the strikers. They helped the local Council of Action to organize strike meetings. They also bicycled round the Oxfordshire villages distributing leaflets. One of the most active undergraduates was Hugh Gaitskell. Although he steered clear of the Union while he was at Oxford, he threw himself into the Labour Club's efforts in the General Strike.

A rumour spread that undergraduates would be called up to take part in strike breaking. The Labour Club held a protest meeting in Hannington Hall, now part of St Peter's College. A large number of opponents turned up to disrupt the meeting and in the brawl which followed John Parker, who ended his political career as Father of the House of Commons, had his glasses broken.

Although the University decided against conscripting undergraduates, the Vice-Chancellor and the Heads of Colleges did encourage them to volunteer. The theory was that they were standing by to help prevent the collapse of national life. They were not, however, to do this in any acrimonious party spirit, since the University should not and would not take sides. In practice, a wholesale exodus from Oxford took place as young men rushed to drive trains or move food at the docks. Final examinations were postponed as mortar boards were exchanged for peaked caps. For most of those taking part, it was an adventure which they enjoyed thoroughly. Those who sympathized with the strikers saw matters rather differently. Goronwy Rees remembers sports-jacketed undergraduates descending on South Wales to assist in 'breaking the threat to their way of life represented by miners who, up in the valleys, had emerged from their underground kingdom to claim a share of the wealth which had been so generously bestowed upon these oafish and arrogant youths.'

The Union itself staged two debates on the issue. In early May, it passed a resolution expressing a hope that negotiations between the Government and the TUC would be continued. Later the members decided by 214 votes to 141 that the Government had disastrously mishandled the coal situation.

The Union seems, nonetheless, to have been of only peripheral importance to the undergraduates who were most concerned by the issues raised by the strike. The same year, though, it made one of its comparatively rare incursions into relations between undergraduates and the university authorites. The names of two undergraduates involved in circulating communist propaganda had come to the attention of the Government. Lord Birkenhead, now Secretary of State for India, but as ever the member of the Government who took the most interest in Oxford University, asked the Vice-Chancellor Dr Wells to send them down. Dr Wells decided that he did not have the power to do this. Instead, he extracted a promise from them not to express their political opinions in public. At a special meeting, the Union passed a motion 'respectfully but firmly protesting', although subsequently a poll was demanded of life members who reversed the result.

In spite of signs of change at the Union, it still preserved many of its old traits. Lord Hailsham, a committed Conservative from the outset, remembers the Union being a little frivolous still in the late twenties. He considers that young people are bound to be frivolous, because they excel in form and lack in depth of experience of thinking. When in 1930, however, the *Daily Express* published articles by three former Union Presidents under the heading 'Has

Socialism failed?', the paper said 'we welcome their contribution as a wholesome sign that the youth of Great Britain have thrown off the malaise of the post-war period, and are facing their responsibilities with clear-eyed earnestness and vigour.' There was a feeling that the wildest excesses of the twenties had been left behind.

The pressure for more serious debates came from the socialists. Michael Stewart and John Parker of St John's together with Roger Wilson from Queen's mounted a campaign to make the Union tackle the main issues of the day. In 1929, they attempted to stop a debate about duelling in which Osbert Lancaster was taking part in favour of a motion about nationalizing the mines. When the Union did turn to a subject like unemployment, it was not to everybody's taste. After the debate on the issue in 1929, the *Isis* critic was moved to write, 'it is hard to imagine any less profitable way of spending an evening than listening to a set of callow and perspiring youths discussing so technical and difficult a subject.'

Many Union members seem to have felt that the problems of the British economy were altogether too humdrum a subject for them to bother with; they wanted to tackle the broad horizons, the world stage. Mussolini was duly condemned again in 1926. There was a new generation too to do battle on the disarmament issue. When in 1928 the Union passed by 157 to 78 votes a motion regretting that the Government had not pursued a more drastic policy of disarmament, there were two future Conservative Cabinet Ministers on the losing side. Quintin Hogg pointed out to Labour supporters on the other side that the Labour Government had begun the construction of cruisers. Now, he said, Britain's fighting forces had been cut down to rock-bottom. John Boyd-Carpenter claimed that Britain's security had already been endangered by too much disarmament. Again, the pacifist ideals of the proposers won the day.

Looking back, Lord Hailsham remembers a genuine wave of pacifist feeling at the time. It was based, in his view, on the belief which still exists to some extent that the First World War was caused by the armaments race, whereas he would claim that the armaments race was an effect of the factors which led up to the conflict.

When the Union debated abolishing military training in schools, they could, for once, talk with some first hand knowledge of the issue. Yet another future Tory Cabinet Minister was in the fray this time. Derek Walker-Smith was a Liberal as an undergraduate, a strong opponent of public schools, and particularly scathing about the Officers' Training Corps. It was a ridiculous and mischievous mockery, he told the House, to claim that they had any educational value. The Training Corps were one of the worst features of the public school system.

The Conservatives found themselves in a minority again in another debate about Russia. In 1927, the Union carried a motion which said that Europe was in greater danger from America than Russia. Quintin Hogg spoke on the losing side, provoking the *Isis* reviewer to comment that he was apt to show signs of rabies at the mention of the Soviet Union.

There were fears that the Union might provoke an even more rabid response when they carried a motion in favour of birth control as a national policy. This was the first time they had dared to be so frank about sexual issues. The main undergraduate speaker for the motion was the writer Edgar Lustgarten. Immorality, he said, was caused by economic circumstances, not birth control. His opponents were in favour of abstention, but that ignored the love and symbolic side of marriage. On the other side the future judge Lord Diplock argued that continence was not harmful. There was a danger that sexual indulgence might become purely hedonistic, an end in itself. That would destroy the beauty of marriage, whose dignity depended on its moral worth.

Lustgarten became President of the Union in 1930, defeating John Boyd-Carpenter. He was a clever phrase-maker, witty and forceful as a speaker without the passion for politics which afflicted many of his contemporaries. For most of his generation at the Union, the Society was a stepping stone towards the House of Commons. Dingle Foot was the first there in 1931, joining his father on the Liberal benches. He only switched to Labour after the Second World War. Quintin Hogg was elected in 1938. Then, in 1945, a whole cluster of new MPs emerged from the Union stable, including Michael Stewart and J. P. W. Mallalieu on the Labour benches and John Boyd-Carpenter and Derek Walker-Smith on the Conservative side. Roger Wilson, like many other leading members of the Labour Club, ended up in academic life.

Many battles joined in the Union at this time continued in the House of Commons and are still being fought today in the House of Lords. Over the years, the antagonists have built up a certain respect for one another. Michael Stewart finds he can admire John Boyd-Carpenter's unshakeable commitment to Toryism and his capacity for hard work. He says he has great qualities of humanity, though somewhat disguised by his rather light-hearted manner. John Boyd-Carpenter in turn pays tribute to Michael Stewart's precise and accurate approach.

Fifty-five years is a long time in which to sustain a friendship, longer still to sustain political rivalry. Critics of the system might suggest that it is altogether too cosy, evidence of a ruling establishment which is drawn from far too narrow a base. In defence, it could be argued that there is nothing wrong with a bit of mutual respect across the party divide. In any case, the Union is not an automatic passport to success. Michael Stewart argues that people who are successful at the Union do not necessarily go on to success in politics because of their Union triumphs; it is simply, he believes, that people who have above average gifts and a keen interest in politics are likely to do well both in the Union and afterwards.

In the 1920s, mutual exchanges of compliments were not much in evidence. Instead, the leading lights of the Union seem to have worked long and hard at devising original ways to be rude about one another. If you could not get your jibe in during the debates, there were always the Union columns of the undergraduate journals, which were nearly always written by Union performers themselves.

Quintin Hogg was twice defeated for the Presidency before he was elected in 1929. He is generally acknowledged to have been a very able, if arrogant, speaker. When he spoke on free trade in 1928, the *Isis* critic wrote that he seemed 'a little more contemptuous of other people even than usual, and, as usual, far more than was justifiable'. Hogg's father was ennobled to become Lord Chancellor in March 1928. The undergraduate Quintin Hogg had mixed feelings about the event, since inheriting the title would debar him from the House of Commons. Nevertheless, he could speak in Union debates with the authority of one who moved in Government circles. 'Mr Hogg,' said the critic describing another debate in 1928, 'had been told a lot of things in confidence by some Great Statesman, and it wasn't really fair to let the little boys play with such a big fellow.' Sometimes the comments on Hogg's speeches seem inspired by more than a smattering of jealousy, a vice to which Oxford Union politicians are even more prone than more mature ones. 'The superior way in which he regards his opponents, and his conviction of the infallibility of the Hon Q. McGarel Hogg makes me long for the day when he will be effectively squashed in debate.' It was not long before someone was describing the future Lord Chancellor as 'Quintin McGarel God'.

Looking back now, Lord Hailsham remembers the Union as a

place for rhetorical fireworks. He also believes it taught the art of debate and civilized debating manners, a role for which there ought to be room in any free society.

Michael Stewart was not a speaker in the traditionally flippant Union manner. In fact he expended a great deal of effort trying to make the Union less flippant. When he did try to make concessions to the prevailing style, it appears he was not wholly successful. 'I had heard all Mr Stewart's jokes before several times, so I liked him better (though not much even then) when he was serious,' ran one criticism. 'Mr Stewart made a speech which I am told he has made seventeen times already', said another critic. 'Mr R. M. M. Stewart has modelled his style on Mr R. M. M. Stewart and that is his chief disability' ran yet another put-down.

Nevertheless, the same R. M. M. Stewart was moving steadily up the Union ladder, partly, as he admits himself, because of the loyalty of members of St John's College to their fellow undergraduates. The Labour Club had helped to build up a St John's machine which turned a large proportion of the College out to vote in Union elections. All the same, by the summer of 1929, Michael Stewart was being described as the best debater in the Union. 'It is presumptuous, but if we must go seeking future Prime Ministers and so forth, I should tip Mr Stewart.'

Even Quintin Hogg saw Michael Stewart as leadership material, although he did not relish the sort of leadership which he imagined him giving. Once Hogg pointed to Stewart in the Union and said, 'The Ex-President from St John's would hang me on his lamp-posts.' Stewart replied, 'They won't be my lamp-posts; they will be the State's.'

John Boyd-Carpenter attracted his share of rude comments in the undergraduate journals too. 'Mr Boyd-Carpenter leant on the dispatch box in a Victorian photographic manner,' said *Isis* in 1928. 'He reads quite distinctly.' On another occasion, it reported, 'Mr Boyd-Carpenter made a speech marred by occasional excursions into prep-school jargon and a confident approval on the part of the author of the merits of his own sublime jokes.' By 1929, however, Boyd-Carpenter is called 'surprisingly good', and criticism of his speeches concentrates on the ideas expressed in them rather than on his oratorical talents. In the summer of 1929, he moved a motion which asserted that Conservatism alone had anything to offer young men. In his speech, he attacked Conservative Central Office for their preference for aged and infirm candidates. 'His Utopia,' said *Isis*, 'would seem to be a house of twenty-five-year-old last ditchers.'

Boyd-Carpenter was twice defeated for the Presidency. The first time, he went down to Edgar Lustgarten, the second time to the rugby international and future Labour Minister J. P. W. Mallalieu. On the third attempt, he defeated John Foot, later the only one of the Foot brothers to remain in the Liberal Party. Boyd-Carpenter was a Union speaker of the old style. During the term in which he was President, *Isis* claimed that here was Philip Guedalla living on in the spirit.

The Liberal Party had its champions in the Union during this period as well. Dingle and John Foot were the outstanding figures during the late twenties. Another brother, Hugh, was President of the Cambridge Union. When Dingle Foot became President of the Union, the magazine congratulated him on his sporting as well as his oratorical successes. 'His most glorious athletic triumphs,' it said of the future Labour Solicitor-General, 'have been gained in playing soccer for the Liberal Club against the Labour Club, where at centre-half he has been able to express in tangible form his contempt for socialism.'

Dingle Foot had a memorable brush with Lord Birkenhead when he was an undergraduate in the Union. In a speech which he was making, Foot related the story that when Sir John Simon and Birkenhead were undergraduates they decided that, as no political party was big enough to hold them both, they should toss up to determine who should join the Conservative Party and who should become a Liberal. 'The noble Lord lost', he added. 'This remark,' retorted Birkenhead, 'has all the characteristics of a Liberal joke. It isn't funny, it isn't true and it is calculated to give offence. I don't care a rap what the honourable gentleman thinks of me. But what will Sir John Simon say when he learns that his young follower believes that he subjected his political career to the vagrant eccentricities of a penny?'

When John Foot was President of the Union in 1931, he was involved in issuing a manifesto protesting against the weakness of Parliament and 'the inadequacy and ineffectiveness of our elders'. The manifesto called for the reorganization of Parliament and a policy of national reconstruction. It was signed by three other prominent Oxford liberals, Arthur Irvine, later a Labour MP, and David Renton and Derek Walker-Smith, both to become Conservative MPs.

Walker-Smith had a dislike of Conservatism at the time which rivalled his dislike of public schools. In a debate in 1930, he suggested that the Conservative Party was 'at one with all the harmlessness of the serpent and all the wisdom of the dove'. He did not always find favour when the debates in which he took part were written up. 'Mr Walker-Smith seemed sleepy and wore fawn shoes. He also had a healthy prejudice against sex and athletics,' ran the account of one of his speeches. Later, he was attacked for writing overfavourable accounts of his own Union contributions as the Union correspondent of *Cherwell*. Other references to him, however, place him in a more charitable light. He was elected Secretary, but failed to climb any higher up the Union hierarchy. This, according to *Isis*, was due to his politics rather than his abilities. 'But for political prejudices, Mr Walker-Smith should have attained a position more compatible with his undoubted talents.'

There were others who, despite their undoubted talents, never rose as far as Secretary. Angus Maude was defeated twice for the office; he also stood twice for Treasurer and was beaten, although he gained the last place on the Standing Committee one term before losing it again. 'Mr Angus Maude,' said *Isis* of a speech in 1930, 'endeavoured to achieve cold, clear logic. It may have been cold; it certainly was not clear.' Lord Maude is in good company in the *Isis Salon des Refusés*. 'Mr A. J. Ayer,' suggested the magazine describing a speech in 1930, 'must speak more slowly.' Later students of the philosopher may sympathize with the criticism. 'He did not improve his speech,' *Isis* said later the same year, 'nor I think impress those few members who remained, by making a prolonged gurgling noise which he announced to be a foreign tongue into which he had inadvertently dropped. Mr Ayer is a good enough speaker not to need to indulge in such intellectual snobbery.' On the same debate, the *Oxford Magazine* remarked, 'Mr A. J. Ayer certainly has the makings of a debater, but loses much in effect by a certain affectation both of manner and of matter.' So much for Oxford's leading philosopher.

Britain's future judiciary were not treated with total respect either. Sir W. J. K. Diplock, now Lord Diplock, was elected Secretary in 1929, but failed to rise higher. 'W. J. K. Diplock is my good friend and I hope to borrow money from him in the near future, so I shall make no attempt to report his speech,' sounds at best a double-edged compliment. Later, Diplock is considered to have 'an airy manner of youth and self-confidence', but 'he needs to speak up'. Another future judge, Peter Pain, who strictly belongs in the next chapter, is given shorter shrift, at least for his first efforts in the Union. 'Mr P. R. Pain' said *Isis* in 1932, 'should do something about (1) his pullover and (2) his trousers.' This somewhat inadequate comment on what was no doubt intended as a great display of oratory is followed up the following week. 'Mr P. R. Pain has still seen neither to (1) his pullover or (2) his trousers.'

Randolph Churchill was another aspirant to office in the Union who never achieved his ambition. When he went up to Oxford, he made it known that he intended to reach the Presidency faster than anybody had ever done before. His first paper speech was against the treaty giving Egypt full self-government. His mother Clementine Churchill was in the gallery. According to *Isis*, he seemed a shade disconcerted by the monster of publicity which he had summoned up; but he made an excellent and businesslike speech. The *Oxford Mail* praised his pleasant speaking manner. He was not, however, to find life easy in the Union. 'Young Mr Randolph Churchill,' wrote Robert Bernays in the *Daily News*, 'who made his debut at the Oxford Union this week, will not become President just because he is the son of Mr Winston Churchill.'

In the next debate in which he made a paper speech, Randolph Churchill made a bad mistake. He told members that he had studied the question of how to make the Society laugh. The debate was on India, and Randolph Churchill took his father's line. England, he said, had done an inestimable amount of good to India and little harm. He would be the last person to thwart the country of self-government when it was ripe for it. At the same time, a people who spent their spare time burning policemen in kerosene could not be considered fit for self-government. The Union had always taken a progressive line on India, and this kind of argument failed to go down well.

Randolph Churchill soon tired of the Union and of Oxford itself. He did not stay there long enough to take a degree. His presence as an undergraduate did, however, lead his father to take a special interest in Oxford. He came down to the Union twice within the space of three years, first in 1928 when he was Chancellor of the Exchequer and then two years later in 1930 when he was an opposition spokesman.

The 1928 debate was on a motion of no confidence in the

Government. The presence of the Chancellor on the opposition side ensured that it was defeated by 355 votes to 454. The opposition, as was the wont of even left-wing undergraduates at the time, had been somewhat deferential in the presence of so powerful an opponent. The *Oxford Magazine* even claimed that Churchill was a little disappointed by the moderation shown by the other side. 'Mr Churchill was, of course, excellent, but one felt he would have been even better if the attack on the Government had been a little more acrimonious.' *Isis* said that 'his manner was so charmingly genial, relieved by flashes of kindly humour, far remote from any suggestion of superiority.'

Lord Hailsham witnessed one of Churchill's performances at the Union, sitting as a member of the audience on the front bench. The speech, he said, was rapturously received. Afterwards, Churchill came and sat next to the young Quintin Hogg, not knowing who he was, and turned round to him and said, 'You know in this country we always pride ourselves on not being very emotional. But if you can speak in this country, you can do anything.'

When Churchill came back in 1930, he was out of power and the motion was 'that this House prefers the last Government to the present one'. Again, he carried the House with a substantial majority, after a speech which dwelt at length on the lessons of the General Strike as the main part of his case against Ramsay Macdonald's Government. It was a Government founded on socialism, he said, and socialism was a foreign doctrine, a doctrine of class war and class hatred and economically disastrous. However, he did not grudge the Labour Party the education they were receiving, and since they were His Majesty's Government, it was only honourable to take it for granted that they were doing their best for the country.

The famous Red Clydesider Jimmy Maxton of the Independent Labour Party came to the Union to represent the opposite end of the political spectrum. He confronted the Liberal leader Herbert Samuel over 'this House would welcome a Liberal Government'. 'To his opponents,' said the *Oxford Magazine*, 'Mr Maxton's tall, stooping figure and dark keen face seem almost sinister, but he has a soft Scots accent which makes him most attractive to listen to.'

Maxton defended the Labour Party against the charge that nationalization meant too much red tape. Because capitalist parties could not own public concerns without red tape and blunder, he said, there was no reason why public ownership should necessarily mean stupidity. As for Liberalism, that was merely a form of Conservatism; any steps forward in the past under Liberal governments had been due to working class pressure.

In the eyes of the Union, Samuel's speech did not match up to Maxton's 'Sir Herbert's speech was a model of clarity and competence,' said *Isis*, 'but had not the inspiration of some political leaders.' Samuel argued for gradualism. The face and soul of the country would be changed, he told the House, by facing problems one by one and dealing with evils piece by piece. Maxton carried the day, no doubt with Conservative support, by 184 votes to 118.

Later, J. H. Thomas came down to give the Union a taste of a socialism which was rather less red in tooth and claw than Maxton's in a debate about the Government's handling of unemployment. Thomas was Lord Privy Seal at the time, with special responsibility for unemployment, rising fast in 1930. Labour were in trouble with their own backbenchers, as well as with the opposition parties on the issue. Lord Boyd-Carpenter, who spoke in the debate as an undergraduate, remembers it well. 'Thomas got up to speak to the cheers which greet all distinguished visitors. he beamed. "'Ow different" (conscientiously dropping his aitches as he always did as part of his image) "'Ow different from the 'Ouse of Commons." After the debate at the President's supper, I somewhat unnecessarily asked him to have a drink. "I'll tell your father of you" (he was in fact a friend of my father's). "First you give me 'ell, then you give me a drink." It was all rather endearing.'

Most of the politicians who came were prepared to flatter the undergraduates by debating with them as if on equal terms, and understood too that the Union liked speeches sprinkled with at least a few jokes. Not so Sir John Reith, Director-General of the BBC, who came down to speak against a motion which regarded the BBC with distrust and its policy and practice with disapproval. This was clearly, in Reith's view, *lèse majesté* on an appalling scale. According to *Isis*, 'it seemed as though he were taking the matter far too much to heart. His manner is unfortunate, being somewhat like that of a schoolmaster whose temper is frayed.'

Despite these reservations about his speech, Reith did carry the House with him. He defended the BBC against the charges of being ignorant or partisan, saying it was giving democracy a chance which it had never had before. It had all the advantages and none of the disadvantages of a state-owned concern.

The autumn of 1931 was a watershed in the history of the

interwar period. The crisis over the gold standard, the collapse of the Labour Government and the formation of the National Government, and the rise in unemployment gave a new and sharper focus to Britain's domestic problems. A period of relative peace internationally was broken by the Japanese invasion of Manchuria, and soon Europe was to become preoccupied with the rise of the dictators. Undergraduates began to change too. They became more interested in politics and international affairs, less preoccupied with style and outward appearance. There was some leavening of Oxford's traditional public school intake with undergraduates from poorer homes. The left gained ground rapidly. The thirties proper had begun.

CHAPTER FOUR

THE RED THIRTIES

1931–1940

For Oxford, for the Oxford Union especially, the 1930s were the decade of the left. A large part of the University intelligentsia were swept up by a tide of socialist fervour. In part, the undergraduates were playing their normal role of being agin the government, whatever the government's political complexion. The 1931 election had given Macdonald's National Government a huge majority; they had 521 seats to Labour's 52 and the Liberals' 37. Labour had elected a new leader, George Lansbury, who took the party leftwards, and seemed an attractive figure to sympathetic undergraduates.

There were willing proselytes at Oxford for the left's big campaigns of the 1930s. With unemployment up to nearly three million by 1933, the National Unemployed Workers' Movement had many sympathizers for their hunger marches. The activities of Hitler and Mussolini, and later of Oswald Mosley at home, created an active anti-fascist movement in which undergraduates participated eagerly.

There were books to read too to stimulate socialist ardour. From John Strachey's *The Coming Struggle for Power* in 1932 to the flood of publications from the Left Book Club in the later thirties, there was no shortage of new left-wing titles for the college servants to dust on the bookshelves of progressive undergraduates. For the more literary-minded among them, there was the new committed poetry to read as well, from Auden, Macneice, Spender, Day Lewis and others smitten by a Marxist muse.

At Cambridge, the spies nurtured by the Apostles were already going forth and multiplying. At Oxford, Communists flourished too, but more openly. In December 1931 the October Club was founded, with the purpose of 'studying Communism'. By January 1933 it had three hundred members, and it picked up more during the year with its campaign against Officer Training Corps. The next year, 1934, the Communists of the October Club, after a bitter battle and with many cries of foul from the other side, achieved fusion with the Labour Club. In effect, the Labour Club was Communist-dominated for the rest of the decade.

The Oxford Communists admired Russia almost uncritically. Indeed, as the Union debates show, sympathy for the Soviet Union still extended beyond the Communist ranks. There were many undergraduate Communists in the cells in the University who were prepared at least in theory to take orders from Moscow.

These were more disciplined revolutionaries than their counterparts in the 1960s. The 1930s Communists did not go in to the same extent for shouting slogans or howling down visiting speakers of opposing views. Many were prepared to go to the Union to argue their case, although there were some who condemned it as bourgeois and boycotted it.

Although the Communists did not dominate the Union in quite the same way as they dominated the Labour Club, the Society did lean to the left all the same. Among the socialist officers of the decade were some who retained the views they formed then for the rest of their lives, but others who have modified their outlook, sometimes drastically. The Labour Club contributed to the Union such diverse names as Anthony Greenwood, David Lewis, Christopher Mayhew, Philip Toynbee, John Biggs-Davison, Leo Pliatzky, Nicholas Henderson, Roy Jenkins and Anthony Crosland.

The left did not have everything its own way. The Union had several Tory Presidents during the 1930s, among them Edward Heath and Hugh Fraser. The tradition remained that voting was on merit as a speaker, not on the candidate's politics, although politics inevitably played a part. The Liberals as usual remained stronger in the Union than they were in the country. The outstanding Liberal President of the period was Michael Foot. Another future Labour leader, Harold Wilson, was prominent in the Liberal Club without going to the Union at all.

As in the generation at Oxford before the First World War, some of the most dazzling performers were not to survive. On the socialist side, Bill Shebbeare would, by general consent, have found himself in the 1964-1970 Government, if not at its head, had he not been killed. Among the Conservatives Alan Fyfe, who also lost his life in the War, was tipped to go equally far.

There was no question that the times at Oxford were changing. The outward manifestation of the seriousness and commitment of the 1930s undergraduate was his dress. The dandyism of the 1920s had all but disappeared. 'Oxford is always at its best when dress concerns it least,' said an *Isis* leader in mid-decade. 'Look up and down any Oxford street. Rarely do you see a man who is trying to make himself ostentatious by his dress. All undergraduates dress in much the same way. Some are a little smarter than others; some are a little shabbier. That is all there is to it. Here and there a man appears in a green shirt and corduroy trousers: but his type is fast dying. Modern Oxford has no time to waste in dressing either conspicuously or fashionably.'

The gourmet breakfast was disappearing too, to be lamented at the time of Munich in the pages of *Isis* by the cricketer C. B. Fry. All the same, life was still far from being all austere even for the earnestly political undergraduates who were so much more numerous than usual. Oxford was no more immune than the rest of the nation's youth from the new pleasures on offer during the decade. Talking pictures and gramophones caught on amongst the dreaming spires as much as anywhere else. *Top Hat* at the Super Cinema in the first week of February 1936 drew much bigger crowds of undergraduates than the Union's counterattraction, a debate on the Hoare-Laval Pact.

Many of the themes which the Union took up during the 1930s were familiar; originality in choosing motions had never been a strong point of the average Union President. There was, nonetheless, a change in tone which gradually became more and more apparent. In the autumn term of 1931, the Union returned to the subject of the Soviet Union. The motion was 'whereas other countries have pasts, Russia is the only country in Europe with a future.' The proposer Anthony Greenwood was the son of Arthur Greenwood, who had been Minister of Health in Macdonald's 1929 government but had refused to go into the National Government. The son became known in Oxford as 'the young Adonis of the Labour Party.'

Anthony Greenwood was full of admiration for Russia. In the

big European ports, he claimed, the docks were at a standstill, while in Leningrad ships were always coming and going full of goods. The general economic improvement in Russia would succeed because of the spirit throughout the country. Social developments were going ahead ápace too. 'The Soviet system of creches,' he pronounced, 'is unparalleled anywhere else in the world. The godless country of Russia has done more than all the Christian countries in the world to put down prostitution.'

According to *Isis*, Greenwood's was a poor and wearisome speech in which statistics played a disproportionately large role. Nevertheless, he had plenty of support. O. C. Papineau, a former Treasurer, said he would rather live in Russia than in England, for liberty in the capitalist world was merely the liberty of the fortunate to take advantage of the unfortunate.

Among the opposers Angus Maude made a powerful speech, claiming that no country could exist, as Russia was attempting to do, without religion or emotionalism. How did the Communists reconcile the ultra-nationalism of the Five Year Plan with their cry of 'Workers of the World Unite', he wanted to know. 'If only Mr Maude could acquire a more stentorian tone,' said the *Oxford Magazine*, 'he would be a first class debater.' Maude was attacked by a later speaker on the other side of the House, Frank Hardie, who was soon to become President. There was a religion in Russia, he asserted, the religion of freeing one's fellow men from poverty. British anti-Russian propaganda was as virulent as Russia's anti-British propaganda. The motion was lost in the end, but only by the narrowest of margins.

The socialists went down to defeat again in May 1932 when the House decided that it thought the idea of a class war preposterous and, in the words of the motion, utterly declined to countenance it. Again, Anthony Greenwood was the champion of the left. He was not advocating class war, he told the Union; he was saying it was a reality. Again, Angus Maude had the task of rebutting him; class war was not logical, hardly decent and possibly not wholly moral in his view. This time, however, Angus Maude had a powerful ally against the socialists, a slight eighteen-year-old who was rapidly making his mark as the most promising speaker the Union had seen for a long time. His name was Michael Foot.

'Patriotism,' said Foot, 'is a much stronger feeling than class hatred. The Labour Party has always been a propaganda party, and its talk of class war is merely another addition to a long list of catchwords. The working class are better fed, better clothed and better housed than they have ever been before. The socialists, after their forty years in the wilderness, reached the land flowing with milk and honey. For two and a half years they blew their trumpets for the walls of Jericho to fall down. Then they turned round to rot in the wilderness. Are we really to sweep away with Marx law, religion, morality in the name of class hatred?' Mr Foot's peroration, said the *Oxford Magazine*, convinced us that we were not. 'Mr Winston Churchill has sometimes spoken rather like Mr Foot,' The Magazine added. *Isis*, on the other hand, felt that Mr Foot's strong feelings about the Labour Party had caused him to stray away from the point of the debate. 'Mr Foot was good, but expended his energy in attacking the Labour Party rather than in dealing with the class war.'

Entertaining though it is to find the future leader lambasting the Labour Party in such a trenchant manner, it would not be true to say that Michael Foot's views have had to undergo a complete metamorphosis since his Union days. Gladstone travelled far further over the political spectrum a hundred years before him. Foot's father was a radical Liberal, and Michael Foot, like his brothers, adopted his father's views when he began to take an interest in politics. While he was at Oxford he became friendly with several socialists, and made common cause with them over many issues. Among his friends were Anthony Greenwood and John Cripps, son of the future Chancellor of the Exchequer Sir Stafford Cripps, who soon was to play a large part in persuading Foot to join the Labour Party.

Michael Foot's *Isis Idol* profile said he described himself as an uncompromising radical. 'He hates the jingoism,' it went on, 'which he attributes to the Tories as much as he dislikes the attack on individual liberty which he believes to be inherent in socialism, but he never sneers at the views of his opponents. That is why his friends come from all parties. The three main tenets of his faith are a genuine pacifism and conscientious objection to the use of arms, a hatred of poverty and inequality, and a passionate belief in liberty and democracy. He is, in fact, in the best tradition of radical beliefs, with a sympathy and a tolerance which make him loathe oppression, and which, if they were not confined to the Michael Foots of this world, would make it impossible. He is a great colleague. He will be a great leader.'

Sometimes Michael Foot's speeches in the Union presage the

sentiments which he expresses in the 1980s. In a debate demanding the immediate withdrawal of Great Britain from her European entanglements, *Isis* said that Michael Foot called on the Government to take risks for disarmament, risks for peace.

Another theme of Michael Foot's as leader was party unity. In the 1930s, his father was experiencing the traumas caused by the splits in the Liberal Party. When the National Government was formed in 1931, there were three Liberal factions. Lloyd George and the other members of his family in Parliament stayed out of the Government altogether, because they claimed that their Free Trade principles were incompatible with membership. Sir John Simon and a group of his supporters went into the Government willingly. The third group, under Herbert Samuel, gave the Government more conditional support. As a Samuelite, Isaac Foot became Parliamentary Secretary at the Department of Mines in 1931, but with Samuel he soon resigned over the Free Trade issue.

Michael Foot had a chance to echo his father's views in a debate at the end of 1931 on the motion that 'this House already buys all the British it can'. He spoke for the motion, saying that the Buy British campaign was hindering the cause of internationalism. *Isis* said that the boredom which had descended upon the House 'only lifted for a brief moment when Mr Michael Foot proved a flame of Lloyd George Liberalism when night had quenched any sign of fire the debate ever had.'

Another preoccupation of the father echoed by the son was India. Isaac Foot, extremely pro-Indian, had been a member of the round table conferences set up by William Wedgwood Benn, who was Secretary of State for India in Ramsay Macdonald's 1929 Government. These conferences had been boycotted at first by the Congress Party. Early in 1932, the Union debated whether it preferred the Indian to the American Congress. Michael Foot said that he sympathized with the aims of the Indian Congress, but he deplored its statesmanship and deplored its policy. The epitaph of the American Congress would be that written on the grave of any common criminal. That on the tomb of the Indian Congress would be 'But yet the pity of it, Iago! O Iago, the pity of it, Iago!'

There were some notable visitors to the Union around this time. At the end of 1931 Oswald Mosley, fresh from the humiliation of his New Party in the General Election, came down to speak in favour of 'the return of the National Government is not enough'. Mosley gave a strong hint that, having failed by the parliamentary route, he was considering extra-parliamentary ways of gaining power. 'That a modern movement must come to this country I am more certain than I have been in the whole of my political life. We have tried to start a modern movement, and it has suffered a heavy defeat at the recent election. Looked at through parliamentary spectacles it would appear to be a knock-out blow, but looked at through the spectacles of modern development it is passing through an inevitable phase of its progress.'

This visit took place before Mosley founded the British Union of Fascists. He had left the Labour Party earlier the same year and founded his own party because of Labour's refusal to accept his economic proposals; his plans embraced many of the ideas of the New Deal years before the New Deal was put into effect. Mosley was not yet a bogeyman to progressive opinion. He was certainly well received in the Union. 'Sir Oswald's speech was as interesting as it was informative,' said *Isis*, 'and the whole audience was grateful to him.'

In the autumn of the following year the hero of the left George Lansbury came down to do battle against the politician who was their chief villain at the time, Duff Cooper. Cooper was Financial Secretary at the War Office, and later to become First Lord of the Admiralty and to resign over Munich. His offence in the eyes of the left was that he had said in the House of Commons that he hoped the University authorities would know how to deal with the undergraduates who had walked with the hunger marchers. The Union was still on the whole polite and deferential to its guests at this time, but, by the standards of the day, Duff Cooper was given rather a rough ride. Anthony Greenwood challenged him over his remarks in the Commons. 'It was a vile thing,' Cooper replied, 'to encourage these poor people, under-fed, ill-clothed, to set out in bad weather, marching the roads to London, knowing perfectly well that they would get nothing when they got there. In a university with traditions, it was a suitable case for the authorities to interfere with the young fools who lost their heads and their sense of proportion.'

The left hissed. Irrespective of the rights and wrongs of supporting the hunger marchers, they did not like the idea that the university authorities should have the right to curtail their political activities. 'You can always tell when you tread on a snake,' retorted Duff Cooper, 'you can hear it hiss.' *Isis* considered that Duff Cooper had made the most brilliant Conservative speech that the

Union had heard for some time. They seem to have preferred Lansbury's all the same. He said he was glad that Christian charity existed among the undergraduates. It was capitalism that was at fault. 'If the present system can do nothing for its victims, then that is the greatest condemnation of the system that can be uttered.'

The *Oxford Magazine* praised Lansbury for his obvious sincerity, the force of his delivery and his delightful joviality. The motion was 'this House believes that in Socialism lies the only solution to the problems facing this country.' It was passed by 316 votes to 247, a sign of the rising strength of the left in the Union as well as of Lansbury's popularity.

The next term, the Union elected another socialist as President, Frank Hardie. In the Lansbury-Duff Cooper debate he had questioned the right of Oxford undergraduates to have £2000 spent on their education while others were pitch-forked onto the labour market at the age of fourteen. The other officers all leant to the left, although they were liberals, not socialists. David Graham was Librarian; Michael Foot was Treasurer; and the Secretary was an Indian, Dosoo Karaka. This team had to face the storm which broke over the best known episode in the Union's history, the King and Country debate of February 1933.

Pacifism and disarmament had been favourite themes for Union debates throughout the century. In 1914 the Society had passed a resolution condemning what they called 'the unnecessary and unnatural policy of the Triple Entente of Britain, France and Russia against Germany.' Motions about disarmament in the context of the League of Nations were common throughout the 1920s.

In the early 1930s, the peace and disarmament movement was gaining adherents throughout the country. The best-known of the anti-war, anti-heroic books about the Great War had recently been making their appearance, Remarque's *All Quiet on the Western Front*, Robert Graves' *Goodbye to All That* and Siegfried Sassoon's *Memoirs of an Infantry Officer* among them. The pacifist movement looked back to the First World War with a determination not to repeat the experience. Max Beloff, who acted as a teller in the King and Country debate, to his subsequent regret, believes that the mood had no relationship to events at the time. Hitler had only just come to power. What he would do remained uncertain and indeed unguessed at. The disarmament conference was still sitting. The extent of Germany's clandestine rearmament was unknown except to a few specialists. 'What we were really saying was that if we had been old enough to fight in 1914-1918, we would somehow have found a way to avoid that war.'

It was entirely natural therefore that the Union should decide to hold another in what was almost a routine series of pacifist motions in the Hilary Term of 1933. The difficulty for the President was in finding an original way of framing the motion and one which would ensure that there would be a good debate. The idea came up at the first meeting of Standing Committee of the term, when Hardie asked the members for suggestions for motions. It was the Librarian David Graham who suggested 'that this House will in no circumstances fight for its King and its Country'. 'This is a very good motion,' Hardie told him, 'but you can't really suppose you will get anyone to speak in favour of it.' Graham suggested that they could always whip up a few people from the Labour Club.

The sequence of events which followed has been exhaustively reconstructed by Dr Martin Ceadel of New College in an article for the *Historical Journal* in 1979. As he points out, Hardie did indeed have some trouble in finding a guest speaker to support the motion. There was nothing especially unusual in this; Union Presidents frequently have difficulty finding the right man for the right subject on the right day. None of the four people who refused did so because of insuperable objections to the motion. Sir Norman Angell, the anti-war propagandist, had a prior engagement; Beverley Nichols was off to Geneva; Bertrand Russell said he always refused speaking invitations outside London; John Strachey had colitis.

The fifth choice was C. E. M. Joad, now head of the philosophy department at Birkbeck College. After a spell in the ILP and a brief period as a member of Mosley's New Party, Joad was now a leading champion of absolute and unconditional pacifism. Hardie felt that the nature of the motion called for a speaker of substance against it. His choice was Quintin Hogg, now aged twenty-five, a Fellow of All Souls, and newly embarked on his career at the Bar.

The debate, said *Isis*, was the best attended of the term. Fifty-seven members had told the President that they wanted to speak, and 428 took part in the vote. This was a respectable turnout, but it did not come near the numbers present on the really big occasions when the House was packed out. The debate between Lansbury and Duff Cooper the previous year had, for instance, attracted 563 members, and this in turn was little more than half the turnout when Lloyd George had been attacked with mangel-wurzels in 1913. There were no demonstrations outside. In the debating hall itself, the *Isis* account gives no hint of either an especially great or an especially notorious occasion. 'Mr Joad and Mr Hogg delivered very fine speeches. None of the undergraduate paper speakers, on the other hand, were quite at their best as regards the substance of their speeches, but in some cases they counteracted their lack of material by a certain impassioned eloquence which at least commanded one's attention.'

The first speaker, Kenelm Digby, was a left-wing socialist from an aristocratic family reading PPE at St John's. 'It is no mere coincidence,' he said, 'that in the only country fighting for the cause of peace, Soviet Russia, is the country that has rid itself of the war-mongering clique. The justification urged for the last war,' he claimed, 'was that it was a war to end war. If that were untrue, it was a dastardly lie; if it were true, what justification is there for opposition to this motion tonight?' Digby, said *Isis*, had 'a tub-thumping style of oratory which would be more appreciated in Hyde Park than in the Union.'

He was followed by Keith Steel-Maitland, son of the Conservative MP Sir Arthur Steel-Maitland, speaking, according to *Isis*, with a vivacity which tended quite effectively to cloak the inadequacy of his arguments. Russia, he told Digby, had a million men in arms. The Labour Party's talk about a class war was hardly compatible with their desire for peace. As for himself, he was proud to defend the King. 'I profess a wish for peace not always popular in the party to which I belong, but I do resist the smug suggestion that all those who vote for this motion will not in any circumstances fight for their King and Country.'

The next speaker was David Graham, the Librarian who had suggested the motion. He was a Liberal, but his views were strongly influenced by his religious beliefs. Like many undergraduates at the time, he was a member of Frank Buchman's Oxford Group, the controversial evangelistic movement which later became Moral Rearmament. His speech was too coloured with Buchmanite phrases and ideas for the taste of most members. With Britain on the brink of war, he argued, it was necessary to pledge ourselves to peace. Life-changing on a large scale was the only hope for civilization.

Quintin Hogg claimed that the policy of the movers of the motion would cause, not prevent, war. The government of 1914 had been made to fight by popular feeling. That would not happen now, he admitted. But the time would come when people would wish to fight again. A moderate policy would prevent this. A powerful England was a factor for peace rather than war. A disarmed Britain would have no more influence for peace in Europe than she had in the Far East, where Japan had invaded Manchuria. Taking their argument that it is never right to fight for your country, Hogg asked his opponents, 'What would you do if you saw a man raping your wife? Would you interfere, or would you confine yourself to a polite invitation to desist?' *Isis* complained that Quintin Hogg's speech was too long, and as a result slightly ponderous. The magazine conceded, however, that he was the only speaker on his side of the House to put forward any really constructive plan.

There was no doubt that the second guest speaker, C. E. M. Joad, had the better of the argument as far as the members listening were concerned. In reply to Hogg's question about rape, he quoted Lytton Strachey's appearance before the military service tribunal which was vetting his application to become a conscientious objector. He too was asked what he would do if he saw a German raping his sister, and he replied in his famous falsetto voice 'I should try and come between them.' The story appealed to the Union audience, and Joad went on to deliver a *tour de force* of pacifist rhetoric. What the motion really meant, he said, was 'this House will never commit murder on a huge scale whenever the Government decided it should do so'. Directly they turn from the individual to the nation, men's minds are beglamoured and befogged in some strange way so that they cannot appreciate the real issues.

Joad went on to put an argument often echoed in today's debates about nuclear disarmament. His case was that, although in the past limited wars might have been justified, the scale of destruction which modern weapons could cause was so great that war had now become unthinkable. The sentiment was not entirely confined to the left. Baldwin had told the Commons the previous year 'the bomber will always get through'. Joad put it this way. 'During the last war we brought down 4.8% of the total number of enemy aeroplanes that crossed our frontiers. In the last raid, when the forms of defence were much more efficient, we brought down six out of twenty-two. Suppose in the next war the forms of defence are twice as efficient as they were after four years' practice at the end of the last one, and bring down twelve out of twenty-two, or rather 600 out of the 1200 which within twenty minutes of the declaration of war with a West European power would be across our frontier; what consolation is that if a single bomb can poison every living thing in an area of three-quarters of a mile?'

Joad ended by putting the case for Gandhian non-violent resistance. 'We fought a war to end war, with the result that we are now spending £116 million a year in preparation for the next war, £40 million more than we spent in any single year before we terminated war by ending it altogether. There may be something to be said for trying a new way. History proves that nothing good comes of the old way. The way I would suggest is the way of non-resistance. An invading army met with no resistance would appear ridiculous to the military mind. All orders given by the invaders would be systematically disobeyed, and although a few leaders would be shot, the casualties would be infinitesimal compared with those in a war.' *Isis* called Joad's contribution a witty and whimsical speech to which it was a pleasure to listen. It reads now as an interesting example of the case for pacifism in the 1930s, with its massive element of wishful thinking.

It is notable, in view of the uproar that followed, that there was little reference to Marxist or Communist ideas in the debate, with the exception perhaps of Kenelm Digby's contribution. The October Club in fact was holding a rival meeting the same night, addressed by Wal Hannington, the leader of the National Unemployed Workers' Movement. Doubtless few Communists forsook the chance to go and hear one of their heroes to attend a run of the mill Union debate instead.

At the end of the debate, the vote was 275 for the motion and 153 against, a comfortable majority which probably reflected to a large extent the impact of Joad's speech. Hardie told Graham as they left the debating hall, 'I hope this gets into the press.' He had no idea of the extent to which it was to do so.

At first, the response was not out of the ordinary. The *Oxford Mail* ran a leader about the debate the next day saying that the sensible position on the issue lay somewhere between the line taken by the proposers and that taken by the opposers. Apart from a straightforward short account of the debate in the *Morning Post*, that was the only Press reaction.

The next day, the Saturday, the controversy began to flare up. The *Daily Mail* had a leader about the debate, saying that the vote recorded the real or affected sentiments of a number of posturers and gesturers, not of the genuine Oxford undergraduate. The paper suggested that it was a mistake to take it too seriously, but the piece showed that the affair had been noticed in Fleet Street. The same day the *Daily Telegraph* published an anonymous letter which did much to fan the flames. The letter writer signed it 'Sixty-four'; he was later to be unmasked as a sixty-four-year-old leader writer on the *Daily Telegraph* itself called C. H. Firth. It was Firth who started the red scare about the Union. 'I fear it was not only a foul joke but a serious declaration of foul opinions,' he wrote. 'Older generations of Oxford men have heard with increasing dismay of the Red tendencies at work there, and of the gathering strength of Communist cells in the colleges.' Firth went on to suggest that action should be taken to reverse the vote. 'Decently minded young Oxford should demand the opportunity for another vote.'

On the Monday, the Beaverbrook press took up the theme of the red scare. The *Daily Express* ran a piece entitled 'The White Flag of Youth'. 'There is no question but that the woozy-minded Communists, the practical jokers, and the sexual indeterminates of Oxford have scored a great success. Even the plea of immaturity or the irresistible passion of the undergraduate for posing cannot excuse such a contemptible and indecent action as the passing of that resolution.' Just to ram the message home, the *Express* sent a special correspondent to Oxford to seek out the Mayor's views on the subject of the goings-on in St Michael's Street. As luck, or a fine piece of imaginative writing, would have it, the *Express*'s investigative reporter found Alderman and Mrs Brown 'sitting in front of a log fire reading their Bibles together in their little home. "I am speaking for the people of Oxford," he said, "when I say that it was a sad day on which those words were spoken and voted for in our university. I sincerely believe that if all the great men, the lovers of England, the great soldiers and fighters who have studied in past years in the University were alive to know what these young men are doing to the noble traditions which they passed down, then they would call these young men of today traitors. Even last November while I was marching to the war memorial a crowd of these young men walked alongside, waving red flags and shouting and displaying nothing but sheer hooliganism and irreverence. I saw then the beginning of Communism in Oxford!"' The *Evening Standard* joined in the hunt, with a column blaming the Union's conduct on a 'confederacy of internationalists'.

The Times the same day took roughly the line which the *Daily Mail* had followed the previous week. A leader with the headline 'The Children's Hour' suggested that there was no reason to regard the motion as a symptom of decadence. That was to misunderstand Oxford, the limited part which the Union played in its life, and the kind of paradoxical theses which 'it is the age-long habit of youth to propound in its debating societies'. The Union, *The Times* went on, was in no sense representative of the University; it had always been liable to fall into the hands of a little clique of cranks.

By this time, people were beginning to respond to Firth's appeal for an effort to reverse the King and Country resolution. Randolph Churchill drafted a circular letter to Life Members of the Society, announcing that he and a group of like-minded people intended to go to the Union on 2 March to move the adjournment and, if possible, to expunge the motion from the records of the House. 'The ephemeral undergraduates who permitted this disgraceful motion to be carried,' said the letter, 'constitute but a tithe of the Oxford Union: they are merely temporary trustees, and they have lamentably failed in their trusteeship.' The other signatories were, like Randolph Churchill, all young men in their twenties. They included Quintin Hogg, Edgar Lustgarten, Alan Lennox-Boyd and Lord Stanley of Alderley.

On the Wednesday, a box containing 275 white feathers arrived at the Union. A second box followed. Hardie announced at Thursday's debate that the feathers were available for all members who voted for the previous week's motion at the rate of two per member. 'It may be possible to increase the number in the next few days,' he added. At the opening of the debate on 16 February, twenty undergraduates rushed the Secretary's table and tore out the minutes from the previous week. Karaka, who was an accomplished boxer, offered no resistance. It emerged later that the twenty, including some professed members of Mosley's Fascists, had decided on the plan on the towpath of the river that afternoon. They tore the minutes into pieces which they displayed round the colleges before ceremonially burning them at the Martyrs' Memorial.

The press campaign continued. The *Daily Express* reported calls from Cambridge for the cancellation of the Boat Race, and quoted an official of the Cambridge Union saying 'the undergraduates who pass these resolutions are what we call the game gaffers – the men who play draughts and dominoes, who wear their hair long, and wool next the skin in warm weather.' Lady Houston, who had sent one of the consignments of white feathers to the Union, said for the benefit of the *Daily Sketch* that those who voted for the motion should be treated as untouchables. 'College education – pah! I would rather that my children were ignorant of all that Oxford could teach them if they had the spirit of patriotism, loyalty and self-respect, qualities that Oxford does not seem able to inculcate.'

The correspondence columns seethed with outrage at young Oxford. They had besmirched with a trial of somewhat nauseous slime ideas which we, and better men before and after us, had come to consider worth cherishing, according to a correspondent in the *Morning Post*, 'I doubt if 275 boys from the slums could be persuaded to assent to such a motion.'

Opinion was not, however, completely hostile. George Lansbury sent the Union a telegram expressing a thousand thanks and congratulations to young Oxford on their splendid lead for peace. The *New Statesman* claimed that the vote was genuinely symptomatic of a remarkable movement of the left now going on in Oxford. 'What these elderly Oxonians will not even begin to understand is that the younger generation really has pacifist and internationalist convictions.' The *News Chronicle* quoted A. D. Lindsay who suggested that the vote had been misunderstood. 'The feeling of those who voted for the motion was not that of disloyalty to King and Country, but one of protest against the prevalent idea that King and Country should be used as motives to make them fight.'

The Union's officers tried to put across the same case. Hardie wrote to the *Daily Telegraph* in reply to the letter from 'Sixty-four'. He pointed out that there was not intended to be a jibe at loyalty and patriotism in the motion, and that nobody had taken it this way during the debate itself. 'It is far from being an outrage upon the memory of those who gave their lives in the Great War,' Hardie went on, 'that we of a younger generation should seriously consider how best to prevent some future repetition of the loss of so many valuable lives.' Michael Foot told the Oxford Central Women's Liberal Guild, 'The reason for the Union passing the motion was because people are tired of the failure of statesmen to provide a solution for war and peace. I believe we accepted the motion because we would accept any new method to save us from the disaster of another Great War.'

It would have been wholly uncharacteristic of Oxford, even in its 1930s mood of comparative *gravitas* and in the middle of a great controversy, not to exploit the comic side of the events which were taking place. *Cherwell* frequently reported the activities of a fictional Viennese called Dr Curtius Bohl. Much to the delight of the undergraduates, the *Daily Telegraph* printed, as if genuine, a letter from Dr Bohl about the debate. 'Though a former enemy of your country,' the hoaxers made Dr Bohl say, 'I have always held strong admiration for the courage and spirit of the British lion, and I am confident that this spirit is not dead.' A fortnight after the King and Country debate Michael Foot parodied the *Daily Express* to a receptive House. The Union had passed a motion declaring that it had no faith in Liberalism. It had done so, Michael Foot suggested, because it was full of woozy-minded intellectuals, yellow cowards and sexual indeterminates.

Meanwhile, Randolph Churchill had enlisted his father in the campaign to have the motion formally expunged from the Minute Book. Winston Churchill brought his full powers of invective to bear against the perpetrators of the motion. 'That abject, squalid, shameless avowal was made last week in the debating society of our most famous university. We are told that we ought not to treat it seriously. I disagree. It is a very disquieting and disgusting symptom. My mind turns across the sea. I think of Germany with its splendid clear-eyed youth demanding to be conscripted into an army burning to suffer and die for their Fatherland. I think of France, anxious, peace-loving, pacifist to the core but armed to the teeth, determined to survive as a great nation in the world.' The sentiments seem to have gone down well with Churchill's audience at an anniversary meeting of the Anti-Socialist and Anti-Communist Union.

Within Oxford, however, the argument had moved on. As the date on which the expunging motion was due to be debated drew closer, the question became not so much whether the Union had been right or wrong in deciding that they would not fight for King and Country as whether life members of the Union had any right to try and undo a decision made in a debating society which belonged primarily, by tradition, to the current generation of undergraduates. Opposition to Randolph Churchill's efforts came not only from those who had supported the original motion but also from members of the Conservative Association, who resented outside interference. Another handicap for the expungers was the low standing of Randolph Churchill personally in the eyes of many undergraduates. *Cherwell* printed an open letter to him:

'For less than the customary period you were an insignificant undergraduate. You left Oxford to make an insignificant tour of the United States and returned to the insignificance of a young man of society, brightened only by infrequent mentions of your name in the gossip columns written by your friends. It is not surprising that, overwhelmed by your failure as a publicist, you should take the opportunity of self-advertisement that the pacifist motion of the Union has offered you.'

The expunging debate was far better attended than the original debate. Admission was by ticket only; a thousand tickets were distributed. The mood inclined heavily against Randolph Churchill and his allies. Several undergraduates donned false beards, to disguise themselves in satirical fashion as life members. Others wore white feathers in their buttonholes. Churchill himself had a police escort. The Vice-Chancellor had previously summoned Hardie to tell him that he had already done great harm to the good name of the University and that he had seriously considered banning the meeting.

In the event the House was unruly, but no violence broke out. Lord Stanley was the first speaker for the motion. The opposition soon cast him as a figure of fun, and as the interruptions flowed, his speech faltered and collapsed.

The next speaker, Frank Hardie, aimed to avoid being drawn into debating the original motion all over again, but instead to defend the Union's constitutional right to have held the debate, from which it followed that it was unconstitutional to expunge the original motion. He called the expunging motion childish and absurd. His intention was to provide motions which were as provocative as possible. The success of King and Country was shown by the fact that equal numbers had asked to speak for and against it. There had been no intention to cast any slur on the King, or on the dead of the First World War. As the President sat down, prolonged cheering made it clear that he and the other officers would not have to carry out their promise to resign if the vote went against them.

By contrast, there was a full minute of boos for Randolph Churchill. 'If you want to show any resentment against me or my friends,' he said, 'you can chuck me in the Cherwell afterwards.' Churchill could see which way the debate was going. 'You will be as much misunderstood this time as last time if you defeat the motion. We have tried to afford an opportunity for you to demonstrate that you were wrong.' Churchill survived barracking and a stink bomb, but his presence did not win him many converts. At the end of his speech he walked out of the debating hall, leaving it to his supporters to say that they wished to withdraw the motion. Hardie was prepared to allow this, but a member objected that he could only do so with the permission of the House. The House declined to allow the motion to be withdrawn. Hardie then put the question. Quintin Hogg, still a firm supporter of the expunging motion, protested that this was premature; there had been no floor debate. Someone shouted out, 'Isn't it said of an Englishman that he never knows when he is defeated?' Hardie overruled Hogg, and the motion went down to defeat by a huge majority, 138 votes to 750.

Randolph Churchill, as he had feared, was pursued after he left the Union's premises. General Sir John Hackett is one of those who can remember the chase. 'Although I was only visiting Oxford at the time,' he recalls, 'I willingly took part in the attempt to corner him and, if possible, remove his trousers as a mark of disrespect.' The attempt, however, failed, as Sir John relates. 'As far as I remember, he went to ground in a public lavatory, which is an odd place to keep your trousers on, but that's what helped him to do so.' One further indignity awaited Randolph Churchill, this time at the hands of the Oxford police who had gone to such lengths to protect him earlier in the evening. He was fined two pounds for obstruction because he had parked his car illegally.

The King and Country motion, which became known as the Oxford oath or the Oxford pledge, was taken up by other universities around the country. The London School of Economics, Manchester, South Wales, Birmingham, Aberystwyth and other student unions all voted for the resolution or others like it. The next year, a popular cleric called Canon Dick Sheppard founded the Peace Pledge Union; within a year eighty thousand people had pledged themselves on postcard not to fight in a war. At around the same time, the Leage of Nations Union organized what became known as the Peace Ballot. On a house to house canvass, they obtained over eleven and a half million replies. Over ten million people answered in favour of disarmament. The result, however, reflected the confusion in many peoples' minds at a time when there was considered to be no incompatibility between support for pacifism and disarmament on the one hand and the League of Nations and collective security on the other. A final question asked whether an aggressor should be stopped by economic measures and if necessary by war. To this, six and three quarter million said yes; over two million said no.

Another vote in the same year as the King and Country debate was taken as an expression of pacifism. This was at the East Fulham by-election, where Labour overturned a Conservative majority of 14,000 to win by 5,000. The voters may well have had domestic rather than defence issues uppermost in their minds when they voted, but the result was interpreted as a vote for disarmament.

Taken together, these indications of pacifist feeling undoubtedly had an impact on the British Government, and they may have influenced the dictators too. How far the Oxford Union resolution alone, however, had any direct influence is another matter. Winston Churchill claimed after the Second World War that 'as a result of this ever shameful motion, in Germany, in Russia, in Italy, in Japan, the idea of a decadent, degenerate Britain took deep root and swayed many calculations.' Churchill believed there was proof of Mussolini being so affected by it that he definitely came to the conclusion that Britain might be counted out. Certainly fascist propaganda in Italy did come to represent the vote as the unanimous opinion of British youth, and Mussolini appeared persuaded that this was so.

Others however doubt that the debate had much influence on the dictators. Lord Beloff believes the idea that it was an important factor to be in defiance of history. Lord Hailsham's retrospective view of the debate is that it was terribly boring and silly; that it was about pacifism at a time when it had the same disastrous role in British life that CND was likely to have now; that it reflected an entirely bogus sentimentality about a very important subject. Nonetheless, he concedes that the debate was very unlikely to have influenced Hitler's judgement at least. 'I think that his judgement was the worship of the Devil. And this was a talking point which the Devil used, but I don't think it altered the course of events in Germany.'

Martin Ceadel argues that Mussolini only came into the war after Britain's youth had proved that they *were* prepared to fight Hitler. In any case, he says, Mussolini cited all sorts of other unlikely reasons for Britain's decadence, including the use of birth control and the surplus of spinsters. Churchill, he points out, had something of a personal axe to grind about the issue after his son Randolph's humiliation in the expunging debate. The Nazis may have known about the King and Country decision, but they never used it in any of their propaganda. Ribbentrop was not yet Ambassador in London, and none of the Nazi newspapers reported the debate. All in all, the activity or inactivity of the British Government is far more likely to have influenced Hitler than a decision by a few hundred Oxford undergraduates six and a half years before the war.

Ceadel's view, that of most historians, is supported too by Sir Hugh Greene, who was the *Daily Telegraph*'s Berlin correspondent from 1934 to 1939. 'Obviously one did not have the opportunity of discussing the matter with Hitler personally,' he has written, 'but one did talk from time to time with high Nazi officials and members of the German armed forces. I am sure that the subject was never mentioned. Why should Hitler concern himself with Oxford undergraduates when he could base his thinking on the attitude of British Ministers?'

Most people who remember the debate or the controversy which followed it, irrespective of the side they upheld at the time, believe now that the importance of the affair was exaggerated beyond all proportion. Sir John Hackett says that he thought of it as another piece of by no means disagreeable silliness. 'When it was blown up into a matter of national interest, one really wondered whether the press had got their values right. What was surprising was that it impressed people as an indicator of the way opinion was going. One knew silly people who would speak and vote that way, like the folk whom one used to see propping up the Berkeley Buttery in the old days, young men with hair just a little longer than the drill sergeant major would like in amiable, casual, flippant conversation. One knew very well that these young men like the young men active in the Union at that time when things got rather different would be found being shot at with a lot of other people. And indeed they were.'

The term after the King and Country debate Anthony Greenwood became President, and the term after that the torch passed to Michael Foot. Foot won the election in his sixth term at the University, which is fast going. He followed his brothers Dingle and John to the Presidential chair at Oxford, while his brother Hugh had been President of the Cambridge Union. 'No election to the Presidency of the Union has been so popular as that of Michael Foot,' said *Isis*, 'but few people thought to congratulate him. His election was too obvious for that.' One contemporary remembers him as far more impressive as an undergraduate than as Leader of the Labour Party.

The term in which Michael Foot stood for President, he spoke against a motion 'that this house prefers fascism to socialism'. According to *Isis*, he trampled upon fascism and socialism in turn, choosing as his special victims Sir Oswald Mosley and Mr G. D. H. Cole. Neither fascists nor socialists, he said, regarded problems from an international point of view; failure to do so would inevitably lead to war. The rejection of the motion would be a victory for Liberalism. 'The Liberal Party in Oxford is safe whilst the Librarian is at the helm,' said *Isis*. The *Oxford Magazine* was not bowled over to quite the same extent. 'Mr Foot's speeches are always full of bright remarks which delight the House, but he would do well to pay a little more attention to the serious parts of his speeches. At present he seldom really deals with the subject.'

The next week Michael Foot spoke in a light-hearted debate in favour of the motion 'that this House flatly declines to view anything with concern, apprehension or alarm', and was hailed by *Isis* as the best all-round speaker in the Union. The only sign that anyone thought there were any limits at all to the heights to which Michael Foot might rise came in a mock description, written in the spring of 1933, of political events in 1973. Here Anthony Greenwood is cast as Prime Minister, while Michael Foot appears merely as Minister of Health.

The Presidential debate, in which Michael Foot and his rival David Graham spoke on the same side although in competition for the office of President, was appropriately enough on the motion that Toryism offers no solution to the nation's economic and social problems. Michael Foot attacked the Government for crippling consumers with a stultifying attack on wages. The motion was carried by 144 votes to 129, but the attention of the members was somewhat distracted from the debate by the presence in the hall of Professor Einstein, as a non-speaking guest. When the President Anthony Greenwood led Einstein into the hall, the entire House, according to the *Oxford Mail*, gave him an overwhelming ovation.

Michael Foot won the election easily, by 219 votes to 106. The themes which he chose for debates while President reflected an increased concern on the part of undergraduates about the activities of the dictators. His first motion, which was narrowly defeated, suggested that the revival of Liberalism offered the only safeguard against war and dictatorship in Europe. Later in the term, the Union debated 'that this House strongly disapproves of Hitler's action in withdrawing from the League of Nations and the Disarmament Conference'. This debate provides a snapshot of opinion at an early stage of Hitler's rule in Germany. The motion was actually defeated by three votes, 187 to 190, largely because there was still a strong feeling that Germany's justifiable grievances had caused the Great War, and that the way to prevent another war was to redress Germany's current grievances. At the same time, few people had much notion of Hitler's full potential for evil.

The proposer, Michael Addison from Balliol, clearly found it hard to take Hitler seriously. 'Hitler is trying to get Germany to take up a pugnacious attitude by doling out cheap uniforms and encouraging young men to wear small moustaches, to sit at large desks covered with papers, and to think themselves important militarists.' He did go on to strike a rather more solemn tone. 'In the schools of Germany today, it is being taught that war is the highest human achievement and the noblest human ideal. It is an attitude which is going to involve us in another war.'

The opposers' case was that this was not really a debate about Hitler, but a debate about the German nation. Peter Glenville from Christ Church claimed that Germany had not been allowed to rise to its feet after being knocked down in 1918. 'She has tried hard to secure peace, world-wide peace, through the medium of the League of Nations, but all her claims have been refused.' The seconder for the opposition was a German undergraduate, Adolf Schlepegrell, later a strong anti-Nazi. 'It has been suggested that Germany wants another war,' he said. 'But even if she does – and I do not for one moment admit it – she is not in a position to have one. When Hitler left the League of Nations and the Disarmament Conference, he was serving the cause of peace, for he was showing the world how rotten its statesmen were.' In retrospect, Schlepegrell says, 'I was certainly always opposed to the Nazis and feared that they might eventually destroy Germany: first morally and then through a policy of mad conquest. But I was at that age naturally reluctant to admit the incredible as it slowly dawned on me and to believe that my native country was about to turn its back on civilization. I hoped that it might all blow over and therefore tried to "interpret" the uninterpretable as long as possible.'

Schlepegrell clashed with Michael Foot over Hitler in the columns of *Isis*. In a review of *The Brown Book of the Hitler Terror and the Burning of the Reichstag* compiled by the World Committee for the Victims of German Fascism, Schlepegrell wrote that the book was written with hatred and malice, and that a large number of statements in it were obviously incorrect or misleading. Foot attacked this review in a joint letter with two socialists, David Lewis and John Cripps. They defended the *Brown Book*, citing an array of proof, such as the simultaneous occurrence of acts of terror in different places and the organization of concentration camps, which made nonsense of the excuse that the terror was merely the usual accompaniment of revolution. 'In parts, no doubt,' they argued, 'it may be described as hysterical, but a feeling of hatred against those responsible for the outrages is appropriate and excusable.'

Around the same time, there was a visit to Oxford by a group of Nazi students. As a guide to the climate of the times, the almost gushing report of the affair in the *Oxford Magazine* is revealing. 'Among our Whitsun visitors, we have welcomed to Oxford a body of Nazi students, fresh from the glories of their revolution. It is always instructive to be brought face to face with one's critics, particularly the hostile ones; and undoubtedly our guests gained greatly from the feeling which was borne in on them throughout their visit, that there may be implications in the *Volkstamm* theory and the practical measures to put it in force, which need to be thought out more fully, if not actually revised, after the dust and heat of the present struggle have had time to clear away. Equally, the Oxford element gained greatly in appreciation both of the fervent and unselfish enthusiasm that has been generated by the Nazi movement, and of the excellent personal qualities of many of its supporters. Friendships established may have good results of mutual relations between Germany and England.'

Michael Foot was preoccupied with the dictators earlier than most. He took time off when he was President to go with his friend Dosoo Karaka to take part in a debate at the University Women's Debating Society. The motion 'that life is just a bowl of cherries' was essentially frivolous, but it gave Michael Foot a chance to air his current preoccupations. 'Look round the world,' he said, 'and you see the disastrous and muddled state everywhere – tyranny in Germany, tyranny in Italy, chaos in China, Japan on the point of war, free speech in Oxford and free fights at Cambridge.' Speaking on the other side, Karaka teased his friend. 'The President of the Union is only a boy of nineteen [actually Foot was twenty]. What does he know of life? Whatever he does know he owes to me.'

Back in the Union, the left still could not always guarantee a majority. When Michael Foot invited down his father's old rival Sir

John Simon to support maintaining the National Government, Simon's presence was enough to carry the day easily for the right. In the debate, Dosoo Karaka called on Sir John, who was now Foreign Secretary, to repudiate the call at the Conservative Party Conference for rearmament. Simon, however, did not let himself be drawn into foreign affairs, to the disappointment of the undergraduates. Instead, he contented himself with stating that peace should not be made into a party issue and went on to defend his own position as a Liberal in the National Government on the grounds of principle. Macdonald too, he said, had abandoned his companions in the national cause, while Baldwin had substituted national duty for party ambition. Simon particularly impressed the Union by speaking entirely without notes.

The next week, Michael Foot was moved to deliver a magisterial rebuke from the chair to a speaker called Spender who was visiting from Cambridge. The motion was 'Western civilization is decadent and doomed'. Spender began a sentence, 'For every man that keeps a blonde chorus girl round the corner, there are hundreds . . .' The President rang his bell for order, and said, 'I must ask the honourable speaker not to harp on topics which may be very fitting in the Cambridge Union.' The unfortunate Spender turned out to be reading for the Ministry at Wycliffe Hall, Cambridge, and was clearly embarrassed when his brush with Michael Foot reached the ears of the *Daily Mail*. 'This total misunderstanding has put me in a very awkward position,' he told them, 'and the result may be to affect my future. Had I been an ordinary layman it would not have mattered so much, of course.' Michael Foot commented, 'At Cambridge, I believe that they are allowed to say such things as Mr Spender said, but I will not allow that sort of thing at Oxford. I think it is against good taste and manners, though I quite appreciate that it was a misunderstanding and one which is not likely to occur again.' His Methodist father must have been proud of him.

Michael Foot was prepared to indulge his own more proper sense of fun in some of his other debates. In the middle of the term he put down the motion, 'that this House refuses to swim the Channel, fly the Atlantic, climb Mount Everest, or squat on a pole'. This was carried easily. For his final debate, he devised the motion 'Borstal and Eton are a couple of fine old schools'.

We have two further glimpses of the future Labour leader as a liberal undergraduate. In a piece which he wrote for *Isis* in 1934 called 'The Rooseveltian Touch', he called for a champion of

English radicalism to emerge to rival Roosevelt in the United States and to stand up to the dictators in Europe. 'The real menace to democracy,' he wrote, 'comes from the possibility of a dearth in its stock of great men. Hero-worship is a well-nigh universal instinct, and in politics it has a vital part to play.' Michael Foot has always believed in heroes. He was soon to find his own in Aneurin Bevan. It is interesting to find him confirming his belief so clearly at the age of twenty-one.

The same year, Foot was prosecuting counsel in a mock trial of Winston Churchill. This was the Union's revenge for Churchill's hostility at the time of the King and Country debate. Quite apart from what he had said on that occasion, Churchill was an obvious butt for left-wing undergraduates, who regarded him as being on the extreme right, particularly because of his views on the question of India. The charge was 'that he has constituted and does constitute a menace to the world.' Michael Foot quoted Churchill's comparison of young Oxford with 'the clear-eyed youth of Germany burning to die for their country'. His indictment of Churchill was extremely savage. 'If the day ever comes in England when Fascism sits enthroned in the seat of power, I prophesy you will see seated there as the Goering or the Goebbels and possibly the Hitler of that revolution the same person who said he liked the spirit of the Blackshirts.' One hundred and seventy-five voted for the prosecution, with 55 for the defence. The sentence of the court was that Churchill should be recommended for elevation to the peerage.

The next term Dosoo Karaka was elected President, the first Indian to hold the office. By his time, the racial prejudice which Bandaranaike had felt within the University had almost disappeared. Certainly in leftist circles it was an advantage to be an Indian. Outside the University, feelings were rather more mixed. In an editorial which could have had them in court today, one of the Fleet Street papers said, 'Now that an Indian has been elected to the office of President of the Union, it will no longer be held in such high esteem.' In his farewell speech as President, Karaka acknowledged that he had been well-treated by the Society and by the great section of undergraduates at Oxford, though he did allege that the Oxford Carlton Club was prejudiced against non-whites. But he went on to say that this gave him an opportunity to speak out for others who had not had his advantages. 'There are hundreds and thousands of men for whom the colour bar has been a living hell.'

A year after Karaka, David Lewis became President. His

background was very untypical of that of most undergraduates: he was born in Poland. When he was twelve, his family emigrated to Canada. He went to McGill University in Toronto and came over to Oxford on a Rhodes Scholarship. There he became one of the leading lights in the Labour Club, pleading the socialist cause with rather more first-hand knowledge of deprivation than most of his contemporaries. *Isis* said of him once that he had 'moments when he would like to butcher duchesses in their beds'. A later, more serious assessment of him as President of the Union described him as the least Oxonian person ever to lead the Society, a grim antithesis to all the suave, slightly delicate young men who for generations have sat on the Union rostrum. 'Tolerance comes hard. He cannot help attacking hypocrisy, snobbery and muddled thinking with a scathing, merciless sarcasm.'

Oxford politics were dominated by two issues in the middle and late thirties. First, there was the slow decline of pacifism and the emergence of an anti-fascism which accepted that the dictators had to be opposed by all means available, including, if necessary, force. Secondly, there were the wars within the Labour Club between the Communists and the anti-Communists. The Union provided a stage, although not the only stage, for arguments which showed an uncharacteristic passion in the university.

Tories, socialists and Liberals alike threw themselves into the arguments about the threat to peace in Europe. In 1936 Winston Churchill overcame his dislike of Oxford to come down to speak to Conservative undergraduates in the Union debating hall about the case for rearmament. At the election the previous year, the National Government had been returned by a majority of 324 to 180 with a commitment to a modest rearmament programme; Labour, now under Attlee, still held that collective security was an alternative to rearmament. Meanwhile, the dictators were demonstrating their attitude to peace. Mussolini attacked Abyssinia and Hitler marched into the demilitarized Rhineland. The League's efforts to stop Mussolini proved completely ineffective; there was no resistance to Hitler's move at all.

Churchill was still an isolated voice campaigning against the weakness of the Government's response to events. It was standing room only in the debating hall for his visit. Unprovoked aggression in Europe could only be prevented, he told the undergraduates, if Britain's armed forces were strengthened. Only rearmament would enable the League of Nations to carry out its ideals of collective security. 'I would build up a League of Nations representative of nations so strong and ready to attack an aggressor that there would be no aggression.'

Edward Heath, one of the undergraduates present, remembers the occasion vividly. 'He made a tremendous speech,' he recalls. 'The Union was absolutely packed. You couldn't have got another person into it. And afterwards some of us went back to Professor Lindemann's flat in his college at Christ Church [Lindemann was Churchill's scientific adviser]. Churchill came there and talked until very late into the night, far past the time when we ought to have been back in college. He went finally at about 2 am and said, "I must now go and stay at the ducal palace of Blenheim." And off he went.'

The same month, Edward Heath took part in a debate in the Union about whether Germany's former colonies should be returned. The argument was between those who recognized the nature of the Nazi regime and those who still argued that Germany had legitimate grievances. The vote, however, showed a decisive switch in opinion since the debate in 1933 about Hitler's withdrawal from the League of Nations. The Union decided that the colonies should not be returned by 191 votes to 94. Edward Heath pointed out that Germany could not seriously argue on economic grounds for the return of the colonies; Hitler's colossal expenditure on armaments vitiated the claim. Returning the colonies would not help to preserve world peace. 'Paying Danegeld never did pay and never will.'

This was Edward Heath's first paper speech. *Isis* said that the twenty-year-old future Prime Minister made a thorough and informed contribution, but that he should find some way of connecting his paragraphs other than the words 'now, sir'. By contrast, the opposer J. R. J. Kerruish, who was later to take holy orders, sounded extremely defeatist. 'Britain cannot hope to win a war with Germany. We should placate and conciliate Germany, not shut the door of conciliation in her face. Otherwise we play "Rule Britannia" on our fiddles while Europe burns.'

Politically minded undergraduates were also greatly exercised by the Spanish Civil War, which broke out in 1936. Philip Toynbee and Edward Heath were among several undergraduates who visited Spain, although not many actually fought in the war. Oxford did not produce a martyr of the status of John Cornford, the twenty-one-year-old Communist poet from Cambridge who was killed in the early months of the fighting. In February 1937 the Oxford

Labour Club held a memorial meeting to Cornford. They organized a food dump for Spain and collected money for the dependents of people killed with the International Brigade.

Spain and Abyssinia were very much in the Union's mind when it debated reform of the League of Nations at the end of 1936. Christopher Mayhew, who won the Presidency on the strength of his speech, attacked the sham of non-intervention in Spain by the fascist powers, and warned that they might take the opportunity to 'non-intervene' in England in the same way.

The Liberal leader Archibald Sinclair, later to become a member of Churchill's War Cabinet, came down to help Mayhew defend the League. Sanctions had not been a complete failure, he claimed. The problem with the League was not its machinery, but its leadership. Sinclair still saw the League as a body capable of resisting the dictators. Lovers of peace and freedom, he declaimed to the Union, could not stand idly by when they saw the horrors of the persecution of the Jews in Germany; a League of Peace had the right to defend democracy against the rubber truncheon and the concentration camp.

The following year, the Union heard from one of the leading champions of appeasement, Samuel Hoare. In 1935 Hoare had resigned as Foreign Secretary, after his secret pact with the French Foreign Minister Laval had been revealed, a scheme which involved ceding large parts of Abyssinia to Mussolini. Now Chamberlain's Home Secretary, he was in Oxford to defend the Government's programme of rearmament. On the other side was the disarmament campaigner and Labour MP Philip Noel-Baker. Hoare went to great lengths to prove that the Government was not in a belligerent mood, and was doing its best not to provoke anyone. It was not prepared to intervene in Spain because its one great aim was to prevent the division of Europe into two opposed sets of powers. The peace-loving countries, he claimed, supported the Government's programme, but more belligerent people must not be forced into military alliances.

Noel-Baker accused the Government of holding back when most nations were prepared to disarm. Britain had refused a scheme of qualitative disarmament which Italy and Germany had accepted *in toto*. The National Government had saved the bomber and wrecked the disarmament conference. There could only be one end to the present arms race. The opponents of the rearmament programme carried the day, but only narrowly.

The belief remained that collective security through the League of Nations, without rearmament, was possible. In another debate in 1937, while the League stood by unable to raise a finger to help the Chinese against a fresh Japanese invasion, the Union decided against a motion that recent history proved that collective security could not be effectively applied to the present situation in the Far East. The mover C. W. Maclehose said that the only way to stop Japanese aggression was by war; people were not prepared for such a desperate measure. Nobody on the other side of the House said he was prepared to fight against the Japanese.

The left by now nearly always carried the day in the Union. They succeeded in defeating a resolution saying that the House preferred Chamberlain to Attlee, and when Anthony Eden resigned as Foreign Secretary over the question of how much ground to give to Mussolini, the socialists joined pro-Eden Tories to carry the motion 'that Mr Eden was right' by a very comfortable margin. The motion was moved by Nicholas Henderson from the Labour Club. Eden, he said, stood for the view that it must not be possible to get concessions from Britain by force. Chamberlain had acted behind the Foreign Secretary's back, leaving him with no option but to resign. The issue between Chamberlain and Eden was that Chamberlain wanted to show that Mussolini was right in his view of how to treat this country. The opposer was Patrick O'Donovan, a Tory and later a distinguished journalist. He claimed that Chamberlain was a realist, who refused to divide nations into sheep and goats. At one point during the debate Chamberlain's supporters were hissed and earned a reprimand from the Secretary, Edward Heath, who was temporarily in the chair.

These debates were rather more substantial than the point-scoring and rhetorical fireworks which have characterized most of the Union's history. It is not surprising that the speakers took the subject matter seriously; they knew war was likely, and they realized too that if and when it came they would be the people required to fight. An issue which affected them particularly was conscription, and understandably therefore they debated it three times within a year. In April 1938, when Philip Toynbee was President, they rejected it. Toynbee's bizarre choice of guests consisted of Henry Bird, the Society's Steward and an old soldier on one side, and John Gollan, the secretary of the Young Communist League on the other. The undergraduate case for conscription was put by two future Conservative MPs, Hugh Fraser and

Julian Amery. Fraser told the House that it was a matter of self-preservation. But a speech on the other side of the house from the socialist Richard Symonds showed that the pacifist tradition was not dead. If there was compulsory national service, he said, the Government would find it hard to deal with the hundred thousand pacifists in the country without wholesale imprisonment.

In June 1938 the Union declared itself for a Popular Front Government to replace the National Government, at a time when the idea of Liberal and Labour collaboration against appeasement was gaining support nationally. Edward Heath was still prepared to give Chamberlain the benefit of the doubt. The Prime Minister was right, he said in the debate, not to have given Czechoslovakia a written guarantee of British assistance; that would only have made her overconfident and unwilling to solve her problems. A Popular Front Government might find agreement on foreign policy, but would certainly be divided on home affairs.

Munich changed Edward Heath's attitude. With some other Conservatives in the University, he decided to support a Popular Front candidate at the Oxford City by-election which followed the Munich agreement. This is his account of the campaign. 'It was not as difficult to defy the party then as it would be today. We were supporting Anthony Eden, Churchill and the rest of them who were opposed to Munich. And so it was the natural thing to find a candidate. We were not prepared to take the Labour Party candidate, who was Patrick Gordon-Walker, but he was prepared to give way. The Liberals were prepared to give way as well, and finally they chose the Master of my own College, Balliol, A. D. Lindsay, who in 1926 had had a great deal of publicity because he supported the General Strike. He was an academic socialist, but what he concentrated on was very much the moral issues raised by Munich, how to handle the dictators, and what you do when they take over other countries.

'Harold Macmillan came down to support him, and I remember hearing him address an open-air meeting at which I was present. We did a great deal of canvassing. Quintin Hogg was the official Conservative candidate at the time, and of course spoke brilliantly on every occasion. I think he was somewhat irritated when he found little bill posters across his main posters saying "Love me, love my Hogg", which he thought was slightly unfair. But there was a good spirit maintained throughout it all. In those days, we had the Carlton Club in Oxford, which was an undergraduate club. It was on the corner, just opposite Balliol. We used to go there and lunch every day before going out canvassing. On one side we had all the Churchill/Edenite young Tories, and on the other side we had the Chamberlain/Hogg young Tories. So we used to sit there at lunch and pass rude remarks across the gap in between. It was all very good humoured.'

Lindsay and Hogg both gave *Isis* a statement of their policies. Lindsay said he deplored the irresolution and tardiness of a government which never made clear to Germany where this country was prepared to make a stand, and he said that rearmament should be tackled as a truly national effort. Hogg claimed that Chamberlain had shown 'real courage, real wisdom, real goodness and, above all, real understanding. It must never be said that we ever fought in a cause which was not wholly just, or that we refused to hold out the hand of friendship while there was even a possibility of it being grasped in good faith.' Hogg won the by-election; but Lindsay had made an impact, and shortly afterwards a second Popular Front by-election candidate, Vernon Bartlett, defeated the Conservative to win Bridgwater.

The Union voted against Munich by a majority of 320 over 266, in a debate attended by 800 undergraduates. Edward Heath joined forces with Christopher Mayhew to lead the attack on Chamberlain. Heath was said to have astonished his fellow-Conservatives with his bitterness against the Prime Minister. His policy was muddled, he said, and he had been largely responsible for bringing the country to the edge of disaster. Hitler could not be trusted: that was clear to everyone save Mr Chamberlain. Christopher Mayhew described Chamberlain's policy as '*reculer pour mieux reculer*'. He had just returned from a visit to Czechoslovakia. He pointed out that Britain had been much better placed to stand up against Germany before the crisis. We had lost half a million Czech troops, formidable fortifications and millions of pounds in trade. The position was now hopeless. Britain should have taken a firm stand, for Hitler was not prepared, still less was the German staff, for a war against four countries with the probable opposition of others later on.

The next month, the Union finally set its face against pacifism. 'War between nations can sometimes be justified' was a chance to overturn the King and Country vote. Despite the siren voice of C. E. M. Joad against the motion, it was carried by 176 votes to 145. Nicholas Henderson, the mover, said that pacifism was quite unthinkable in view of the menace of the fascist powers. The fascist leopard could not be expected to change his spots when confronted only by a sheep. Joad's speech was a less effective repetition of the 1933 performance. Another war, he said, would produce even more disastrous results than the last one; the upshot of that had been that four-fifths of Europe was writhing under the stranglehold of autocracy.

Munich was still the most pressing issue when Edward Heath contested the Presidency against J. R. J. Kerruish. This was his second attempt; in the previous term he had been defeated by an Australian Liberal called Alan Wood. The Presidential debate reflected Edward Heath's hostility to Chamberlain; the motion said that 'this House has no confidence in the National Government as presently constituted'. The Government, he said, was an organized hypocrisy, composed of Conservatives with nothing to conserve and Liberals with a hatred of liberty. As for Chamberlain's foreign policy, it could only be described in the maxim, 'If at first you don't concede, fly, fly, fly again.'

Edward Heath's arguments were buttressed by the former editor of *The Times* Wickham Steed, now strongly at odds with the paper's policy. The Government, he said, was leaning towards the butchers of human freedom and the crushers of human personality. Kerruish asserted in reply that war had now been averted, and there was a chance for it to be averted for all time. Edward Heath carried the day in the debate, and carried off the Presidency by 280 votes to 155.

Heath took the President's chair for the first time in January 1939. The same month, an *Isis* leader suggested that the question facing the country was no longer whether it was right to go to war, but whether it was right to go to war this year or next. 'If the call comes,' it went on, 'we shall all troop out and die like heroes.' It was natural therefore that the new Union President should put the issue of conscription back on the agenda. Again, Hugh Fraser championed the idea. Britain could only be properly rearmed, he said, when it had a large reserve of manpower for immediate use. The present voluntary system lessened efficiency, and put the responsibility on employers, who could not be expected to throw away profits unless all their competitors also allowed their workers time for training. Julian Amery's father Leo Amery came down to support the motion. Democracy could never be saved if we were unprepared and divided, he argued; Constantinople had fallen when it could have withstood, simply because of religious squabbles within the city. The victor of the Bridgwater by-election, Vernon Bartlett, argued the other way; any government which tried to force through compulsory National Service would completely split the country just at the time when we required national unity. Conscription lost by nineteen votes.

The next week, the motion was 'that this House deplores the recognition of General Franco'. The proposer was an extreme left-winger John Biggs-Davison, now a Tory MP. He accused the Government of cold-blooded malice and hypocrisy. The Republican Government, he claimed, still controlled almost a third of the country. 'Who are we to say that the people of Republican Spain should abandon their fight in the cause which they consider to be just?' *Isis* said that it was a good speech except for the fact that it savoured too much of the stock clichés of the left. Biggs-Davison was supported by another up-and-coming socialist, Anthony Crosland. He said that Spain would be yet another name inscribed on Chamberlain's heart after death, provided he had a heart and provided there was still room. For all Julian Amery's arguments that recognition was inevitable, the motion was carried by thirteen votes.

In the summer term, with the war only a few months away, the Union returned to the issue of conscription yet again. This time a packed House welcomed national service by 423 votes to 326. Julian Amery spoke on the winning side. John Biggs-Davison was again pitted against him. He condemned conscription as militarily useless. Instead of collective security, he said, Britain was building up without Russia a scheme of crazy and indefensible alliances.

A. P. Herbert, now Independent MP for Oxford University, arranged a pair in the House of Commons so that he could come and listen to the debate. He wanted to find out what young people thought before deciding how to vote on the issue in Parliament. 'I wish that this episode was as well remembered as the silly King and Country affair,' he comments in his memoirs.

In case there was any doubt left about their attitude towards the Prime Minister, the Society went on to demand 'that Chamberlain must go'. The fiery left-wing Labour MP for Jarrow, Ellen Wilkinson, came down to make a particularly ferocious attack on Chamberlain. 'Mr Chamberlain is essentially the narrow party leader. He has never understood what Fascism is. He has put his class interests and his party interests before the interests of the British Empire.

He smashed the League of Nations and the result is that no small nation today trusts Britain's word. Mr Chamberlain is not a crook or a scoundrel; he is a much more dangerous thing at the head of the British Empire – a thoroughly frightened man.' On the other side of the House, John Peyton, later to be Edward Heath's Minister of Transport, was only lukewarm in support of Chamberlain; the alternative to him, he said, was extremely doubtful. It was left to former President Christopher Hollis to sound enthusiastic about the Prime Minister. 'The story of appeasement is not yet ended. No one knows how it will end, but it may well have been that Mr Chamberlain was triumphantly right in making his gesture.'

The debates about the dictators reached a much higher standard than the Union's average. Christopher Mayhew has a point when he claims in retrospect that the undergraduates were eloquent because they were well-informed. For many who took part in these debates, life was all about politics. Edward Heath confirms that the tone was serious. 'We had the dictators. We all thought a war was coming. And that wasn't anything to joke about.'

On the whole, the debates about the dictators went the way of the current Labour Party line, although Conservatives and Liberals were quite often elected to office on their personal merits as speakers. Christopher Mayhew remembers that the members of the Labour Club were encouraged to take part in the Union's activities, despite the bourgeois nature of its gentlemen's club atmosphere. 'It was part of our crusading, a way of getting members into the Labour Party, intimidating the Tories and getting publicity.' The Labour Club had as many as fifteen hundred members. By comparison, its activists considered the Tories to be amateurs and snobs. They felt a special distaste for the members of the Bullingdon Club, whose idea of a good evening's entertainment was to pelt captive hawks with champagne corks.

The Labour Club believed in campaigning outside the University. In the summer of 1934 they bought an old lorry, painted it and fitted a loudspeaker on the front, then drove it around in the Clarion Rural Campaign. Later Nicholas Henderson remembers going on a camping tour of Dorset with John Biggs-Davison and holding socialist meetings on street corners. The Dorset locals who heard them would no doubt have been surprised to learn that the young comrades addressing them were to become respectively HM Ambassador to the United States and a pillar of the Conservative right.

With Labour dominant, much interest centred on faction fighting within its ranks. The Communists were constantly being accused of fiddling and manipulating votes, notably the vote which led to the fusion of the October Club and the Labour Club. Nicholas Henderson believes that the goings on in the Labour Club in the 1930s taught him a great many lessons about communist tactics which stood him in very good stead in later life. The prevailing view, however, was that there were no enemies to the left. The Communists denounced revisionists like Christopher Mayhew, Roy Jenkins and Nicholas Henderson as social fascists. Christopher Mayhew, tipped by many at the time as a future Prime Minister, was the champion of the Labour right against the Communists. He founded a Democratic Socialist Group, which boasted a special red tie with three arrows through it. Philip Toynbee, a leading Communist, commented at the time: 'Its charm is only to be rivalled by its exclusiveness.'

There was always a certain element of self-delusion about the University Labour Club. Richard Crossman once began a talk to one of its meetings with the words, 'working class chaps like you and me'. Although Oxford was now recruiting undergraduates from a wider social mix, many of the Labour Club's members had been to public schools, like Crossman himself. It was easy to poke fun at them. *Isis* reported that the large Oxford contingent for the May Day demonstration in 1937 was particularly popular with the crowds 'because of our Boat Race victory, no doubt'.

Nonetheless, the Labour Club members thought of themselves as more adult than their predecessors, and much more in touch with the working class movement through their canvassing and the camps which they ran for the unemployed. The old undergraduate anarchist-socialism-cum-sexual communism expressed through velvet ties, suede shoes and extravagant speech, according to one of the club's leading members writing in *Isis* in 1937, was a thing of the past.

The Communists were supposed to do as they were told by the party. Whereas earlier generations had ignored their academic work, the 1930s Communists were told to take it seriously. 'Few of us,' wrote Philip Toynbee, 'are allowed by the party to do more than a bare minimum of political work during our last year.'

G. D. H. Cole was the great guru of the Labour Club. With his pipe, his ascetic looks and his willingness to give generously of his time and attention, he appealed greatly to young Oxford socialists.

The Cole Group, an inner circle of Labour Club members which met once a week in his rooms, was at its zenith in the 1930s. As a left-winger opposed to communism, he had some success in restraining some of the undergraduates from joining the Communist Party. Lured to a debate in the Union in 1934, he spoke about the class-struggle, prophesying a double aggravation of the class-war, the spread of class consciousness among workers and the ultimate abolition of capitalism.

The right had a mentor too in Dr Hugh Dalton, a frequent visitor and talent spotter for the party. He helped Christopher Mayhew among others to find a seat in Parliament. Dalton spoke at the Union in 1937 in favour of Labour's Immediate Programme to tackle unemployment. This was one of the rare occasions when the Labour Club were defeated, thanks largely to a speech on the other side from Edward Heath, who suggested that Dalton's knowledge of the working classes had been gained on the playing fields of Eton.

Clement Attlee himself paid some attention to developments at the University. He wrote an article in *Isis* contrasting the large and active Labour Club of 1936 with the situation in his day. 'No doubt,' he wrote, 'this party has drawn support from those classes who were hardly represented in the Union of my time, but it also increasingly draws adherents from the comfortable classes who question not only the ethical, but also the rational foundations of their comfort.'

The Conservatives, for all the aspersions cast on them by Labour, were holding their own. The Conservative Association rallied round to meet the socialist challenge with periodic bursts of activity, particularly under the chairmanship of first Ian Harvey then Edward Heath. The progressive wing of the party tended to dominate. Alan Fyfe wrote in *Isis* that they were ashamed of the conditions in which many of their fellow citizens lived. They wanted social reform, but did not believe that they had to smash up everything. Edward Heath, who like Fyfe belonged to Balliol College, always a bastion of the left, had many socialist friends. He used to be invited out to lunch on Sundays with Roy Jenkins by Jenkins' father, who was a Labour MP. The antithesis of the shire conservatives, he even took part in a march and demonstration against Franco's Spain. Yet he was never tempted by socialism. He says he always believed that the way to solve the social problems of the country was not by authoritarian means, and he saw the socialists as authoritarians.

The Liberals had lost their preeminence in Oxford, but they were still a strong force in the Union. In 1936 they carried a motion which said that a Liberal revival was the only safeguard against dictatorship and war. Alan Wood, an Australian who became President of the Liberal Club and the Union, argued in *Isis* that unlike the other Oxford political clubs, the Liberal Club had a definite voice in the formation of the party's policy. Its members also had a better chance of being selected for favourable constituencies, he believed. After all, a quarter of the Liberal MPs in the House of Commons had been at Balliol College alone.

Red Oxford still predominated, its tone reflected particularly in two debates in 1936. Speaking on a motion about Russia, even Christopher Mayhew forsook his normal anti-communist stance to praise the concept of the dictatorship of the proletariat as a means to an end. Russia, he said, had a tremendous cultural programme as well. 'He then,' said *Isis*, 'gave a vivid account of the Leningrad Park of Culture and Rest and laid it down as a maxim that the best things should be shared by everyone.' To some extent, of course, any debater has to make out the strongest possible case for his side, even if it means suppressing his doubts and even distorting his own views. There is no doubt, though, that extravagant praise of the Soviet Union still found favour with a great many undergraduates, even though the anti-Soviets just carried the day by eight votes.

The Union did, however, carry the motion 'that this House recognizes no flag but the Red Flag'. Oxford expected the reverberations to be as great as those for the King and Country debate. The vote was reported as far away as France; *L'Éclaireur de Nice* announced '*L'Union des étudiants d'Oxford a adopté, hier soir, par 67 voix contre 57, one motion déclarant qu'elle "ne reconnait pas d'autre drapeau que le drapeau rouge"*'. Apart from this the controversy did not echo much beyond the dreaming spires. *Isis* claimed the vote bore out the belief of the average Oxford undergraduate that the Union was a meeting house for socialist cranks. Certainly Union membership had fallen off considerably after the King and Country debate, mainly because parents were not prepared to pay subscriptions for their children to join such a subversive body. Not for the first or last time the Union found itself in financial difficulty as a result. *Isis* suggested that a new University debating society should be set up, to get away from socialist domination. The idea, however, was immediately attacked by leading lights in the Union of all parties, and it never got off the ground.

There were limits to the lengths to which Oxford's socialists were prepared to go. For a time, some of the socialist officers of the Union discarded evening dress to show solidarity with the working classes. In 1936, the Union put the question of dress to the vote. Setting aside a suggestion that socialists should wear suits, Liberals dinner jackets and Conservatives tails, the House insisted that all officers should wear tails, and the socialists thereafter for the most part conformed.

Although feelings ran very high in the 1930s, on the whole the Union was reasonably well behaved. The nearest it came to disorder was when the legendary Harry Pollitt, General Secretary of the British Communist Party, was invited to speak. Edward Heath remembers that a college rugger team went up to the gallery armed with bags of flour. Half way through Pollitt's speech, the bags descended. They all missed him; but they broke around him on the floor and covered him with flour. Christopher Mayhew recalls having alerted the police to the possibility of trouble, with the result that the offender was caught. The *Manchester Guardian* reported that the gallery was overrun by members of the Union wearing red ties and that there was a bit of a scrimmage. The debate ended quietly, however, and the incident was not repeated.

The progressive Conservatives had one of their champions down to the Union as well. Lady Astor told the undergraduates that she was a born social reformer. 'I am not in the least interested in keeping things as they are – I want to see them a jolly sight better. If I thought socialism could do one quarter of the things it promised, I should be a socialist.' Many of the undergraduates were suspicious of Lady Astor because of stories about the Cliveden set. That was an imaginary Lady Astor, she told the Union. 'I should like to meet the Lady Astor who was the leader of the Cliveden set, who makes and breaks Ministers, and who seems to be a combination of Cleopatra and Jezebel. That has gone all over the world, which shows the power of a communist lie.' The motion 'that the future of the working classes lies with progressive Conservatism' was defeated narrowly, by 164 votes to 169.

The earnest political young men were not earnest all the time. Christopher Mayhew led an Oxford Union rugby team, which went down to defeat at the hands of the Cambridge Union. The match was notable for the number of players who were sick on the touchline at half-time. Afterwards, Oxford were the hosts for a debate on the motion 'that sport is either murder or suicide'.

In 1938, the Union carried a motion 'that this House deplores the decline of frivolity'. *Isis* noted the occasion for Edward Heath's maiden funny speech. 'We must realize the importance of not being earnest,' he said. 'The watchwords today should be "liberty, fraternity, frivolity".' The speech was a success, although its composition had given Heath trouble. 'I remember the problem of making a humorous speech about humour, which was far more difficult than I had imagined when we had the motion. Sometimes you can make a speech about another subject and have amusing things to say, which lightens it; in fact one ought to try to do that. But when you start to discuss humour itself, then the tendency all too often is to become very solemn.'

Of his generation Edward Heath has risen the furthest in British politics. Impressions of him as an undergraduate differ. Some saw him as industrious, sensible and hardworking, but uninspired and sometimes boring as a speaker. 'Very competent, but without the ebullience of youth', 'efficient, not outstanding, in no way very brilliant' are among the judgements of people who knew him then. There were several other Tories, many believed, who were more likely to make it to the top. Others, however, remember another side of his character; he was extremely confident, they say, and very affable, with none of the aloofness which some have seen in him in later life. 'He smiled all the time,' according to one contemporary. 'He was very jovial and humorous, always shaking with laughter. No one would say that of him now.'

On the whole, the *Isis* descriptions of Edward Heath's oratorical efforts are favourable: 'an extremely forcible maiden speech'; 'Mr Heath has plenty of confidence: he must be careful not to appear too aggressive'; 'Mr Heath spoke with sincerity and moderation.' His *Isis Idol* began, 'Teddy Heath was born some two months before the tank. Lacking the thickness of skin characteristic of this early rival, he soon outstripped it in charm of manner, and has since proved its equal in force of utterance and ability to surmount obstacles.'

Apart from the debates on the international situation during Edward Heath's term as President, his programme reflected a wide range of interests. One week, the House debated 'that a return to religion is the only solution to our present discontents'. Rather surprisingly for a body which was apparently so anti-establishment at the time, the Union passed this motion by 279 votes to 94. Heath was disappointed that the obsession of the Union regulars with politics had left them incapable of thinking properly about more profound matters. 'The weaknesses and failings of a University education,' he wrote in *Isis*, 'all the superficiality, the shallowness, the sterility of undergraduate thought, were revealed unmercifully as speaker after speaker tried to find something to replace the political clichés with which he can normally get away. Over sixty people wanted to speak: not six of them were worth hearing.'

Another disappointment for Heath during his term was a last-minute cancellation by Sir Thomas Beecham. Heath had persuaded Sir Hugh Allen, the Oxford Professor of Music, to get Sir Thomas down for a comic debate on the motion 'that this House would like to appoint a dictator'. The night before the debate was due to take place Sir Thomas lost his nerve, and sent a telegram to say that he could not come. The critic James Agate, who was to have opposed Sir Thomas' mock bid to make himself dictator, agreed to change sides and make the case for a dictatorship by himself instead. The debate seems to have been a great success notwithstanding the last-minute change of regimes. Reinforcing other people's impressions of how much he enjoyed life at the time, Edward Heath wrote in his description of the debate in *Isis*, 'Any omissions in this report of the above speeches are due solely to the fact that the President must have been laughing so much at the time that he forgot to make a note of the point.'

As President, Edward Heath tackled the Union's financial problems by expanding the Society's social activities. 'We had the first Oxford Union Ball,' he recalls, 'and that was a wild success, because the Union has got lovely rooms. To be able to enjoy oneself there, to dance there and to have supper was very pleasant. The other thing I did was to say that if we really want to encourage undergraduates to become members of the Union, then we must improve the dining room and the bars and we must allow credit there. This was wildly acclaimed. Everybody was absolutely delighted, except for the Senior Treasurer, who found that at the end of my term none of them had paid their bills and that the credit was still there. Anyhow, they sorted that out.'

Other Presidents of the period had more of a mixed press than Edward Heath. The most controversial of all was the late Philip Toynbee, then a Communist with an anarchic lifestyle. He was once described in the Union as a man who needed a nurse, while she, poor lady, would need a chaperone. His worst faults, said his *Isis Idol*, were incompetence and a fugitive love of luxury. However, it went on to attribute his election as the Union's first

Communist officer to his popularity, as well as to the growing influence of his party. 'He has no enemies,' the piece claimed, 'and remembering his passionately held political views, this is a remarkable feat.'

Max Beloff, then a right-wing socialist, was considered very unlucky to have missed the Presidency. He was beaten by fewer than thirty votes by Bill Shebbeare, partly, it was thought, because he broke ranks with the Labour Club by defending evening dress for Union officers. As a wit, Beloff was claimed to equal Ronald Knox. 'With a malicious little twinkle in his eye,' reads one review, 'he commenced to fill the air with Belaphors and Maxagrams.'

The Union meant great opportunities for those who reached prominence in it. Edward Heath met Churchill. Christopher Mayhew and Roy Jenkins got to know Hugh Dalton. Nicholas Henderson debated against Lady Astor, and was briefly swept up into her social circle and introduced to Bernard Shaw. It all made these young men feel very important. Not all their contemporaries, however, shared their own view of themselves. The detractors of the Union were as numerous as ever. The Union was all but moribund, wrote one of the critics in *Isis* in 1937, without a trace of humour or spontaneity. The jokes smelt like stale haddock, and the only other ingredient was a continual flow of vague, badly expressed political theories. For the left, their weekly denunciation of fascism was as confession to a Catholic; they could then begin a fresh week with the sins of their personal capitalism purged from them.

Another thirties undergraduate who did not take part in the Union's activities has recently made a critical assessment of the Society. Lord Grimond has written, 'It is absurd to generalize about the Union – its great figures have been of many types. But it could – I put it no higher – encourage that view of politics which expresses itself in clichés suitable for speeches or articles. It has been a little responsible for the superficiality of much political comment, the sneering, the desire to appear on the inside and claim a spurious intimacy with political figures even if you have never exchanged a word with them.'

Against that judgement the Union has its ferocious defenders, foremost among them Edward Heath. 'I think the Union does help you an enormous amount. I remember when I first went into the House of Commons in 1950, I felt I was coming home. It was perfectly natural. It wasn't the present Chamber because we were then meeting in the House of Lords, but that didn't make any difference. I think we avoided all the strange feelings which many new members have – how do I settle down here? How do I handle that?

'The other thing which the Union does is to teach you – or force you if you like – to think very quickly on your feet. Because in any speech you can be interrupted by any of your contemporaries who are there at union debates, and you very quickly fall down if you haven't got the answer, directly you are interrupted. So I think that is another asset of the Union. Again, it makes you prepare a speech which is going to influence people. You cannot just stand up in the Union and produce any sort of speech, because again you very quickly get shouted down. So it means you have got to concentrate on the structure of the speech, decide what you want to say, how you're going to say it, and then try to influence people there to support you, because at the end of every debate, you've got a vote. That is a very salutary thing to bear in mind. In the Union, you have not got whips rushing around telling people which way they have got to vote. You really have to persuade people.'

When the Second World War broke out all four of the members who had been elected to office left Oxford on war service. Unlike the generation of 1914, those who remained at the University decided that they would try to keep the Union going. Nicholas Henderson, as the highest ranking member of a Union committee left, took over as President without an election. The next term another group assumed office, again without an election. The President in this first term of 1940 was Madron Seligman, now a Member of the European Parliament. The Treasurer was Anthony Crosland ('he will warm the Treasurer's chair to good purpose', said the *Oxford Magazine*) and the Secretary was Roy Jenkins ('he has a fine control of language and is a convincing debater').

One of the Union's first actions after the outbreak of war was to adjourn in sympathy with Czech students who had been murdered by the Nazis. Edouard Benes, President of Czechoslovakia before Munich, sent Nicholas Henderson a telegram to thank the Society. 'Deeply moved by action of Oxford Union Society adjourning in sympathy with undergraduates of Czechoslovakia,' it read. 'Brutalities committed surpass in extent cruelty all reports reaching world public. Nazi Pan-Germanism wishes destroy future of Czech nation by destroying flower of its youth and depriving rest of all possibility of higher education. This new Nazi crime contradicts all principles humanity and must finally turn against its authors. News of your action reached Prague in our broadcasts and will harden our people in their resistance to barbarian domination. Pray accept and convey members Oxford Union my warmest thanks.'

Benes came down to Oxford the next term to take part in a debate on the motion that 'this House has no faith in liberal Western democracy as a basis of Government'. Roy Jenkins was the proposer. Edward Heath came back to Oxford to join Benes in opposing. Benes' reception reflected the admiration which the Union felt for him and their guilt at the way he had been let down by Britain.

The first months of the war changed the perceptions of many politically-minded undergraduates. Anthony Crosland set the trend for many others to desert the left, though earlier he had almost joined the Communist Party. Handsome, self-assured with an inclination towards arrogance, Crosland had been an ex-public schoolboy in full revolt against the system.

The Nazi-Soviet pact began to shake the faith of many on the left, but at least in public, Tony Crosland at first was prepared to defend it. He spoke against a Union motion in November 1939 'that this House considers that recent Soviet policy has not been in accordance with socialist principles'. 'The German-Soviet pact had been made in self-defence,' the *Oxford Magazine* reports him saying, 'after the Poles had refused to allow Russian troops on their soil. This was the best speech Mr Crosland has made in the Union. His sang-froid was useful against interruptions.'

Roy Jenkins spoke on the opposite side. The son of a Labour MP who was Parliamentary Private Secretary to Clement Attlee, he was never tempted by the prevailing Marxism in the Labour Club. He had already developed an appreciation of wine, and one contemporary remembers assuming that he was the product of an Asquithian country house when he first met him. He was not unduly anguished about having to put on the capitalist rig of white tie and tails. Over two years younger than Crosland, at this stage he cut a less authoritative figure than the red firebrand from Trinity. 'He was not prepared to accept the dictates of Moscow as infallible reason,' said the *Oxford Magazine*. 'Socialist principles will never be served by the forcible annexation of a country or part of a country. Mr Jenkins made, as usual, a very sound and sensible speech; but he should try and get his arguments home by using more emphasis and thrust at the right moments.'

Despite this clash Jenkins and Crosland were becoming close friends. The Russian invasion of Finland set the seal on Crosland's break with the left, and the two Union officers played a leading role in the battle which followed against the Communists at Oxford. When Labour's National Executive disaffiliated the Marxist-dominated Universities' Labour Federation, the Croslandites attempted to disaffiliate the Oxford Labour Club in its turn from the ULF and reaffiliate it directly to the Labour Party. They were outvoted by 182 votes to 108, and so instead formed a new breakaway club called the Oxford University Democratic Socialist Club. This was only one in a long series of splits and fusions which have characterized Oxford Labour politics, but it was useful practice in breaking the mould for the founder of the SDP.

It was one thing to deplore the Russian invasion of Finland, another to support the idea of an Anglo-Finnish expeditionary force to go to Finland's aid. When the Union debated the issue in January 1940 most of the Labour Club were against diverting the anti-fascist effort to anti-Soviet ends. A Communist undergraduate called Stuart Schultz attacked the Finnish commander Marshall Mannerheim as a Nazi German puppet. The Finnish Ambassador Gripenberg came down to defend his country. In the middle of the debate, the President Madron Seligman recalls, 'there was a scuffle in the gallery over my head. I couldn't see what was happening, but a riot broke out in the chamber as a banner was unfolded with the strange device "Hands off Russia!" It was then I discovered that the leading perpetrator of this inadmissible breach of Union etiquette was none other than Tony Crosland. I had a flaming row with him afterwards in which I demanded his resignation and he demanded mine, of all the cheek.

'After order had been restored and the House had divided on the motion, I well remember having to force my way out of the chamber through a crowd of student left-wing agitators, and being kicked in the groin for my pains. It was my first experience of political bully boys.'

The motion, which said that all possible help should be given to Finland, was carried by 295 votes to 141, with Roy Jenkins and Leo Pliatzky from rival wings of the Labour Party both speaking against it. Afterwards, the Finnish Ambassador protested through the Foreign Office that it was wrong for the Union to have divided the House on a subject where Finland was so obviously in the right. Seligman had even more trouble when he tried to persuade the

French Ambassador to come down and debate events in France, where Daladier had banned the Communist Party. The Chancellor of the University summoned him to tell him that the French Government had complained to the Foreign Secretary Lord Halifax; they considered it outrageous that the society which had passed the King and Country motion should presume to debate the policies of the French Government at war. In the end the Union backed down, withdrew their invitation to the French Ambassador and were duly thanked by Lord Halifax.

At the end of this term the Union brought back elections. Tony Crosland and Roy Jenkins were not placed to compete directly with one another. Jenkins regarded himself at this time as Crosland's adjutant, a fact which was to influence their relationship later. Crosland stood for President, but lost to Robin Edmonds, who was later to scale the heights of the diplomatic service. Jenkins was more successful, winning the office of Librarian.

Jenkins put a great deal of effort into the Union, particularly during this term when he was close to the top. His line remained that of an orthodox Labour supporter. In May, he was described as advocating a socialist peace effectively. Then in the Presidential debate that 'without a great growth of socialism, this war will have been fought in vain', he claimed, according to the *Oxford Magazine*, that 'Nazism was a religion: we too must fight inspired by belief in a new world order. The League of Nations has failed because of capitalism's inherent tendency towards war. Capitalists had brought Hitler to power: a Socialist Germany was vital for European peace. The power of the international financier must be destroyed if social justice was to be won.'

The motion was carried, but its mover lost the Presidential election to his rival James Comyn, now a judge. Roy Jenkins was devastated. He confesses that, although his defeat took place between the evacuation of Dunkirk and the fall of France, he considered the three events of almost equal importance at the time. Like others, he regards the Union as the place which taught him to speak.

Roy Jenkins decided to have a second go at the Union Presidency after his first rebuff. He spoke against a motion in October 1940, with which he might have had some sympathy later in life, 'that no single party is capable of dealing with Britain's post-war problems'. Then for his second Presidential debate Gaitskell's future lieutenant was to be supported by Aneurin Bevan. The motion was that 'this House does not want to hear of the Conservative Party again'. 'At home,' said Roy Jenkins, 'the Conservatives' idea of justice is the Means Test; abroad, the strengthening of their potential enemies.' This time he lost the election by a margin of twenty-seven votes to an Indian called I. J. Bahadoorsingh. Jenkins' oratorical efforts during this period are variously described as 'sincere', 'sound', 'sensible', 'fairly forceful'; he may have lacked the maturity and the impact of some of his rivals.

Anthony Crosland survived his defeat for the Presidency, not to mention distinguished service in the war, to come back to the Union in 1946. Later in life Crosland used to be rather disparaging of the Union, but one friend testifies that he could recall every detail of all the debates in which he had taken part. In this pre-war phase, he is remembered as outstandingly well-informed and a daunting debater.

In 1941 the Union offered its despatch boxes to the House of Commons to replace those which had been lost in the bombing, and of which they were copies. The Speaker wrote to thank them, but suggested that the offer be left in abeyance until after the war, because it would not be right to risk the loss of a second set of despatch boxes. For the Union's leading members, this would have been the most natural gesture in the world; as far as many of them were concerned, they were to all intents and purposes members of the House of Commons already.

CHAPTER FIVE

AUSTERITY, ANTICS AND ANGRY YOUNG MEN

1940–1959

The Union carried on after a fashion throughout the war. Attendances were often small, and many undergraduates did not remain in Oxford for the full length of a normal degree course. Nonetheless, keeping the Union going formed part of the effort to preserve civilization as it was known in the face of the German menace. The members duly went through the motions; in fact, the motions they went through closely resembled ones which had been debated in happier times. It was considered inappropriate to debate the conduct of hostilities. Taking themselves as seriously as usual, the members worried about the impact which they might have on the national interest. If they had not worried, the university authorities were prepared to worry on their communal behalf. Instead, undergraduates looked forward to the end of the war, and argued whether people should be fighting for a Tory Britain, a socialist Britain or a Liberal Britain.

In 1943 the Union debated the Beveridge Report, deciding in favour of a motion that 'planning of social security by the State must involve the loss of liberty and initiative by the individual'. The next year, the Home Secretary Herbert Morrison came down to speak for a motion (which was easily carried) advocating public ownership after the war. He put the classic Morrisonian case; public ownership of natural monopolies would cut out waste; public corporations like the Post Office had been proved to be efficient; it was in the public interest to control trade agreements; civil servants should be trained in economics so that the State was better equipped to intervene in economic life. His argument was considered moderate and unexpectedly subdued. The first speaker for the Tory minority was an undergraduate called Geoffrey Rippon. His speech was described as being distinguished more in its flashes of humour than in its matter and length. He reminded the house of an old Burmese proverb; 'There are three major calamities, fire, flood and officials.'

Occasionally, the Union did touch on wartime issues. In January 1943 they debated 'that in the opinion of this House His Majesty's Government is doing everything in its power to rescue the victims of Hitlerite terror.' The debate proceeded in the normal way until the guest speaker Victor Gollancz had his say. He told the Union that it was just possible the debate might influence Government policy; more had to be done to give sanctuary to the Jews fleeing from Germany. His persuasiveness induced the movers of the motion to cross the floor, after which it was carried by a huge majority.

The Union took some time to return to normal after the war. The whole of Oxford, in fact, was in a state of upheaval. The half-empty University soon filled to bursting as the demobilized flooded back to finish courses begun before the war or to begin studies postponed because of war service. Alongside them jostled much younger men and women, who had reached the normal age for going to University as the war ended. The mature and the immature tended to drift into two camps. For the college authorities, the 'in loco parentis' principle had to be applied with discretion. It was hard to play the heavy-handed disciplinarian with people in their mid to late twenties who had served in battle. Many of the returning undergraduates were married.

The privations with which people had put up cheerfully during the war increased rather than easing up afterwards. The breakfast indicator sank to an all-time low. Dried egg, and not much of it, represented the standard college breakfast. There was little wine to be had in Oxford. The appearance of the occasional banana was hailed with ecstasy. Rook pie found its way onto the menu in the

Union dining room. True to itself, however, Oxford did from time to time find ways of cushioning itself against the full rigours of austerity. Roast cygnet was once served in the Union, when it became the lucky beneficiary of a swan upping.

All the same, it was, as Lord David Cecil remarked in a debate at the time, an age of austerity undergraduates and utility dons. The colleges were cold, particularly in the interminable winter of 1947. The Union, even when the hot air began to circulate freely again, was even colder. If the body learnt to cope with discomfort, there were privations for the mind as well, for books were in short supply. One post-war undergraduate remembers having to trail around Oxford after the one copy of whichever textbook was in demand that week, taking turns with all the other people who wanted to read it.

The problem of clothes loomed large. The vogue for scruffiness still lay far in the future. If the young gentlemen did not have quite the Woosterish concern for their dress affected by the undergraduates of the 1920s, they still required the standard upper middle class wardrobe, which the restrictions imposed by clothing coupons made it difficult to acquire. The Union's officers still had to wear tails; the young Robin Day for one used up most of his coupons in preparing himself sartorially for the Secretary's chair.

As before the war, the outside world and its concerns were breaking into the ivory towers. Undergraduates were keenly interested in the question why they felt so cold, hungry and uncomfortable; it set some of them wondering why many people outside Oxford were a great deal hungrier, colder and more uncomfortable. Some believed that austerity was necessary, part of the transition to the fairer world which the Attlee Government was creating. Others took the view that the shortages and restrictions could have been avoided, and were instead exacerbated by the incompetence and doctrinaire approach of the socialists. The Tories, one sympathetic undergraduate declared in the Union, wanted to remedy the lack of *joie de vivre* in the population.

It may be hard for some people to imagine, but six wartime years without proper political argument represented a real deprivation for many of the undergraduates who joined or rejoined the Union at this time. As soon as the members had gravely offered their felicitations to His Majesty the King on the occasion of the great victory vouchsafed to his armies, they rejoined the political front lines with zest. It was a zest, though, which did not have quite the

The Union Buildings with the original debating hall, now the library

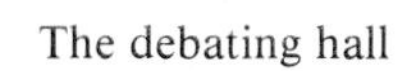

The debating hall

Drawing by G. Gathorne-Hardy, 1898

Interior of the old debating hall, now the library, with Pre-Raphaelite murals

Harold Macmillan at the Union: (*above*) as an undergraduate in 1914; (*below*) launching the Appeal in 1975

Michael Foot at the Union: (*above*) 1933, with the King and Country Standing Committee (third from right; second row); (*below*) the new Labour leader with broken ankle in 1980

Socialism in action at the Union; President Tony Benn helps to wash up after the staff supper

Sir Robin Day coxes the Oxford Union boat in 1950; Tariq Ali dances the night away at the Union ball in 1964

Famous names at the Union: Robert Kennedy, 1967; Michael Stewart facing the demonstrators, 1970; Jeremy Thorpe as Liberal leader in the referendum debate, 1975; Richard Nixon, 1980

Women at the Union: Geraldine Jones is elected first woman President in 1967 and Benazir Bhutto in the President's office

fire and passion of the 1930s, and which left room for rather more non-political subjects than had been debated before the war.

Anthony Crosland returned to Oxford with considerable military experience – he had been a parachutist and air-photograph interpreter, and had served in North Africa, France, Italy and Austria. He involved himself again in the Democratic Socialist Club, which he had helped to set up in 1940 as a breakaway from the Labour Club. Now aged twenty-eight, he was working hard for his degree so it was only with some reluctance that he agreed to stand for President of the Union. He won by four votes, because the second preferences for the third candidate split his way; he had been behind on the first count. His rival Ronnie Brown went on to be President the following term, and eventually to become a surgeon.

Crosland displayed a bit of surgical skill himself in carving up his opponents in debate. Tony Benn made an intervention in one of his speeches to the effect that it was important for Labour undergraduates to discard the taint of intellectualism. Crosland replied that in order for the honourable gentleman to be able to discard the taint of intellectualism, it was first necessary for him to acquire it.

By the time of his Presidency of the Union, Crosland had little of the left-wing firebrand left in him. He preserved the dislike of conventions which he retained throughout his life, but politically he had become the pragmatic egalitarian who was to write *The Future of Socialism*. His *Isis Idol* said, 'it will come as something of a disappointment to those who look upon Socialists either as long-term Trade Unionists or long-haired fanatics to learn that Tony Crosland is neither of these. He is, he says, somewhat ruefully, a very respectable Socialist, coming as he does from a family with a civil service tradition behind it, and having a father who was a senior Civil Servant at the war office.' Crosland was older, more clever and better looking than anyone else in the Union at the time, a fact of which he was not entirely unaware. Contemporaries remember that he could be crushing and arrogant at times; he could also be charming and friendly when it suited him.

Tony Benn, Crosland's pupil for a while, was in the same mould, an ex-public schoolboy with socialist views who was at the same time considered an agreeable enough companion by those with the same background but different beliefs. Unlike Tony Crosland, he came from a radical family: his father had moved from the Liberals to the Labour Party and become Secretary of State for India. He had been at Oxford for a spell during the early part of the war then served in the RAF for two years, but did not see active service. His most memorable wartime achievement, it was said, was winning a camel race in Alexandria two days after V.E. Day.

'What can be said of him as a person?' asked his *Isis Idol*. 'He dresses scruffily, talks too much and is rather boisterous. He doesn't drink, but smokes almost continually. His interests are mainly political (being a rather idealistic Socialist) but he also enjoys discussing a great many other subjects, of which he is even more ignorant. Fortunate in having an extremely happy and vivacious family circle, he is never more at home than when he is with them. He collects pipes, believes in complete social and political equality as between the sexes, gets embarrassed rather too easily for comfort and laughs at his own jokes. Being by nature somewhat unmethodical, he attempts to organize his life with three mechanical devices. A petty cash account (to keep him economical), a job list (as a substitute for an imperfect memory) and a time chart (to give him an incentive to work).

'Of the future, he does not like to think overmuch. He is on the list of Labour Party parliamentary candidates (potential) and hopes to make something of this, when he has had time to supplement his rather inadequate PPE education, by gaining a little first-hand knowledge and experience of some aspect of political activity.'

Tony Benn became Secretary of the Union the term after Tony Crosland was President, and rose effortlessly through the *cursus honorum* thereafter. As President, he was said to have been elected by the 'prevailing seriousness'. One contemporary describes him as 'serious, doctrinaire and totally without humour' at the time. Another likens him to an overgrown boy scout. There was no doubt, however, about his popularity. *Isis* said that his election was surprising only in so far as it was decisive. 'If Mr Benn has made a bad speech in the Union, we have yet to hear it. He has shown himself witty, courteous and forceful in debate and in private business. His political opinions are not alarming to most people, nor are they insincere. Beyond question, his success is well-deserved.'

The mature Benn is acknowledged, even by his strongest opponents, to be one of the most accomplished speakers in British politics. There are signs of his style developing in reports of the debates in which he took part. As Secretary, speaking up for the trade unions against accusations of tyranny, he was said to have given the endearing impression of sweet reasonableness. When interrupted he gave way readily, but did not deal with the points made. 'He continued smilingly where he left off and gave the impression of preferring his own words to the comments of his fellows. With practice, he will be an excellent debater. He should not hold his coattails like mudguards, but ought to continue to say that the wages of sin is death and the wages on the railways a great deal worse.'

There was no doubting Tony Benn's commitment to socialism at the time. Even at Oxford he assumed working-class habits. He used to wear a flat cap and rode about on his bicycle with a haversack on his back. He did however at this stage make use of both barrels of his name as well as his title 'the honourable'. When Kenneth Harris went on a debating tour of the United States with Benn and Sir Edward Boyle, he claimed jokingly that as a mere commoner he had been expected to clean their shoes for them.

In general Benn was a staunch defender of the Attlee Government. He is fond of arguing now how radical the 1945 manifesto was, and it was certainly possible at the time to sound simultaneously left-wing and loyal to the Government. In debates, Tony Benn defended socialist planning, which he said was in the long-term interests of the country; denied that the trade unions tyrannized workers; supported the Government's handling of Indian independence and spoke with appropriate quotations from W. S. Gilbert in favour of a motion which said that the House of Lords was a menace to democracy. A rare departure from the Government line came over Spain. He attacked Ernest Bevin for not withdrawing support from the Franco regime. He defined the attitude of the Government as 'no intervention with the rights of the Spaniards to do as they're damn well told'.

The impression, however, among his contemporaries was that Tony Benn was heading for the Labour establishment. He struck one Union habitué who knew both men at Oxford as far less of a rebel than the young Gerald Kaufman, who appeared on the Union scene a few years later. When he came back to the Union as a young MP in 1951, Tony Benn took part in a debate with his father and his brother on a motion that the foreign policy of the Government displayed too great a dependence on the United States. While Lord Stansgate and David Wedgwood Benn supported the motion, Tony Benn was against it, alongside Lord Hailsham. 'He agreed with much of what was said from the other side of the House,' according to *Isis*, 'but his fear of Communist aspirations made him side, as is right and proper with a fledgling Socialist MP of obvious ministerial calibre, with the Government on this family occasion.'

Tony Benn was certainly not averse as an undergraduate to joining in any extravaganzas the Union was mounting. For the Eights Week debate when he was President he wore hunting pink along with the other officers, and was duly photographed by the *Tatler*. The Tory-leaning officers wore white silk facings on their jackets; the socialists had scarlet ones. The motion which Tony Benn devised for the occasion was 'that this House prefers to travel with its back to the engine'.

In his own speaking, Tony Benn was capable of being witty in a typical Oxford Union sort of way. As Treasurer, he was asked why there had been no cake for tea for some time. The champion of the Cripps austerity programme was able to stand up and tell the House that under the present rationing arrangements it was 'impossible for honourable members either to have their cake or eat it'. After his last speech as an undergraduate the *Tatler* wrote, 'the Hon. A. N. Wedgwood Benn of New College signalled his last appearance with an easy eloquence and display of wit which should make *Hansard* a joy to read in years to come.'

Benn made an energetic and sometimes unconventional Union President. He turned out in a nine-strong Union rounders team to take on a side from the women's colleges. The Union team ungallantly won. He also laid on a supper for the Society's staff, at which he and the other officers acted as waiters. In a further act of *noblesse oblige*, he led the washing up team next morning, although his efforts at the sink seem to have been mainly for the benefit of the photographer. As Treasurer, he invited a group of former German prisoners of war to listen to the famous English sense of humour on display as the undergraduates debated 'that this House fails to see the importance of being earnest'. The group, which included a former U-boat commander, were said to have followed the proceedings with great interest.

Tony Benn proved a staunch defender of the Union's independence as a private society when in 1948 there was a proposal that the Society's assets should be transferred to the University because of the Sharp report on traffic in Oxford. The Sharp scheme entailed not only driving a major road across Christ Church meadow, but also destroying the Union library, murals and all. The Secretary Peter Kirk argued that the Union would not be entitled to sufficient compensation to allow it to rebuild premises on anything like the scale of the original ones; it therefore needed the protection of the University. Tony Benn opposed him. He pointed out that the Sharp proposals were very unlikely ever to be carried out, on which he turned out to be completely right. Even if the Society did have to move, he argued, it was better to be independent with inferior premises than to be subject to the rules and regulations of the University. 'We may have to go back to the difficulties which this Society had in its early days,' he told the House, 'but we shall still be the Oxford Union – free to do as we like.' Tony Benn's view prevailed, and the Union has been free of both planning schemes and the University authorities ever since.

With Tony Benn the rising star of the Labour Club, the most impressive of the young Tories was Sir Edward Boyle. Although a baronet and at Christ Church, always the college for toffs, Boyle did not immediately impress his contemporaries as patrician. He was immensely fat and more than a little absent-minded, often appearing at breakfast in college with shaving soap around his ears, and occasionally without having adjusted vital parts of his dress. He was clever, very well and widely read and had a very retentive memory. His career at the Union was followed very closely by his mother, who attended most of the debates in which he took part, His father, a Liberal MP, had died recently, a fact which increased his mother's concern and ambition for him. Some who knew him say that when his mother died, Edward Boyle's ambition died with her.

Boyle was not a naturally brilliant speaker. He had a tendency, according to some, towards pedantry and verbosity. He was mocked for his habit of saying 'If I may say with respect.' 'Perhaps I should have less respect,' he commented once. In his examination papers he added a footnote stating, 'I am grateful to Mr Hugh Trevor-Roper for making this clear to me,' a gesture which seemed rather pretentious for an undergraduate. The obverse side of this quality, however, was a genuine *gravitas*, rare in a young man, and enabling him to carry off grand statements about subjects like freedom which would sound like trite truisms on other people's lips.

Boyle had another quality which is rare in the Oxford Union, genuine modesty. This among other reasons made him greatly liked and he was elected to office with relative ease. Playing the ever-absorbing game of speculating on the future of young meteors, *Isis* said this of him: 'Though he is too modest to think much about it, his friends are trying to link his waggon to a political star. It will be interesting to see what happens. He will be an indifferent success on the hustings; he is at his best in a high-level debate or giving, in his own time and place, a prepared speech. His pleasant, mellifluous unrhetorical voice delivers clear and well-turned periods. His even tones are well suited to express his loyalty to reason. You can hear him making up his mind, and it makes good listening. Sometimes, too often, his eye leaves the audience and looks at some point in the gallery; you turn round to see whom he is regarding, but there is no one there. Now and again he makes some immature, impulsive gesture; snatches at his spectacles, or awkwardly saws the air with his arm. There is something attractive about his movements, and the spontaneity becomes him. His manner, as he begins the speech, is unassuming, almost deferential.

'His chances of becoming the political figure envisaged by many of his friends depend on how well, and how soon, he masters the human element of which politics are made. The values, the aims, the hopes – these he already has. Singleness of mind, the capacity for remembering to reckon with people and issues not immediately upon the scene, these he may develop. Certainly, he will never capture the crown of leader: he is too lacking in sense of milieu and moment. The scholar in him recoils from the dramatic phrase which will strike through to the common heart. But there are other ways of acquiring power, and he is an attractive man who does not seem to want it.'

The term after Boyle was President, the Secretary's chair was taken by a phenomenon called Kenneth Tynan. Tynan belonged to the generation that was too young to have fought in the war, and so had gone up to Oxford at the normal age. Finding the prevailing attitude too humdrum and too serious, he set out to create an alternative Oxford, which recaptured the atmosphere of the age of aesthetes in the 1920s. The undergraduate Tynan wrote once, 'Oxford consists to all intents of the one-twentieth who live with a flair for abandon. They form an aristocracy on Hellenic lines. Three-quarters of undergraduates are ex-servicemen who talk of Tel Aviv and nationalization and work hard.' For many of his contemporaries in the late 1940s, Kenneth Tynan *was* Oxford.

Tynan's normal garb was a purple doe-skin suit with a gold satin shirt. His contemporary Godfrey Smith remembers him as grievously thin. 'His head was so bereft of flesh that it could have played Yorick in an emergency, and it was crowned with a farouche thatch of butter-coloured hair. His nostrils flared wildly like a doped Derby favourite, and when he was excited his lips were forced back as if by an invisible bit, leaving teeth and gums bare: at these moments onlookers had the disquieting sense that something awful was going to happen. In fact, he was only struggling to defeat his already celebrated stutter. The voice, when it came, had a husky theatrical quality, as if it had been smoked and then bubbled through gin.'

Kenneth Tynan's conquest of Oxford centred on the theatre and the magazine world, but he swept up the Union too as he carried all before him. While he treated theatre audiences to his Hamlet and his Samson Agonistes, he made his debut at the Union opposing, tongue in cheek, a motion deploring the tyranny of convention. The *Oxford Magazine* said that he deplored extravagance in a superbly extravagant speech.

Thereafter, Tynan's speeches in the Union always pulled in the crowds. Sir Robin Day, whom Tynan defeated to become Secretary, recalled the atmosphere surrounding his performances for Kathleen Tynan's biography of her husband. His mere presence meant, he wrote, 'that something shocking, something memorable, something brilliant was expected. The all-male Union then tended to conduct itself with propriety and with deference to the presumed sensitivities of its lady guests in the gallery. Tynan, however, was seen as a licensed shocker, expected to go slightly beyond the accepted bounds.'

One of his notable performances was on the motion that 'this House wants to have it both ways'. He was against it, he said, because it clearly implied that there were only two ways of having it. 'And I know for a fact,' he added, glancing up to the gallery packed with excited young ladies, 'that there are at least forty-seven different ways of having it' [he paused before languidly delivering the punchline] 'not excluding the one on the grand piano.'

Tynan's speeches were a theatrical experience which divided his contemporaries – some strongly disapproved of him; most thought he was marvellous. He spoke in Tony Benn's 'back to the engine' debate, telling the President how glad he was to be back in the draughty old speakeasy. His speech, said the *Oxford Magazine*, reached its climax when he made his one reference to the motion. Tynan returned to commend the motion that sincerity was the refuge of fools; sincere people, he said, were social lepers or martyred prophets. In this debate he made the memorable concession that his own speeches were sometimes criticized on the grounds that an aperitif followed by an aperient was no substitute for a meal.

Humility was a curse, Tynan announced to the Union, supporting 'this House has no confidence'. It was the harbinger of inertia. Where was the confident Englishman of the foreign wireless, in top hat, kilt and spurs? In the Union, to 'er' might be human, but this was an age of dwarfs. The House might have no confidence, Tynan said, but he had plenty. He insisted that everyone in the House should stand up and shout, 'I am big strong and powerful.' Naturally they all did.

Tynan was Secretary when the Union debated that this House would rather be a dustman than a don. He had himself carried into the Chamber in white tie and tails lying on a Corporation dustcart. A Tynan speech was always hard to recapture in print in the cold light of day. One effort, according to *Isis*, ranged through Picasso, his state of health, restoration comedy, puberty, night clubs in Yorkshire, all following one another in a bewildering stream of fantastic, morbid, neurotic craziness. Everyone tried to describe Tynan. He looked and behaved like a bottleneck according to the critic who described his performance in a debate on 'this House deplores the continued presence of Englishmen at Oxford'. 'He ejects a strongly pressurized stream of images so fast that we get the impression that they have all been boiling inside him for weeks and begging to be released.'

While Tynan dazzled Oxford with his wit, Benn with his eloquence and Boyle with his intellect, others who were to shine later made less impression. F. W. Mulley, (Christ Church) said *Isis* of the future Defence Secretary after a contribution on the Palestinian problem, 'is no better a speaker than most undersecretaries'. Women were still debarred from the Union, so that Margaret Roberts of Somerville did not have an opportunity to start her path towards Ten Downing Street there. Not all those who remembered her in Oxford Conservative circles, however, anticipated the extent of her later success. She was, according to one contemporary, able and nice, but had not broadened out at that age. A closer friend does, however, recall that she did talk of becoming Prime Minister. The Labour Club thought that they had a much more likely candidate for the first woman Prime Minister in Shirley Catlin, later

Shirley Williams, who wrote for *Isis*, acted and had most of male Oxford in love with her in between her political and academic exertions.

The period of the first Attlee Government was exciting for anyone with an awakening interest in politics. Sweeping reforms were being carried out, arousing strong feelings. A debate on the Government's domestic policies in 1946 attracted nearly eight hundred undergraduates; the visiting speakers were both good performers, John Boyd-Carpenter and Dr Edith Summerskill, but the issue must have had a great deal to do with the attendance. The arguments typified those being thrashed out during the post-war years. Boyd-Carpenter accused the socialists of producing a 'dull, dumb, dim tourist-third equality in which every person proceeds in orderly fashion, regimented and controlled from the municipal pre-natal clinic to the county crematorium.' Dr Summerskill defended the Government's aims of improving nutrition, housing, open spaces and planning.

Other visiting speakers touched on the same themes. Anthony Eden drew a crowd of over a thousand for what was in fact his maiden speech in the Union in 1946. 'Controls there must be,' he said, 'but they should be applied intelligently, combining the wider knowledge of the state and the wider planning of the state with the initiative of free enterprise, without which our national prosperity cannot be restored.' Eden was lionized by the dominant young Conservatives at the Union because of his stand against Chamberlain before the war. Nonetheless, there was an apologetic tone about parts of his speech, which suggested how far prominent Tories were still on the defensive after the devastating 1945 election defeat. 'We have made many mistakes in the past,' he told the Union, 'and shall undoubtedly make many in the future.' With Oxford Liberals still a force to be reckoned with, Eden talked at some length about copartnership and profit sharing. He addressed an appeal towards the bust of Gladstone. 'What would that grand old man of Liberal politics have thought . . .' he began, whereupon an unseen hand behind the bust moved Gladstone's head round to turn towards the speaker, and brought the house down.

Hugh Gaitskell was also belatedly lured to the Union to defend the Labour Government. 'This country has a genius which will make possible the maintenance of our democratic liberties and at the same time bring about the achievement of socialist ideas,' he told the members.

The Tory majority in the Union could behave roughly. The Attorney-General Sir Hartley Shawcross was on the receiving end of a barrage of hissing and interruptions when he came down to defend the Attlee administration, moving the *Daily Mirror* to comment afterwards that the Union seemed to have 'a queer idea of sportsmanship'. Sir Hartley had a particular brush with a Tory undergraduate from Brasenose called Ralph Gibson. Referring to a point which Gibson had made, he began a sentence: 'Nobody but a child like the honourable member from Brasenose . . .' Sir Hartley had misjudged a house many of whom like Gibson were former captains or majors, and all of whom greatly resented the charge of childishness. There was uproar. Sir Hartley attempted to retrieve the situation by claiming that he had intended his remarks to be taken in a spirit of bonhomie; he had meant that the economic and political outlook of the member was childish. Not a man to be put down by an Attorney-General, Ralph Gibson went on to become a judge.

The Union has always been a difficult audience to humour. Another visitor of the period, Lord Swinton, nearly fell into the same trap as Shawcross, saving himself in the nick of time by turning 'when that young man has as much experience as I have in these matters' into 'that young man with all his great experience will know'. Others made no effort to adapt. Once in a speech to the Labour Club in the debating hall, which had been circulated as a press handout for the benefit of a wider audience, Herbert Morrison absent-mindedly began a sentence 'And so I say to you, Mr and Mrs Consumer . . .' The undergraduates, of course, fell about laughing.

Despite the indignities to which some of their number were subjected, the great and the good continued to come down to Oxford and the Union. Some of them acted as talent-spotters, notably R. A. Butler for the Tories and Hugh Dalton for Labour. Dalton was another of the Government's prominent supporters brought to the Union to defend nationalization.

A voice from the more remote past returned too when Tony Benn as President gave Lord Simon the chance for his Union swansong. Benn himself spoke in the debate and invited Simon to take the chair while he did so, fifty-one years after he had occupied it as President himself. Simon made an appeal for liberty, which he thought was being hamstrung by the Labour Government. 'I think the time has come when people like you, representing as you do the growing youth of the country, should declare that socialist policy and legislation are cramping the springs of energy and enterprise, and that it is only by getting back to the most real enjoyment of the liberties of the ordinary citizen that this country may hope to see the recovery for which we are all striving.'

Dried eggs and coupons were keeping undergraduate attentions on events at home; foreign affairs did not maintain the importance that they had in the 1930s, though there were debates on India and colonial freedom. Perhaps more of an echo of the 1930s reverberated in the row about the Corporate Club. This was a fascist group which Tony Benn and some friends attempted to expose. They wrote to *Isis* revealing that Oswald Mosley had been to visit the Club, and that one of its members had written an article in the Spanish press boasting of the existence of a large reactionary movement in Oxford. Members of the University, they said, should exercise the utmost vigilance in the interest of the country and of the good name of Oxford.

In October 1947 the Union carried a motion deploring legislation to curb fascist activity, by a substantial margin. The news reached the Soviet Union, where students in Leningrad were inspired to send Oxford an open letter, duly published in *Pravda* and broadcast by Moscow Radio. The Union resolution, according to the Leningrad students, was a betrayal of the interests of peace and democracy. 'Fascism is not a subject for discussion. Was it not against fascism that mankind shed an ocean of blood in the last war? Surely this cannot be forgotten after only two years?' The current President of the Union Peter Kroyer replied by inviting the Leningrad students to a debate; of course, they never came.

In 1945, many had felt that there would probably never be a Conservative Government again. Who could desire the return of such an era? Even Conservatives, while fiercely challenging the policies of the Labour Government, had little confidence that their alternative would ever appeal to sufficient numbers of the electorate.

Yet as the 1940s drew to an end the pendulum swung back. At Oxford, the Government supporters went on the defensive against their Conservative opponents. The Tories settled in for a long period of domination in the Union.

At the same time political passions abated further and interests broadened. The love of showmanship and elegance, always a penchant of the Union's, came close at times to seeming its *raison d'être*. One of the most spectacular events was a boat race against the Cambridge Union which took place in 1950. The cox of the Oxford boat, weighing in at sixteen and a half stone, was Robin Day. The stroke was Peter Emery, now MP for Honiton, described at the time as the 'immaculate misconception' because of his faultless dress and his difficulty at expressing himself. Jeremy Thorpe, later Liberal Party leader, rowed at number seven. Godfrey Smith was at number six. Stanley Booth-Clibborn, the current Bishop of Manchester, was number four. Number three was the journalist Keith Kyle and number two was the leading Social Democrat Dick Taverne.

The proceedings were conducted with great solemnity. Robin Day and the Cambridge President Norman St John Stevas arrived for the occasion in a Rolls Royce, from which they emerged in full evening dress, complete with top hats. St John Stevas sported a silk-lined opera cloak, Day an enormous pink carnation and gold-handled cane. By comparison, the oarsmen seemed somewhat underdressed, wearing merely dinner jackets. Their coxes duly inspected them and pronounced them ready for the race. Half way down the course, a rowing boat carrying staff from the Cambridge Union in white jackets met the crews so that sherry could be served. They then rowed themselves incompetently on to the finishing line, which they crossed together. St John Stevas and Day were then both ceremonially ducked.

Back in the debating hall, the barricades of the 1930s had been dismantled and the port was being passed cheerfully across the divide which remained between the parties. Many of the socialists of the time have since abandoned the Labour Party; Peter Tapsell was actually a Tory MP before the decade was out as was another Oxford comrade, Geoffrey Johnson Smith. Dick Taverne abandoned Labour in the early 1970s. Shirley Williams and Bill Rodgers became founding members of the SDP in 1981. Of course, events since their Oxford days had an immeasurably greater effect on most of these people than anything which happened while they were undergraduates; but the climate of the time may well have sent them gravitating towards the centre.

Of the socialists of the period who have remained in the Labour Party, the most notable is Gerald Kaufman. Today one of the most formidable performers at the dispatch box in the House of Commons, he is remembered in his Union days as a dialectician with whom it was better not to tangle. He had a sharp and sometimes bitter tongue, and was regarded by some Tories as having a chip on his shoulder, though that may have been because he tended to get the better of them in argument. Coming from Leeds Grammar School, he was not on the same terms with the Tories as public school socialists like Dick Taverne from Charterhouse and Peter Tapsell from Tonbridge. In Union elections he remained an outsider, never progressing beyond Standing Committee. At least one contemporary, trying to reconcile his ability and his lack of success, attributes it to anti-semitism.

The young Kaufman was once described as having 'a lively, bouncy, raised eyebrow manner, which made his arguments easy to listen to if a little difficult to follow.' He was called a natural debater of considerable promise when he took on a later Commons contemporary Peter Blaker opposing 'the cat is the best answer to the cosh'. He then followed up his success with a speech on the winning side of a debate on capital punishment, for which even the most Tory-dominated Union has never voted this century. 'Mr Kaufman has shown an excitable nature in previous debates', said *Isis*, 'but was mercifully restrained on this occasion.'

Gerald Kaufman's socialism was unflinching. Communism was not the greatest danger facing the world, he told the Union. Capitalism had given birth to the crisis of our time. But he could joke about his politics too. Debating the middle classes, he said that they had lost confidence because the Middle Class International had faded out of existence.

Frustrated in the Union, Gerald Kaufman was rather more successful in the Labour Club where he had the distinction of setting up an investigation into electoral malpractice which resulted in an undergraduate called Rupert Murdoch being disbarred from holding office.

Most people at the Union were keen not to turn either the debates or the elections into straight party battles. In 1950 Robin Day and others wrote to the newspapers to protest against headlines like 'Oxford Union: No Socialist Officers' and 'Labour Defeat at Oxford Union'. There was no political significance in the results, they pointed out, and it was very misleading to attach party labels to the candidates. They were elected on their merits as speakers. If things were otherwise 'nothing could be more disastrous for the future of the Oxford Union Society. It will inevitably lead to the swamping of the electorate by loyal party men who do not attend debates, to wholesale infringement of the salutary rule against canvassing, and often to the rejection of the better men.'

There had been a striking example of this philosophy the previous year. In February 1949 Richard Faber, a Conservative, and Rodney Donald, a socialist, tied for the Presidency. Faber resolved the situation by standing down in Donald's favour, on the grounds that he still had time to stand for the office again whereas Donald was at the end of his Oxford career. Faber was taken to task by the Beaverbrook Press for taking such a soft attitude to the socialist menace, albeit clothed in the white tie and tails of the Oxford Union's Librarian. 'What goes on at the Oxford Union?' asked the *Evening Standard*. 'A Tory and a Socialist tied for the presidency. How to resolve it? The Tory withdrew. No doubt this was a fine, gentlemanly gesture; all the same, it was just nonsense. England's young Tories must not follow the non-combatant methods of the majority of the party's front bench in the House of Commons. Rather they should adopt the advice of the old warrior Churchill and fight on the beaches, in the fields and in the streets.' Appropriately enough, Faber became a senior diplomat.

One reason for the opposition to the stereotyping of prominent Union figures as Conservative or Labour was that many of the most successful ones were Liberals. Robin Day, Godfrey Smith and Jeremy Thorpe, who followed each other into the President's chair in successive terms, all supported the Liberal Party. Robin Day lived and breathed the Oxford Union for almost his entire university career. Although he appears to have taken his Liberalism very seriously at the time, and in fact went on to become a Liberal candidate, his real interest lay in the art of debating itself. His delight in argument has remained with him, to the general benefit of the viewing and listening public and the occasional exasperation of his interlocutors. His proclivities were noticed in his *Isis Idol*. 'One would not be surprised to learn that he had sat up in his pram and championed the cause of Infants' Rights: once he had started, it is certain that no other baby in the neighbourhood would have got a word in edgeways. By the time he went to school, it was clearly hopeless to try to stop him talking, and he became President of the Debating Society there.'

Robin Day made his first paper speech in the Union in favour of reforming the educational system at Oxford. Day's girth as an undergraduate was a frequent butt of his opponents' humour. Later when he was an officer there were questions about the fate of deckchairs in which he had sat. He took to referring self-mockingly to himself as the champion of the small man. Appropriately enough in this first debate he complained that hunger in the age of austerity was sapping the intellectual powers of undergraduates. *Isis* called him smooth and witty, and a master of the art of quotation, though the *Oxford Magazine* complained that, despite his fine imposing presence, he roared like a sucking dove.

Later that year, with due impartiality, the future Sir Robin attacked the Labour Party for its attitude to the Hague Conference on European Unity and the Conservative Party for its lack of a policy for economic recovery. According to *Isis*, he spoke in 'a kindly, urbane manner', drawing attention to the radical side of Liberalism.

By 1949 Day was being called Oxford's most plausible and sizeable Liberal. No longer the sucking dove, he had what was reverently described in capital letters as the Liberal Voice. 'His peroration calling for a strong progressive radical alternative was the signal for another burst of the Voice.'

The next year, the Voice was turned on the churches, criticizing their social record. 'Far larger than life,' said *Isis* admiringly, 'he dwarfed the dispatch box; his hands moved protectively from his stomach to his notes, and he made one of the best speeches the House has heard from him. Communism had grown up, he suggested, because of the churches' failure during the Industrial Revolution.' There was some doubt, however, how long he had spent in historical, philosophical and theological research in evolving this theory. 'Mr Day has become so good a master of technique,' said the *Oxford Magazine*, 'that one would like to point to the few remaining imperfections: in spite of his superb mastery of the House, it rejected some of his antitheses and questions as too glib for a debate of this intellectual seriousness.'

Robin Day debated for the Presidency on the motion that a political and economic policy of the Extreme Centre constituted the sole hope for the country. 'Mr Day has taken a great deal of trouble to tape the Union style. He well realized that if you must argue seriously it is essential to soften the blow with a judicious mixture of relevant or irrelevant humour. And this is perhaps the most important lesson that debaters can learn. But the second is not to be so concerned with the softening process that substance is obscured and detail blurred. When Mr Day was amusing, his point was lost; when his points showed up they leered at and taunted us through a maze of turgid pompous verbosity. This accomplished speaker appeared nervous and distracted; his speech was disjointed; he used the greater part of it to unwind a fabric of specious generalizations which could be used to describe almost any political or economic policy.'

Despite this jaundiced notice from a critic who put down his opponents in equal measure, Robin Day won the Presidency easily, with 263 votes to a mere 93 for his nearest rival Peter Emery, 89 for Jeremy Thorpe making a premature stab at the Presidency and 24 for the *quondam* Labour Minister of Transport John Gilbert.

Apart from the boat race with the Cambridge Union, the most notable event of the Day Presidency was a clash between two great opponents of the 1930s Oxford Union, Cyril Joad and Randolph Churchill. The motion was 'that this House regrets the influence of America as the leading democratic power.' Joad had recently been convicted of travelling first-class on a train with a third-class ticket. Churchill, after consulting Robin Day over dinner about the wisdom of making such an attack, described Joad as a third-class Socrates.

The atmosphere outside the Union helped to recapture the flavour of the King and Country controversy. Rumours of a Communist demonstration brought police and university officials to the premises in large numbers. Churchill attacked Joad for his part in the 1933 debate. 'He's still at his old game with his same old bad advice,' he said. 'He is corrupting and infecting and polluting the relationship between Britain and the United States. I have come here to express my whole-hearted hostility and opposition to the narrow-minded, petty and wrong-headed doctrines propounded by Professor Joad.' Joad chortled in his seat, enjoying all this hugely. When he came to speak he showed that he was still capable of influencing a Union audience, even though this one was much more Conservative than that present for 'King and Country'. The Americans, he said, had only one standard and that was money. 'Today it must be obvious that the nations are heading for hell, and it is America which is leading us there.' Joad ended with his familiar pacifist message. 'It is for us to keep out of war at all costs. It is possible to keep out of another war, and the greatest reason for our entry into another war is our dependence on America.'

For his Eights Week debate Robin Day devised a theatrical ploy to rival Tynan. Without anyone knowing, he hid a group of trumpeters from the Cowley Motor Works Brass Band in the gallery before the debate. As Day led his Presidential party into the hall they were greeted with a tremendous and totally unexpected fanfare.

Sir Robin is only half joking when he says that ever since he was President of the Union he has gone on doing the same sort of thing only for money. Chairing debates between politicians in the Union is pretty useful experience for chairing debates between politicians on radio and television; the path from the Union to the television studios has become as well-beaten as the path to Westminster. The Union's media men have, in a sense, replaced the churchmen of earlier eras, even to some extent playing the same role in the nation's affairs. There is no question which of them occupies the televisual equivalent of the See of Canterbury, even if he does not always have trumpets now to herald his appearances.

Godfrey Smith, unlike the Liberals who came before and after him, never wanted to go into politics; he always wanted to become a writer, which is what he did. His experiences as President, he says, put him off politicians for life. His first debate was on a motion attacking the Labour Government. It clashed with the Conservative Party Conference, which made it difficult for Smith to find a Tory guest speaker. Without consulting Smith, the Treasurer Jeremy Thorpe fixed a Liberal speaker. Smith considered that Thorpe had been usurping Presidential powers in an outrageous manner. He promptly cancelled Thorpe's invitation, only to find on a visit to the Liberal Assembly at Scarborough that Thorpe had nobbled all the available alternative speakers. His next choice was Raymond Blackburn, who had recently left the Labour Party and was sitting in the Commons as an independent.

The day before the debate, Godfrey Smith telephoned the Government speaker whom he had lined up. This was the Parliamentary Secretary to the Admiralty, James Callaghan MP. He confirmed the arrangements with him and told him who was speaking on the other side. Callaghan put the telephone down on him, having told him that if he wanted to know what he thought of Mr Blackburn, he could come and hear it. He added for good measure that he would get in touch with Transport House to ensure that no other Labour MP would speak in his place.

Callaghan was attacked in the press for his action. According to the *Yorkshire Observer*, 'Mr James Callaghan, a fine, vigorous and lively young Minister, has disclosed a raw totalitarian streak in his nature and an ugly picture of how his party controls the liberty of speech of some of its leading members.' Smith, who appreciated that he had been somewhat naïve in failing to realize the strength of feeling in the Labour Party about defectors in general and Raymond Blackburn in particular, sent Callaghan a telegram of apology. Callaghan, meanwhile, had been stung by the press criticism to issue a statement. It complained that a new motion had been substituted for the one on which he had originally accepted to speak, and that a new opponent had been substituted without reference to himself. 'I do not know very much about the practices of the Oxford Union, but in other circles this would be regarded as very unusual and slightly discourteous, especially as Mr Blackburn does not speak for the Tory Party and has little political standing. I therefore declined to go.'

The Union officers decided that they would not take such an affront to their honour lying down. William Rees-Mogg, the Librarian, suggested the obvious remedy, a letter to *The Times*. The four officers drafted a suitably magisterial rebuke which duly appeared in the paper. Mr Callaghan had been less than generous, it said. He had never been told that he was debating against the Conservative Party; the Union Society was not a hustings: it was a debating society.

In the end, Godfrey Smith was able to find a Labour speaker with fewer reservations about debating with deserters, in the form of Anthony Wedgwood Benn. Later, James Callaghan was down in Oxford on other business and made up his quarrel with Godfrey Smith. The Union officers believed that he had been reprimanded by Attlee for overreacting to the undergraduates.

The third in the wave of Liberal Presidents was Jeremy Thorpe. Not popular in the way that Smith and Day had been, he was regarded by some who knew him as overambitious, which is saying quite a lot in the atmosphere of the Oxford Union. It was believed that, although many flouted rules like the anti-canvassing regulations, Thorpe had overstepped the limit. There was a formal inquiry into his activities over the Liberal Assembly at Scarborough. He was also suspected of such devious ploys as organizing canvassing for an opponent so that the opponent would be disqualified if elected. Thorpe's defenders maintain that he did no more than other ambitious Union hopefuls. Jeremy Thorpe himself believes that nothing more than youthful pranks were involved.

Thorpe was certainly talented. His natural Union style, with a turn of phrase, a sense of timing and an ability for mimicry, was bound to go down well with a Union audience. He was a great extrovert. He wore Edwardian clothes, including frock coats and brocade waistcoats, and had a lifestyle to match. When lunching with friends at a restaurant near the Bodleian Library he would so it is said fling open the window there to indulge in what he described as 'addressing the multitude'. He was, in his way, a political version of Harold Acton.

Thorpe's Liberal principles had developed in defiance of family tradition. His father had been a Tory MP. The young Jeremy, however, was evacuated in the war to a school in America where he had become attracted to radicalism, partly in reaction to the Republicans surrounding him. He espoused Liberal principles during his time at Eton, and came up to Oxford determined to conquer the University in the interests of Liberalism, or as some of his rivals would have it, in the interests of Thorpe.

'Here is a personality whose vivacity, wit and easy manner stand in sparkling relief to the drab stage of Oxford life,' said his *Isis Idol*. 'His likes and dislikes are often too violently felt and expressed, and some feel as a future politician he would be wiser to be more discreet. An interesting and stimulating career lies ahead of him, providing he does not let his enthusiasm overreach his wisdom.'

Thorpe's activities at Oxford included a great burst of public speaking during the 1950 General Election. The advantage of the Liberal Party for undergraduates is that they can find themselves playing quite prominent roles at an early age. Thorpe spoke to at least one meeting every night, ending up at Oxford Town Hall on the eve of poll.

His first impact on the Union scene, however, seems to have been made not in a political debate, but on a motion deploring the fall of the House of Stuart. The President, Uwe Kitzinger, was piped to the Chair to the strains of 'Speed Bonny Boat'. The historian Michael Maclagan identified the nub of the debate by pointing out that the Stuarts and the Hanoverians were equally immoral, and the question was which of them were immoral in the more agreeable way. Thorpe's contribution to this profound argument was hailed as promising. 'He was interested in legitimacy and fascinated by illegitimacy. He dwelt on Oxford in Stuart times when disaffected Tories threw chamber pots. It was a time of sentiment and infidelity, of witty hairdressers and of enterprising mountebanks.'

Thorpe shared the preoccupation of politically minded contemporaries with Southern Africa. His interest in the issue at Oxford developed into one of the main concerns of his political career. In February 1950, the future 'bomber Thorpe' successfully moved a motion that South Africa was not worthy of membership of the Commonwealth.

He managed to bring South Africa into a speech about events in Asia at the end of the same year, a bad speech according to *Isis*. 'As a whole it was poorly constructed: the opening slow and tedious – a second-rate ABCA lecture on the history and geography of the Far East, the phrases often infelicitous – "the future is a matter of time." Yet at the end he got a good part of the applause to which he has become accustomed. Why? Because of his self-confident, party manner, his command of gesture, his way with interrupters, his ability to play with the hand – and the signet ring – of a maestro upon the emotions of his audience.'

The same sort of qualities were ascribed to Jeremy Thorpe in the description of his unsuccessful bid for the Presidency against Robin Day, when they both spoke in the debate about the extreme centre. 'He slumped forward, his long face lengthened by excessive gloom, his mind as empty of economics as it was full of wisecracks. He mentioned the motion once to assert that the House in general and he in particular did not want to bother with economic problems. After all, he said, what's all this stuff about inflation, and rate of interest, consumer surplus? They're not important. Let's talk about the election, the visitors, the Liberal Party, or even myself.'

The next time Jeremy Thorpe stood for the Presidency, the debate was about the philosophy of Conservatism. Thorpe did a good imitation of Churchill, and claimed that the Tory party was held together by no better bond than that of fear and self-preservation. The voting won him a majority of 57, with 352 votes, to Dick Taverne's 295 and William Rees-Mogg's 155. For all the reservations which people had about him, Jeremy Thorpe seemed an unstoppable force politically; not long afterwards he turned the talents which he had acquired at Oxford to the difficult task of winning a parliamentary seat for the Liberals.

One of the paper speakers chosen by Jeremy Thorpe was an undergraduate from Balliol called George Carman, who spoke against the proposition that the present values of Western civilization cannot meet the challenge of the modern age. 'It is not the values which are falling short,' he said, 'but we who are falling short of the values.' Twenty-eight years later, Carman acted as Jeremy Thorpe's defence counsel at the Old Bailey.

Thorpe's successor in the Presidential chair was in many ways his antithesis. William Rees-Mogg was as plodding as Thorpe was flamboyant; his speeches were as weighed down by methodically researched and esoteric facts as Thorpe's were unencumbered by attention to detail. Rees-Mogg's conversation, it was said at the time, went naturally with port; it did not fizz like Thorpe's. People laughed at Rees-Mogg, but liked him; they laughed with Thorpe, but were cool towards him.

The young William Rees-Mogg wore clothes which would not have disgraced a Victorian Prime Minister. When he was President, he lived in rooms behind Beaumont Street. 'His walls are hung with portraits,' said his *Isis Idol*, 'and his floors are covered with bits of paper he cannot find room for in his pockets. He rarely goes to bed, but never gets up, and is sure to be at home in the mornings, the wireless tuned to "Housewives' Choice", and the bed covered with a copy of the *Financial Times*.

'By lunch time he is wandering slowly towards the Carlton, dressed in a suit of indeterminate age, shape and colour. His tailor lives in Bath. Although fond of cricket he loathes physical exercise, and prefers to spend the afternoon paying calls. After a quick tea in Somerville he settles down to the day's work, except on Thursdays when he goes to the Union.'

Rees-Mogg, something of an Oxford institution, stood for election for office ten times in the Union; he was rejected for each of the four officers' chairs on separate occasions. He refused, however, to accept defeat and was eventually elected Librarian. The next term, he and Dick Taverne lost the Presidency to Jeremy Thorpe. With finals looming, it became a choice between becoming President and going all out for a first class degree. Taverne and Rees-Mogg discussed the situation together. Taverne opted for his books and duly collected his first. Rees-Mogg had been advised by his tutor that the Presidency would not make a great deal of difference to his academic chances. He stood, won, and ended up with a second.

In retrospect, Sir William feels he made the right choice. The Presidency, he points out, is rarer than a first, and shows evidence of public attributes; it indicates what people can achieve in the rough and tumble of ordinary life. The Union, he admits, took all his time at Oxford to teach him how to speak; but the powers of persuasion which he learnt there have subsequently proved invaluable. Fifty per cent of modern administrative life consists of persuading people in committees, making a case competently and amusingly in a short space of time. The Union taught him all that.

On his way to the President's chair at the Union, Rees-Mogg had a term as President of the Conservatives. He was a compromise choice between an aristocratic faction based on Christ Church and a progressive faction to which, although holding progressive views himself, he did not belong. One of his actions was to affiliate the Conservative Association to an Oxford peace group. This unlikely event took place after a meeting which he had with Shirley Catlin, the chairman of the Labour Club. It was at the time of the Korean War, and Shirley Catlin wanted to stop the peace group being dominated by Communists. By persuading the Conservatives to join she ensured an anti-communist majority, so that while all the other University peace groups were passing resolutions condemning South Korea, Oxford passed resolutions condemning North Korea.

Several undergraduate pens grappled with the challenge of describing the oratory of the young Rees-Mogg. His mixture of humour and pontification when he spoke on coal nationalization was depicted as 'popular and rightly so'. When he spoke on social equality, *Isis* called him a character quite unique and all too rare. 'One knows exactly what to expect. He winds his way by devious, sometimes completely incomprehensible, routes through a maze of personal opinion backed by the odd reminiscence here, the obscure quotation there, and presented with a philosophical old world charm which knows it is right and does not care a bit if people disagree. No one was really surprised when he began quoting from Edward IV's Parliamentary Roll, though I am not quite sure what it really referred to. Still, that did not matter. The burden of the member from Balliol's argument was that Social Equality did not exist, and if it did no one wanted it. One might just as well sell a mermaid to a misogynist.'

Debating Conservatism, it was said, William Rees-Mogg began 'by being indignant and ended up by being quietly soporific. "Socialists had taken us from cheap money to dear money to no money". He paused, readjusted his glasses, pushed back his lock of hair, smiled and became William again, kind, thoughtful, pleading with the sweetest reasoning.'

He took part in the debate on the churches' social record as well. 'The priests of God must be tribunes of the people,' he told the

House. 'He took a drink of water, his thumb vanished into his waistcoat pocket, his hands spread out, expressively, before him and he made a quick amiable and informed survey of various churches returning to England in time to hear the Lords debate Contraception and single out a long quotation from Disraeli which left the way completely clear for that vigorous bird of prey.'

Interviewed on the eve of his Presidency, William Rees-Mogg was asked about his ambitions. 'In Oxford I hope, as we all do,' he told the interviewer, 'to obtain a good degree and go down in the odour of sanctity. I have not set my heart on becoming Prime Minister. But I should be willing at any time to accept the portfolio of the Chancellor of the Duchy of Lancaster.'

It was perhaps easier for contemporaries to predict the career of Stanley Booth-Clibborn. There is little surprise that he has progressed from the Secretary's chair to a bishop's throne. 'There is a touch of the earnest young curate in him,' noted the *Manchester Guardian*, in a description of a debate in which he took part against R. A. Butler in 1949.

Booth-Clibborn is a descendant of General Booth of the Salvation Army. An idealistic socialist, he has held to his political as well as his religious beliefs. 'His arguments are always sincere,' *Isis* once said, 'and he is allowed to make statements which, coming from someone else, would infuriate the House. Some would argue that his faith in the social conscience is at least a little misplaced. Fifty years ago he would have been a great and valuable crusader for a new party. Today he tends to ignore issues which his fellow politicans find more pressing and more serious. A party, he maintained, ought, before it is fit to lead the country, have a social conscience, faith, courage, a consistent set of principles and the support of the people as a whole. All these the Labour Party had.'

The ecclesiastical tradition also lived on in the Union in the form of the redoubtable Canon Claude Jenkins, the Regius Professor of Divinity, who served with distinction as Senior Librarian for twenty years. One term, the proofs of the Standing Committee photograph were unusually slow coming back from the photographers. On enquiring, the Union officers discovered that Canon Jenkins had been sitting in the front row exposing a line of brass flybuttons. The flashlight had created an ethereal glow around these flybuttons which had considerably distorted the picture. With judicious touching up, canonical dignity was restored, and the photograph joined the others up the Union's back staircase.

Norman St John Stevas, who also became Secretary of the Union, had all the makings of a rather different kind of bishop from Stanley Booth-Clibborn. His beatific smile, *Isis* once said, prevented any offence being given by those acid touches which tradition demanded in welcoming visitors to the Society. He became and remains the only person who has ever held office in both the Cambridge and the Oxford Union. He described himself when he first spoke as a Cambridge virgin on the brink of an Oxford Union. Oxford made gentle fun of his origins. When he attended the opening ceremony for the new Union bar, *Isis* wrote of him, 'The only freshman there – Mr Norman St John Stevas – was busy making a good impression. He was thrilled to be at a University and excited at the sight of champagne.'

In the Union, St John Stevas rivalled the wit and flamboyance of Jeremy Thorpe; but he impressed with knowledge rather than energy. 'His superb diction, together with a certain lack of emphasis, gave the impression that really he considered a climax rather beneath him,' someone wrote of one of his speeches. Nonetheless, he argued lucidly, firmly and indefatigably. One notable contribution came in a speech in favour of electoral reform in 1951. 'With our present electoral system, you blame the other party for the ills which beset the country. The present system deprives us of the cooperation and unity which is so necessary today.' The motion was carried.

Norman St John Stevas' ambition was to become President of both Unions. Not everyone approved; Robin Day in particular felt that he was pot-hunting for the sake of it and, with his experience, had an unfair advantage over the younger and greener Oxford undergraduates with whom he was competing for office. Day conducted a campaign of harassment against St John Stevas, interrupting his speeches at every possible opportunity to try and prick his bubble. The campaign began almost as soon as St John Stevas arrived as a member. Day made an elaborate introduction from the despatch box. 'One has only to visit his elegant rooms in Christ Church,' he said, 'to see that there is a man of taste, of refinement, a man of society. There on the mantleshelf are 100 invitation cards: some accepted, some rejected, many of them quite genuine. Here on a table are carelessly strewn cultured periodicals and books – books about art. You know Mr President, those big books about art. And there on the side board are the bottles, the bottles of a man of discernment: Chateaubriand '32, Chablis '27, and Chanel Number 5.'

Later Day changed his tactics. While Stevas was speaking, he feigned complete boredom. Eventually Stevas expressed surprise that nothing he had said had brought Day to his feet. Day rose soporifically, made his way wearily to the dispatch box and said, 'I'm prepared to go to any lengths in order to make the honourable member's speech a memorable one.'

In the event, Stevas was beaten for the Presidency by an American from Illinois called Howard Shuman. He had been in the audience when Tony Benn, Edward Boyle and Kenneth Harris had visited his university on a debating tour and became enchanted with the idea of the Oxford Union. Tony Benn had done much to help him come to Oxford. For one debate, he was persuaded by Robin Day to adopt the role of the stage American claiming to come from a place called East Whistlestop, and sporting a loud multi-coloured lumber jacket with a red baseball cap. By the time he became President, however, he had adopted what he called the English 'striped trouser technique', and held great store by the importance of the office. 'If I can get President of the Oxford Union,' he announced, 'I can get President of the United States.' He became instead Administrative Assistant to Senator William Proxmire.

In that self-confident era nobody questioned the institutions of Oxford; most of the Union activists enjoyed themselves there, and believed that their activities marked the prelude to glittering careers. The President after Howard Shuman, Patrick Mayhew, was comparatively modest about his aims. Where William Rees-Mogg had aspired to the Duchy of Lancaster, Mayhew claimed he wanted to be First Lord of the Admiralty. He became President ninety-nine years after his great-grandfather G. J. Goschen, later a Chancellor of the Exchequer. Although he was also a descendant of Edmund Burke, Mayhew's oratorical talents were not always appreciated. 'Monotonously cadenced,' *Isis* said of an early effort, 'it seemed like a poor imitation of Churchill, without the whistle of false teeth and the warm liquidity that make that statesman's speeches so easy on the ear. It is a mistake for any speaker to use the word 'finally' more than seven times.' As time went on, Mayhew made his reputation more as a wit than as a politician; his imitation of William Rees-Mogg was considered outstanding. His *Isis Idol* suggested that his rambling stride and venerable mood of oratory would seem to make him a fairly easy target for affectionate satire, even in the Union which cherishes the old-fashioned.

Some of the more serious political figures of the day did not bother much with the Union. Peter Parker, thought of by some as a future Prime Minister, was Chairman of the Labour Club, President of Lincoln College Junior Common Room and Hamlet in the Dramatic Society production. His attendance at the Union was rare, though he did appear to make a speech deploring the modern movement in poetry and the fine arts. The artist, he said, must give the average man the chance to understand and feel for himself; artists were too isolated from the community.

Another figure from the theatrical world lured to the Union for a single performance was Tony Richardson. He began his speech on the motion that the British stage was empty by firing a blank cartridge into the gallery. His speech, said *Isis*, was eagerly awaited by the strong contingents from the dramatic societies who came to see their long-haired Samson among the Philistines. 'Seeing him had to be sufficient, for he delivered a tirade with such speed and gusto that it was almost impossible to hear most of it; nevertheless, his performance was marked by many gymnastic and dramatic highlights. When he had finished, he returned to the trapdoor from which he had sprung earlier like a pantomime demon king, having spoiled by his delivery what might have been an extremely good speech.'

It all made a change, anyway, from the political debates. The Union's politicians were being subjected to the criticisms that earlier generations had suffered. Robert Robinson contributed a piece to *Isis* in 1950 which he called 'Dull Dogs and Hollow Men':

'Politics in Oxford is a pale flood of unaerated detail, a zestless melange of dull but accurate information, a turgid infusion of inhibited politeness towards opponents, and a flaccid obedience to party doctrine. In the Union, in the political clubs, in the magazines, there is not one personality to be found: instead, politics in this University continues to exude a filtrate of thick-tongued youths, tight-crammed with every debating point ever recorded in *Hansard*, and more resembling articulate catalogues than human beings.

'Where are the idealists? The champions of lost causes? The leaders of proud minorities? Oxford should teem with these. Have they all gone into the dark, to be replaced by a synthetic race of cheer-leaders, of touch-line supporters of the game as played professionally?

'The Oxford politician is ponderous. Young men of twenty-one are to be seen straining to adopt the comportment, the gestures, the facial expressions, the phraseology and the inflections of old port-poisoned buffers who have spent forty years in the Athenaeum behind *The Times*. Perhaps they imagine any rebelliousness at Oxford will be held against them when they come to try their luck outside: perhaps they have a picture in their minds of an Eton-cropped female with elastic-sided boots in one of the lesser ministries, who is noting down avidly their comments for future reference.

'But one thing is clear: they must do something. For at present they are as dusty a bunch of old grandmothers as ever verified a reference. They have no notion of the excitement of their task, nor of the adventurousness of the politics they should offer. Rot them to a nasty, logical, piddling little grave, for *they* have no business with ways of life.'

At least the prematurely port-poisoned young buffers of the Union enjoyed each others' company. This was not a period which relied excessively on outside visitors, although there were the regulars. Richard Crossman and Robert Boothby could be guaranteed to put on an effective double act. They came down more than once together to argue about Communism; the Cold War had become the major political preoccupation. Both had the Union manner. Challenged in a debate on Tory foreign policy to say whether in any of his speech he would actually refer to the subject of the motion, Boothby replied 'Yes – in a very moving, brief peroration.'

Crossman describes one of his many Union visits in his diaries. 'At the Union they hold a very grand dinner in the old-fashioned style before the presidential debate. There were lots of beautiful girls in evening dress and the two Proctors were also in attendance, both of them taught by me, which shows how old I am growing.

'The motion was "that the Western powers have failed since 1945 effectively to meet and understand the challenge of Communism." As I was speaking for the motion, I had a relatively easy time. I was in full spate, talking about how the Tories always send a cruiser somewhere at the beginning of a Tory Conference, when a young Conservative rose and asked me whether I would acknowledge my debt to Mr Ian Mikardo, who a fortnight ago had made the same joke. This, of course, brought the house down, and there were uproarious demands for "Answer" and 'Withdraw'.

'I wish I was as comfortable in the Commons as I am in the Union. I merely scratched my nose and said, "The important thing for us Bevanites is who gets down to Oxford first." For some unknown reason this was regarded as a most brilliant reply. So I proceeded to my peroration about the Copernican revolution – the solar system, with the white centre of Europe in the middle and the dark satellites going round it, has been irrefragably broken etc etc – only to be told that Harold Wilson had used this the week before. Since the first joke was one of George Wigg's, which I had told Ian, and I had invented the other, I felt more coordination was necessary.'

Boothby and Crossman scored effortlessly off each other. Once, when Boothby knew he was going to lose the vote, he said, 'I have an overwhelming sense of having won the argument.' In his speech, Crossman countered, 'Mr Boothby has an overwhelming sense of having won the argument – but of having won it for whom?' When they went on a debating tour of the United States, Robin Day and Geoffrey Johnson Smith felt that this example of the cut and thrust of British debate would go down well across the Atlantic, and they used it frequently. One night, they had had a quarrel; Day, knowing that Johnson Smith was not listening to a speech which he had heard several times before, left out the prearranged Boothby line. When Johnson Smith came out with the Crossman reply about the opposition claiming they had won the argument but for whom, Day intervened and accused Johnson Smith of putting words into his mouth, throwing him hopelessly off his stride.

Attlee came down in early 1952, the year after he had lost power. He was given the loudest and longest ovation which the Union has ever heard, according to the President of the day, although that did not stop the Society, with its Conservative majority, from voting for the motion which he was opposing. Attlee had perhaps riled the Tories by suggesting they were uneducated. He had received a letter, he said, from one of them containing the three most profane words in the language, all of which were misspelt.

Dr Edith Summerskill, with two children at Oxford, was another regular visitor of the time. 'Erect and formidable, with metallic streaks of grey flanking her coiffure, she seemed the embodiment of militant feminism,' according to *Isis*. Vera Brittain also came to speak. 'She is Shirley Catlin's mother,' said *Isis*, 'and that is quite enough to make the House love her. It is rewarding to hear a speech delivered in a tone of cheerful, friendly commonsense without rapture or rhodomontade. She is a feminist and she said so. The need to get back to Somerville before the gate was locked at

11.15 saved her from going on too long.' The gallantry of Oxford journalists towards eminent women visitors knew no bounds. Lady Violet Bonham-Carter was said by the *Oxford Magazine* to have had the entire House at her feet. 'One felt that there was none who would not have jumped into the Isis at her bidding.'

After Churchill returned to power in 1951 the Union remained Tory-dominated. Life at Oxford grew steadily more comfortable, with good jobs to be had almost for the asking at the end of the three year idyll. Oxford had known such good times before, but not for a while, and the ex-national servicemen who were replacing the war veterans were little inclined for the most part to question their good fortune.

The Conservatives were still split in two. The aristocratic faction centred on Christ Church, went in for a great deal of hunting and shooting. Some of them kept spaniels in their rooms. When they made the occasional speech in the Union they were open to barbs like that of *Isis*: 'In the intervals between huntin' and shootin', Mr Maxwell-Hyslop has learnt enough about speakin' to get by, but one cannot see him inspirin'.'

The floppy young men in cavalry twills frequented the Carlton Club, which maintained an atmosphere of pre-war opulence very much to their taste. They were a snobbish lot, and when an ambitious undergraduate called Michael Heseltine from Shrewsbury School arrived on the scene it was clear that he was not sufficiently blue-blooded to enter their circles. Instead, he organized his own rival Conservative grouping, the Blue Ribbon Club, which was designed to appeal to progressive, non-Old Etonian Tories.

Michael Heseltine knew exactly where he was going. He used to eat regularly at a restaurant by the station called Long John's, run by a man called Silver, with his friend Julian Critchley. Here they would amuse themselves by writing out lists of the offices which Heseltine was planning to achieve, starting with the Blue Ribbon Club, moving up through the Conservative Association, the Oxford Union, Parliament and the Cabinet to Number Ten Downing Street, together with dates by which these ambitions would be fulfilled. He has remained more or less on course.

His achievement in becoming President of the Union was remarkable, in that he was never a very good speaker and he did not know very much. He was, in fact, something of a late developer. An early reference to one of his debating speeches says that he overran his time, a vice to which he is still prone as a much more successful and skilled orator. Patrick Mayhew wrote rather patronizingly in the *Oxford Magazine* about a later performance that he had shown great improvement on his past form. 'With a bit more warmth he will be very good.' The next year, however, the *Isis* critic complained that he spoke in a monotone, far too quickly, and was very difficult to hear from the back.

Michael Heseltine spent many hours at Mrs Stella Gatehouse's speaking classes to improve his technique. Mrs Gatehouse, the wife of a parson with a parish near Bicester, used to make her services available to the City Conservative Association and to undergraduates. Heseltine became something of a favourite of hers. One Sunday, he was even invited to preach in the Reverend Gatehouse's church. Despite a strict injunction not to mention politics, he treated the congregation to a disquisition which bore a striking resemblance to one of his Union speeches, although he threw in a passing reference to God.

With all this effort, the *Oxford Magazine* noted that he was beginning to resemble a regular Hyde Park orator. 'He can answer interruptions very effectively, look breezily confident at times, and at others quiet and confidential.' His real flair, though, was as an organizer. He did much to redeem the Union's ever-precarious financial position. He was Chairman of the Committee which ran the Union Ball at Christmas in 1953 and helped to persuade the Union to run a debate for the BBC Television cameras. As Treasurer in the summer of 1954, he attempted a salvage operation on the dining room, and turned a loss there into a profit. 'If one really wants to see human happiness in existence one has only to enter the Union dining room to see Michael Heseltine,' his friend and rival Anthony Howard wrote at the time. The Union, Heseltine announced, was now a commercial undertaking.

Other innovations followed. A television set was installed. Then Heseltine persuaded his committee to convert the cellars for dancing. The walls which had reverberated to fledgling oratory for so long were to be shaken by Michael Heseltine's jazz bands and to echo to the sound of his cash tills; but without his efforts they might not have survived at all. He did at least provide a venue which would be used a few years later by a promising undergraduate jazz musician called Dudley Moore.

Meanwhile, despite Mrs Gatehouse, Heseltine's oratory was still receiving only mixed notices. 'An agglomeration of futilities ("I am not talking in high intellectual terms; I am dragging in reality" "Human nature is at the bottom of this motion", "We must be quite honest about this") was garnished with absurd gestures and uncontrolled delivery.' An unexpected appearance in favour of a motion criticizing the Tory Government's foreign policy turned out a damp squib, according to the *Oxford Magazine*. Heseltine rather surprisingly argued for a reduction in Britain's standard of living and in spending on armaments in favour of economic expansion in Britain's colonies and the creation of a Third World Force. He was heckled for this act of apostasy, but ploughed on. 'Rapid delivery and undistinguished phrasing,' declared *Isis*, 'need not accompany sincerity nor even prove its existence, and they tend to forfeit the audience's attention.'

Heseltine did rather better when he spoke against the motion that 'this House refuses to be alarmed and despondent at the prospect of 1983'. This was the Presidential debate. Heseltine put forward a progressive Conservative case with what was described as an unaccustomed neatness of phrase; he had in fact had considerable help from friends in the composition of the speech. In its struggle for freedom, he said, the West was in grave danger of sacrificing the very principles it sought to preserve. Could anyone honestly say that he was not alarmed at what the future held for Southern Africa? Within the Commonwealth we found the evils we detest and which we fought in the last war. In America, the cult of McCarthy had become the curse of democracy. He had, said *Isis*, presented the case for liberty with force and conviction. 'It is irrelevant to say that he has not got the Union manner, and that his voice is too loud for the Hall.'

Michael Heseltine won an easy victory over his nearest rival. He could not, wrote Anthony Howard in his *Isis Idol*, owe his success to his oratory, nor to his popularity. 'He has never, as he is the first to own, been considered "a nice chap" by those who know him only from afar. It has always been "that man Heseltine".' His secret, it is suggested, was rather persistence and pertinacity. 'When Michael has been seriously opposed in Union elections, he has fought as though for his life; and it has, in fact, quite literally been his life for which he was fighting. Yet it was not an unhealthy longing – this longing of his for the Presidency, for it was not primarily a selfish one. Admittedly, he is always making frightful remarks like "We're all here for what we can get out of it". But he doesn't really believe it as he says it; and no one who has worked with him, or rather worked under him (for Michael, whose father is a colonel, is very much the G.O.C.), ever could. His loyalty to, and affection for, the Union is the most genuine thing about Michael. It is possibly a rather possessive form of affection, for it relentlessly requires that the Union shall conform to his plans. Two terms ago people laughed at those plans: today Michael, as the chief advocate of the Brighter Union Policy, can afford to smile, if not to laugh at those who opposed him. He has toiled for the Union as has probably no other undergraduate in the whole of its history.

'Lots of people, of course, disapprove of Michael. They dislike his irreverence, his irresponsibility, and quite frankly his ignorance. But most of them, if they know him at all, still cannot help liking him; and those who don't have to keep themselves constantly up to hysteria pitch to prevent it happening. Michael has all the roguish honesty, the sudden reckless humility, and the rakish charm to be the hero of a picaresque romance.'

Even as a senior Cabinet Minister, Michael Heseltine remembers his Union achievements as a pinnacle of his career. 'President of the Union is top of the pile. There's nowhere else to go. In your own context, in your own generation, that is it. There are twenty Cabinet Ministers, a hundred other Government Ministers, and in commercial terms thousands of people reaching senior positions. But the President of the Union is something different again. It is something you pay rather a price for in the period immediately afterwards; you reach a pinnacle far too early in life for the scale of opportunity it represents. But when you're there, in the eight weeks for which it exists, then the world is at your feet and it is a privilege beyond price.'

From the other side of the political fence, the Labour Club produced a clutch of fifties' Presidents, Bryan Magee, Tyrell Burgess, Jeremy Isaacs, Anthony Howard and Brian Walden among them. As usual, ideological splits in Labour's ranks mirrored the social divisions among the Conservatives. Labour supporters divided between the Bevanites and the right, and later between the supporters of CND and those who believed in going clothed into conference chambers.

Most Labour supporters, right and left, were happy to go to the Union. There was reckoned to be a Labour block vote which could be mustered to elect socialist undergraduates to office. The Labour Club was the largest of the political clubs at the time, and its members usually turned out for elections, although they seldom voted the Tories down in debates.

Labour undergraduates were most preoccupied with colonial questions, in particular South Africa, the Mau Mau in Kenya and Cyprus. The Bomb featured prominently as well. Anthony Howard made an unsuccessful attempt as early as 1954 to mobilize the Union behind banning the Bomb. Aneurin Bevan himself was lured down to speak to the Labour Club in the Union debating hall, although he was not now prepared to address as bourgeois a body as the Union Society itself.

In general, however, it was still not a time of great political controversy. 'There is no longer much discontent for a roving passion to feed upon,' pronounced one contributor to *Isis*. 'We are rapidly approaching a state of moo-cow happiness when colonial policy is about the wickedest thing we can think of and politics generally is losing its appeal for those who might otherwise be among its champions.'

It was largely to stimulate interest in the Union in a summer term when other attractions seemed rather more alluring that Anthony Howard decided to invite Sir Oswald Mosley to take part in a debate. Standing Committee, led by Jeremy Isaacs, were outraged and forced Howard to cancel. Three years later, however, Brian Walden issued another invitation to Sir Oswald, and this time the visit went ahead. He faced hostile questioning about the invitation, but defended his decision on the grounds of free speech. 'If I am going to be asked to exclude guests from the Society just because certain people find their views odious, it will be the dangerous end of a very unpleasant wedge,' he said.

Another stratagem for increasing interest in the Union was to turn its attention to religion. In the mid-1950s, as again in the mid-1970s, something of a religious revival flowered in Oxford, harnessed for the Union in particular by Anthony Howard, himself the son of a clergyman. When he was in the Chair the Union decided by one vote that it regretted the approval given by the Churches to the Billy Graham crusade. Jeremy Isaacs had the members debating the Roman Catholic Church. The motion that the world would be a better place without its political power and influence was narrowly carried, after a battle between the champion of birth control Marie Stopes and the leading Jesuit Father Joseph Christie. Father Christie came back four years later to defend the churches as a whole against the allegation that they could not deal with the problems of the twentieth century. Democracy, liberty and equality before the law all sprung from the Christian outlook, he said.

The impact of press and the media preoccupied the Union in the fifties. Oxford, as usual slightly behind the rest of the Western world, was coming to grips with the presence of television. In 1945 undergraduates caught their first glimpse of a set in the same spirit of astonishment at the wonders of technology with which their predecessors had gaped at aeroplanes before the First World War. A lecture on the new medium at the Junior Science Club was packed out, and most of the audience, it was said, suffered agonies of impatience waiting for the demonstration which was to follow it. The speaker stopped talking in time for the last half hour of the BBC's broadcast from Alexandra Palace. 'The audience, entranced,' reported *Isis*, 'watched a darts match, a demonstration of African art, and a pianist.'

In 1953 the Union decided that it did not welcome the advent of commercial television. Christopher Mayhew came down to speak against the motion, accompanied by a baboon called Beauchamp to back up his case. This was shortly after American television had interrupted the showing of the Queen's coronation with commercials featuring the chimpanzee J. Fred Muggs. 'This animal is greedy and can only gibber,' Mayhew said of Beauchamp. 'He is therefore perfectly qualified to take part in a commercial television programme.'

The Union activists tended by now to be the younger undergraduates who had come up straight from school on state scholarships. The commoners had to do their military service first. On the whole, they stayed away from the clubs and societies, preferring work, sport and pubs, not necessarily in that order.

One of the most precocious of the adolescent meteors was Brian Walden, the son of a plate glazier from the Midlands. In an early performance he attacked South Africa, where the two main parties had been arguing about the appropriate punishment for a group of political offenders. They were both agreed on corporal punishment; the argument was over how much of it to inflict. 'What will the South African High Commissioner say to us?' he asked. 'Why, he will say, what are a few lashes between friends?'

In Parliament Brian Walden gained a reputation as one of the best post-war speakers but meanwhile his Oxford technique was given the inevitable irreverent analysis by his contemporaries. 'His method and gestures are repetitive. Has there been a debate when he has not singled out all his opponents in turn, with his finger, to ridicule and embarrass them? Has there been a debate when he has not tried to lord it over us and lead us by the nose?' Again, 'He breathes controversy as others breathe oxygen. When the Last Trump sounds, he will turn the Day of Judgement into a full dress debate with St Peter'. And, 'He has kept his vitriol, but he applied it in telling little dabs instead of smearing it all over the opposition.'

When Brian Walden was Treasurer of the Union the political mood of Oxford, and indeed of the country, changed. Suez and Hungary dispelled the prevailing apathy, and engendered passions which had not been felt in the University since the 1930s. There were demonstrations for and against Eden. Students from the trade union college Ruskin were prominent in organizing protests against the Government; Tories from Brasenose retaliated by throwing tomatoes at them, singing 'Rule, Britannia' and devising banners with such subtle slogans as 'shoot the wogs'. At a big emergency meeting organized by the anti-Suez forces in the debating hall, Denis Healey, Janet Vaughan of Somerville College, Raghavan Iyer, a former Union President, and Lord Altrincham all spoke.

The Union proper was circumspect about Suez. The Standing Committee decided against an emergency debate, on the grounds that a snap decision in a vote could lead to the sort of outcry which followed the King and Country motion. The funds, it was agreed, could not stand another wave of patriotic fathers refusing to pay their sons' subscriptions. Eventually, however, a debate was held, and the motion 'that this House opposes Great Britain's military action in Egypt' was carried by 352 votes to 206.

Front-line politicians were lined up, but cancelled because of a vote in the Commons. Instead, four recent officers came back to add such weight as they could to the occasion. It was a debate conducted with great passion, in which Bryan Magee branded the Foreign Secretary Selwyn Lloyd as a suburban Machiavelli. Eden, he said, was suffering from delusions of adequacy; his action was lunatic and imbecilic. He had preserved peace by telling the Israelis 'If you don't stop invading Egypt, we'll invade too.' Britain's reputation had sunk, he said, to the lowest level since 1783. The country had lost more than its good name; it had helped perhaps to lose the liberty of Hungary. 'Our action in Egypt enabled the Russians to get away with what they had done at nothing like the price they would otherwise have had to pay.'

Peter Tapsell, now a Tory, opposed. Amidst vociferous heckling, he took the Government line that those who did not support Eden were like the appeasers of Munich. Egypt had provoked Israel; the British Government had aimed to stop the war and they had succeeded.

Jeremy Thorpe followed. During his speech Brian Walden, who was sitting in the Treasurer's chair, passed him a message. 'I have news relating to an old friend,' Thorpe announced when he had read it. 'I can tell the House that Sir Edward Boyle has resigned from the Government.' It was a moment of high drama. The opposition looked disconcerted as Thorpe pressed home his attack. Eden had lied, he said. Tapsell intervened to warn him to beware of slander. Eden had lied, repeated Thorpe.

Then William Rees-Mogg stood up to defend the Government. He, unlike Tapsell, was heard with respect. Britain, he claimed, had averted the real danger of direct Russian intervention in the Middle East. The majority for the opposition point of view was, nonetheless, decisive. This was a very different generation in a very different mood from the undergraduates who had cheered Eden to the echo in the debating hall ten years before.

The political temperature, raised by Suez then Hungary, was kept high by the arguments over the Bomb. Oxford became passionately divided between two camps: those with CND badges and those without. Brian Walden argued at the time that CND consisted largely of the champions of the USSR who realized that their cause could no longer be defended after Hungary, but recognizes in retrospect that many others had been drawn to the movement as a great moral crusade.

Suez and its aftermath had the Conservative right worked up as well. They were always more comfortable, however, in their dining clubs than in the Union, and the successful Union Conservatives of the day tended to be on the progressive wing of the party, among them Kenneth Baker, Anthony Newton and Alan Haselhurst. They looked to figures like Ian Macleod, Reginald Maudling and Edward Heath as their models.

In the Labour Club the gulf was widening between those who were loyal to Hugh Gaitskell and those who admired Canon Collins and Michael Foot. It was a mixture of political and personal differences which led to an epic feud between Brian Walden and the Union's leading left-winger Dennis Potter.

Walden once wrote of Potter, 'On those rare occasions when he crawls out of his cocoon, and faces his Labour Party critics, Potter is often forced to admit that much of what he writes and says is contradictory, that many of his facts are wrong, that his knowledge of a particular subject is slight or non-existent, and his diatribes upon it are therefore somewhat less than fair.' Potter regarded Walden in turn as a party hack. 'Walden's definition of constructive seems to me synonymous with existing Labour Party policies; for not only is it disloyal to criticize these, but unintelligent as well. I readily confess that external contradictions abound in my tiresome rhetoric, and humbly admit that I do not know the answers with anything like the incisive and commendable certainty of my critic. Walden thinks, for instance, that we ought to keep the Bomb, or, rather, he will think so right up to the moment that the Labour Party decides otherwise.'

Walden became President of the Union; Potter later stood for the post and was defeated. Their differences came to a head with a monumental row which spilt into the pages of the national newspapers. The cause was a somewhat obscure incident involving the election for Walden's successor. Potter accused Walden of unconstitutionally trying to use his influence against one of the candidates, at which Walden called the allegation a filthy smear and threatened to sue Potter. There was uproar in the debating hall. In due course, a tribunal of inquiry reported after a considerable lapse of time and to the satisfaction of neither Walden nor Potter. It was one of those affairs which become a complete obsession at Oxford at the time when the personalities involved are regarded as the most important people in the known world. The other characteristic of such incidents is that it is not long before no one can remember what the fuss was all about.

Between them, the two disputants did dominate Oxford politics. Like Brian Walden, Dennis Potter was a working-class boy, but he made more of the fact. According to his *Isis Idol*, he boiled eggs in a tin kettle rather than dine in Hall, and tried every strategem to stop his college servant from calling him 'Sir'. In the Union, he railed against the Tory Government and the Gaitskellites. The Government, he said, had allowed Expresso bars to boom while cotton factories closed.

Dennis Potter admitted cheerfully that he had a chip on his shoulder. In his play *Stand up, Nigel Barton*, his leading character is working-class, torn between his roots in a mining community and Oxford, so that he becomes a bit of a misfit in both. Nigel Barton makes a speech in the Union in which he expresses his contempt for what the stage directions describe as the charade and puerilities there. 'There speaks the eternal voice of Oxford,' says Barton. 'Nothing is worth personal commitment. Nothing should be allowed to disturb the indolence and lethargy of its institutions. Nothing should scratch the old stones or ancient battlements. That we should Not Fight for King and Country is debated and decided with the same juvenile frivolity as the equally momentous proposition that well-bred camels should have only one hump.'

PRESIDENT: One lump, sir. Or two?
NIGEL: Oh, for God's sake.
(PRESIDENT *sits down, abashed*)
NIGEL: The proposer has stated in impeccable, braying cut-glass tones that class no longer matters in Britain. I do not greatly care to hear an Old Etonian tell me that class is of no consequence. His parents have not wasted their money in buying him his privilege, have they?'

Ten years after he went down from Oxford, Dennis Potter told *Cherwell* how he looked back on his Union days. 'Shaming as it was, I enjoyed the drama of those crises. It was pleasing to see the Establishment beginning to panic. It also gave me confidence. The feeling came that if I can do it here I can do it out there.'

With undergraduates like Dennis Potter about, anger was again becoming fashionable as a political emotion at Oxford. The world of the Aldermaston marches began to impinge on the Union, instigating a new vogue for protest and stridency.

The fifties came to an end in the Union with a scene which combined elements of the old world with a flavour of the new. In December 1959, the Prime Minister Harold Macmillan visited the debating hall for the unveiling of the bust of him carved by the sculptor Oscar Nemon. He was the first of the Union's great men to be honoured in this way during his own lifetime. When his words were forgotten, Mr Macmillan said in his speech, he would at least be remembered as an excellent example of Oscar Nemon's middle period. 'This is a very great occasion for me. I have never had it so good. You have paid me an unparalleled honour; you have put me among the immortals. I am deeply touched by the kindness you have shown me and thrilled by the honour you have done me.' Lord Monckton unveiled the bust, reminding the Union that he had given the young Macmillan his first paper speech. 'It is nice to know that you back a winner once in your life.'

Before the debate started, however, the Secretary of the Conservative Association, Phillip Whitehead, moved an adjournment motion to protest at the Government's failure to bring the nationalist leader in Nyasaland Dr Hastings Banda to trial. The progressive Conservatives, who were much exercised by colonial questions, thought the presence of Macmillan, Monckton and Alan Lennox-Boyd in the chamber created an opportunity for protest which was too good to miss. Mr Macmillan passed a message to the President saying that he would leave if the adjournment motion was carried. The President called for a show of hands and, despite the decisive majority in favour of the motion, declared it defeated. There were cries of shame and demands for a count. Another of the officers, Alan Haselhurst, suggested that the views of the House had been heard by the Prime Minister and that it would be discourteous to him to prolong the issue. His view prevailed. Nevertheless, even on an occasion when the Union was basking in its traditions by honouring a great figure from its past, the new stridency had succeeded in breaking through.

CHAPTER SIX

VIVE LA DIFFERENCE

WOMEN IN THE UNION

It is hard to believe that the Oxford Union did not admit women as full members until 1963. Some would say that this only goes to prove what a stuffy, dyed-in-the-wool institution it is. Others would point out that the Union has espoused quite radical views at various stages of its history, its attitude to women merely reflecting how much upper middle-class society in general took male dominance for granted, and how resistant until recently its structure was to change.

In his book published sixty years ago, Herbert Morrah comments approvingly on a Union kept free of feminine influence. He has a clear idea of the proper role for women. 'Ladies have always been welcome in the Union gallery, and on the whole they have been well-rewarded for their tolerance and their patience. Their presence has been greatly appreciated.' Morrah goes on to tell the story of an Eights Week debate, where a questioner asked the President, 'Sir, is the gallery safe?' The President replied, 'The honourable member may be reassured, but should anything happen, the house could only rejoice in the fall of heavenly bodies.'

Prejudice against women in Oxford was formidable. One J. E. C. Bodley, reminiscing in *The Times* in 1923, wrote of the Union jubilee year half a century before, 'Every incident of those radiant months is fresh in my mind. Oxford was almost unspoiled, though ominous signs were looming. Architects were busy at their meddling sacrilege. Royal Commissions had licensed Fellows to marry; and this revolution, with the founding of the women's colleges, was to engulf the lovely city in a suburban wilderness made for housing the invaders.'

Before the First World War there was no question of women joining the Union, although the suffragette Mrs Millicent Fawcett did become the first woman guest in 1908. In 1922 came the first of many motions to allow women to take part in debates. It failed by thirty-four votes, and the arguments of even its proponents did not exactly place the Union in the vanguard of the women's rights movement. D. V. Thomson of Balliol said that members on his side of the House were in favour of women voting in the Union since the fair sex invariably voted for the handsomest candidate. C. H. Pearson from the same college claimed that there was no cause for alarm that male members would be outshone by the women as speakers. Like Rugby football, debating was something at which women could never compete with men. Women would at least make debates more amusing. But the opposers demanded one last refuge from the competition of the opposite sex. They argued successfully that the House should stick to its precious and deepseated prejudices.

Women were now coming to Oxford in increasing numbers. Although very much a minority on the outer fringes of the university, they were perceived by some as a threat. Leslie Hore-Belisha complained in the *Evening News* in 1922 that women were unbalanced in their attitude to education. The article maintained they were spoiling the fun of Oxford by working too hard, an accusation which could be levelled against relatively few male undergraduates. 'At Oxford and Cambridge, the ideal is not the undergraduate who shuts himself up in four walls of books. Women in the universities are ignoring games and are avoiding society. There is no such thing as a woman "Blue", although there are plenty of "blue stockings".' Hore-Belisha feared that women would 'transform the whole character of our society and convert us from a freedom-loving, fresh-air loving, tolerant sportsmanlike people into drudges and experts.' He ended on a positively apocalyptic note. The women's colleges, he alleged, were prejudiced against the sportswoman or the hostess of the future. Unless this was reversed, 'all that we understand by English civilization will fall with a crash'.

The Union stayed, nonetheless, on the progressive side of the suffrage argument. In the 1920s they voted to approve the extension of the franchise to women aged between twenty-one and thirty, although the motion provided another field day for the male chauvinists. One undergraduate argued for the present system as ensuring that only those women interested in politics turned out to vote; a woman would need to be strongly motivated politically to declare that she was over thirty.

Women did have more enlightened defenders; Gerald Gardiner for one. In 1924 he wrote, 'From the rules and regulations which seem to apply to the women students one would suppose Oxford to be the most Victorian and reactionary spot in Europe.' When the first woman President was elected in 1967, Lord Gardiner was one of the hosts at a lunch in her honour.

In 1926 the first woman don to speak in the Union, Lynda Grier, the Principal of Lady Margaret Hall, took part in a debate about education. A woman undergraduate, Lucy Sutherland, was later invited to oppose a motion that the women's colleges should be levelled to the ground, which was passed. Miss Sutherland argued that women were a harmless race, whose pursuits were mild and whose interests were of a homely and reputable nature. Their excitement, she maintained, lay chiefly in the gathering of wild flowers, and their most adventurous expedition was crawling about the floors of country churches brass-rubbing.

In 1930, *Isis* was still peddling an anti-feminist line. 'Women are not intelligent: they form judgements as unfairly as brilliantly, they for ever admit the personal, they would, given their heads, overturn every recognized rule and canon for the glorious individuality of the exception. Here in Oxford we see women at their very worst.'

The Oxford Union was not alone in its attitude to women. At Cambridge, a poll was carried out on the question of admitting women to their union. As a joke, Hugh Foot and Gilbert Harding organized the opposition to the proposal. They circulated an appeal to members purporting to come from its proponents, dirtily stencilled, with the names on the envelopes misspelt. For good measure their circular was couched in ungrammatical English and adopted an unpleasantly superior tone.

Some prominent Oxford women laid plans for their own women's union society in 1931. Its premises would be used for debating, but could double as a place to work between lectures, thus ridding women of the need to retreat to their suburban fastnesses. Mrs Bernard Shaw and Lady Astor both coughed up subscriptions, but the project ended as another of Oxford's lost causes.

In 1934 the wild left-wingers who had just voted not to fight for

King and Country rejected the idea of women being allowed on the Union's premises between four and six in the afternoon for tea. The opposition claimed that the idea represented the thin end of the wedge and would lead inexorably to women being allowed on the floor of the House. 'Let those jaundiced critics of modern Oxford hide their heads for shame,' rejoiced the *Daily Mail*. The Oxford Union had shown, to the great relief of one and all, that it was still capable of good old-fashioned prejudice. 'Was this the act of a bunch of spineless dilettanti? Was the courage of Horatius or the Greeks at Thermopylae any greater than that of the undergraduates, who, heedless of the consequences, stood firm in the face of Les Varsity Girls?

'In the case of the Union this splendid defence of the writing-room, especially between four and six PM, has a practical as well as a moral significance.

'It is in the cloistered serenity of this room that the feasts of rhetoric, later to delight the packed benches of the debating hall, are born and nurtured in the mind of the undergraduate orator. It is the wilderness to which every embryo Demosthenes withdraws to be alone with his thoughts and his *Concise Oxford Dictionary*.

'Were this sanctuary to be invaded by the chatter and demoralizing perfume of the female tea-addict, it is not too much to say that Eloquence would be smothered in the cradle.'

That same year, however, the decision was reversed. Indeed, English oratory was imperilled by the admission of women not only for afternoon tea, but for morning coffee as well. In 1935 the Society took the revolutionary step of admitting women as guests for all meals. The President David Lewis originally ruled that such a huge constitutional innovation required a two-thirds majority, which it did not obtain. Legal advice, however, favoured the opposite conclusion, and all-male eating became a thing of the past.

The next step was to promote women from third-class to second-class citizenship in the Union by making them debating members, an idea championed by Max Beloff and Christopher Mayhew in the mid-1930s. Debating membership meant that women could attend and take part in debates, but would not be allowed to stand for election or vote, or to use the Society's rooms. 'Every political club in the University today has women amongst its most active members,' argued Beloff. 'It will be a good thing to get a new class of debater, someone who is not interested in the motion solely from the point of view of making a good election speech, and to get speeches which are not made solely for effect.'

The arch-opponent of the admission of women was the Treasurer of the day, Ronald Bell, who appropriately enough became the leading critic of the Sex Discrimination Bill in the House of Commons forty years later. 'This Society was built by the subscriptions of men and its traditions were created by men,' he said. 'It would be impossible to admit women as officers of this Society, especially in the office which I hold, because it involves the supervision of the staff. I suggest that the admission of women to the floor of the House will definitely detract something from the atmosphere of the debates.' Bell carried the day.

Two years later, in 1938, Christopher Mayhew had another go at getting women admitted. This time, one of his main opponents was Edward Heath. 'It is but a further step to admitting women to full membership of this Society,' he said. 'Women have no original contribution to make to our debates, and I believe that if they are admitted to the floor of this House, a large number of members will leave.' Philip Toynbee, President at the time, commented that people would not admit women because they were afraid of them, afraid of being shown to be the feeble speakers they were. The proposal was, nonetheless, lost again.

The idea of admitting women was resuscitated and rejected time and time again. The novelist Nina Bawden recalls taking part in a demonstration on one of these occasions in 1944. 'Although I had no real desire to join the Oxford Union (the standard of debate was so low, most of the speakers so deep in youthful self-love they made me feel old and tired as I listened) I threw pamphlets and balloons from the public gallery in support of a motion to admit women because the President invited me to. That was Tony Pickford, who, with his frail, beaky good looks, his style and intelligence, seemed to me the only exemplar in the whole Union of what I had expected Oxford to be; the fact that he was known to be suffering from a fatal disease gave him an added, and awesome, romantic attraction.'

In this debate the opponents of women put forward the view that since a large number of Union members were away serving in the forces, it was the duty of those remaining in Oxford to act as trustees for them and to hand over the Society at the end of the war just as it had been at the beginning. The vote went 127 to 24 against women that time; but when the veterans returned to find their male bastion as they had left it, they confirmed the decision by a similar margin. For good measure, they put down a motion the following year that in the national interest the women of the university should be compelled to take a domestic science degree. It lost, but relatively narrowly.

In the late forties Michael Summerskill emerged as the main champion of women. As the son of Dr Edith, he had little choice in the matter. She sat in the gallery to watch her son present the case in 1949. 'Oh, what will Mother say?' asked the *Daily Express* when the cause once more failed, this time by 311 votes to 98. Anthony Walton, who repeatedly championed male exclusivity at the time, was given to presenting what passed for a reasoned case, but would end with a triumphant peroration: 'We're not arguing with them, we're telling them. We just don't want the women,' to roars of applause from his supporters.

Michael Summerskill's great ally amongst the would-be members was Shirley Catlin. They wrote a joint letter to *Isis* putting forward their case. Keeping women out of the Union, they said, was tantamount to debarring them from full participation in University life. 'We will be told that their voices will not carry – a complaint never made in the House of Commons; that they are not talented speakers – but that is one of the Society's purposes; that men will be unable to attend to the debate – an interesting sidelight on their powers of intellectual concentration; there will be a shower of objections.

'Those opposing this move will gain a wealth of comfort from such arguments; they will be showing by their actions, however, that Oxford's teaching has failed utterly, in them, to eradicate a quite irrational dislike of woman the thinking independent being, as opposed to the subservient, dependent being.'

The letters in reply revealed some of the thinking of the opposition. 'No fair observer,' argued one, 'can doubt that most women are merely passengers in university life; rarely does a woman ask a question at a public meeting; more rarely still does she write anything except bad poetry; even the women's magazine is only supported out of philanthropy, or secret subsidies.' Even many women were lukewarm about the proposal. 'Must this elegant, elderly and reputable Society,' one girl was quoted as saying, 'sink the traditions for which it is deservedly famous, and must women be tendered one more battlefield on which to display the undoubted superiority of their sex?'

In retrospect, Shirley Williams remembers that she was campaigning for the principle at stake rather than out of any overwhelming desire to join the Union. The campaign was certainly less than deadly serious. 'I recollect feeling that the Union debates were rather boring and that the whole of the Union was rather an elaborate business,' she says.

At the time, it was clear that the Oxford Union's vote was not going to stop Shirley Catlin making debating speeches. She set up a women's debating society called OUIDA, which stood for Oxford University Inter-Collegiate Debating Association. Robert Robinson could not resist the shades of St Trinian's in the concept. The first meeting opened, he wrote, to cries of 'you pinched my lakkers stick, you beast', and he went on, 'Miss Shirley Catlin proposed the motion. Simpering prettily, she said she deplored the Oxford system of philosophy which gave her more than one answer to the same question; she coyly suggested that Oxford be left to "the Fellows".'

When Godfrey Smith suggested that he should write an *Isis Idol* of Shirley Catlin, the editor told him that a woman did not deserve a whole profile all to herself; he would have to bracket her with another girl. The piece duly set Shirley Catlin alongside Val Mitchison, another daughter of a famous mother, the writer Naomi Mitchison.

In due course Shirley Catlin became the first woman Chairman of the University Labour Club, leading *Isis* to renew the argument for women in the Union. 'Oxford men covertly believe that a woman's place is on a pedestal, behind a teapot, or in a punt; and men in Oxford are in a majority. Seventy-one years after the foundation of Somerville and Lady Margaret Hall, women have not been assimilated into the life-stream of the University; they act only as occasional injections.

'Very few men seem to want to help them out of this likeness to hypodermics. For example, women are still excluded from the Union. Rightly so, most men would say, mentally picturing tender girls blushing all the way up their arms when called upon to make their maiden speeches. The thought of women in the quiet rooms of the Society is enough to evoke a snarl from even the most liberal-minded. Lovesick virgins would litter the writing-room penning billet-doux to their indifferent swains, sealing the envelopes with hot tears and a surreptitious kiss. Tiny but inept hands would wield billiard-cues, to the permanent damage of the cloth; the telephone-booth would be eternally occupied by nylons, high-heeled shoes and an aura of scent.' What was really needed, the leader concluded, was half a dozen prodigious dynamoes like Shirley Catlin to reverse all the prejudice.

Meanwhile the cause of sex equality continued to be treated as a joke in the bastions of male privilege. When a team from Oxford went over to Cambridge to debate the motion 'that the discovery of atomic energy had been the greatest disaster for mankind since the Flood', a wit proposed that 'Flood' be deleted and the words 'emancipation of women' put in its place.

Nonetheless, women undergraduates spoke more and more frequently as guests in the Union. In 1950 Florence Elliott of St Hilda's caused quite a stir by taking on a Roman Catholic bishop over the issue of birth control. 'Girl argues with bishop about sex' made a natural popular newspaper headline which was repeated with variations throughout Fleet Street.

Gerald Kaufman was one of the male undergraduates who entered the lists as a champion of women. Equal pay for equal work scarcely existed, he told the Union in a debate on the subject. It particularly incensed him that peeresses in their own right could not take their seats in the House of Lords. Against him Rodney Elton, now a Government Minister in the Lords, displayed sheer brilliance, according to *Isis*, in discovering that there was a fundamental difference between men and women. Women were good at caring for babies and dishcloths, his argument went, but quite ineffective as jet pilots, rugger blues and all-in wrestlers. A former Chairman of the left-wing Socialist Club, Caroline Carter, came as a guest speaker. She told the President Howard Schuman, 'In your country, Mr President, you put women on a pedestal. Here you remove them to an even higher level, the gallery.'

Attempts continued throughout the 1950s to persuade the Union to allow women in as debating members, but all were unsuccessful. It was claimed that men would not be able to be as rude to women as they were to other men. Women, it was said, could not be heard because of the bad acoustics in the debating hall. 'There are three types of women at the University,' declared one of the opponents of their admission to Union debates, Lalithe Athulathmudali, 'the beautiful, the clever and the vast majority.'

In 1959 the Union did eventually vote for women as debating members by 380 to 294. The opponents, however, demanded a poll and, with the help of life members, they had the decision reversed.

The margin was 675 to 489. Again in 1961, a vote in the debating hall approved the admission of women only for the change to be blocked by a poll. This time, however, the poll actually came out in favour of the women, but not by the two-thirds majority required.

Later that year two girl students gatecrashed a Union debate dressed as men. They wore wigs, high-necked sweaters and men's jackets and trousers. Afterwards they wrote to the President thanking him for his hospitality and saying that they hoped that they would soon be able to attend without feeling ill at ease in unaccustomed clothing. Their college responded by gating them. One of the girls, Bridget Rose Dugdale, was later to achieve even greater notoriety for her part in an IRA-inspired art robbery.

Finally in 1962 the two-thirds majority was achieved, and women were admitted for debates. 'There may be greater moral justification for excluding women than for excluding Jews or negroes,' said one of the leaders of the campaign, 'and if anyone can explain what this justification is, I shall be only too pleased to listen.' The backwoodsmen went down fighting. Lord Sudeley from Worcester College announced, to wild cheers, that he was proud of his sex. 'Are we not nauseated,' he declared, 'by women who wear trousers?' 'It is not prejudice against women,' said another undergraduate incoherently in the debate, 'it is a feeling.'

Lydia Howard from Somerville became the first girl to speak in the Union as a debating member. Her speech was described as 'rational and unornate'. Then, later in the year, there was a move to make women full members. The opposition argued that the Union would be overcrowded; that it was better for facilities designed by men to be used by men. The proponents retorted that it would be healthy to turn the Union into a social centre instead of a sewer for ratrace politicians. Overcrowding would not be a problem, because women did not buy their own drinks at the bar and not too many women would join anyway because the women's colleges were so far away. The reformers found it necessary to add that they were not trying to turn the Union into a brothel, such was still the misogynist climate of the times.

Once again, the wishes of undergraduates, who voted for women as full members, were flouted by the votes of the life members, although the poll result fell only five short of the necessary two-thirds majority. The reformers felt bitter; the only explanation, one of them said, was that the third who had voted the other way were either scared of females and sex or were 'senile, doddery, and obviously celibate old men'.

Yet another poll in February 1963 finally settled the matter. Even when the names of Errol Flynn (once) and John Vassall (twice) had been eliminated, the votes in favour still amounted to a comfortable two-thirds of the poll.

The poet Philip Larkin has written:

> *'Sexual intercourse began*
> *In nineteen sixty-three*
> *(Which was rather late for me) –*
> *Between the end of the* Chatterley *ban*
> *And the Beatles' first LP.'*

Perhaps it was an appropriate year for the admission of women to full membership of the Oxford Union, while so many other barriers were crashing down at the same time. It is highly dubious, however, whether the Union ever became a great centre of sixties permissiveness. The freezing temperature, the mausoleum quality of the marble and the bust of Mr Gladstone all exerted restraining forces. All the same, as one of the first woman officers of the Union remembers, an element of sexual display did enter into the art of making debating speeches. Romantic liaisons and lovers' tiffs began at the same time to play a part in the petty intriguing amongst the Union's office-seekers.

The admission of women coincided with a vogue for inviting actresses down as guest speakers. Fenella Fielding appeared at the Union in 1964 to support, 'This House prefers the Beatles to Beethoven'. 'I've lived with several great composers,' she told the house, 'and I assure you it's no life.' Diana Rigg, at the height of her fame in *The Avengers* on television, spoke in the Union in 1966 on 'this House prefers fun to games'. 'Don't just say something,' shouted an admirer from the back of the hall, 'stand there.'

Undergraduate women soon found that the male competition was not so overwhelming, though, like most of the men, they found the Union audience intimidating at first. Janet Morgan, who was the first woman to win office in the Society, remembers catching sight of the bust of Harold Macmillan during an early effort and completely losing confidence. She says she put her name up for Secretary as an experiment to see what would happen. In the event, she beat a large number of challengers, including the novelist and former Tory MP Jeffrey Archer, to win the post. She learnt about the result the next day from a placard on a newstand proclaiming 'Oxford Union elects girl'. She had never expected to win.

Janet Morgan's stand was not a radical one. 'Those aggressive feminist type women make me shudder,' she told the *Sunday Telegraph* after the election. 'They frighten me. I joined the Society because I thought I had something to say. But I believe men are better in debate than women and I think we must make our contribution in a womanly way. After all we present enough challenge to men without having to try to be aggressive.'

Janet Morgan set about making her womanly impact on the still very male-dominated society. When she became Treasurer, she enjoyed going to the covered market with the Steward and choosing the food, flowers and wine for the still very substantial pre-debate dinners. She entered a conspiracy with the Steward so that it would appear that she was sitting at the bar drinking large amounts of alcohol with the men while in fact she drank hardly anything. Speculation as to what she would wear on debate nights abounded: purists suggested a black and white female equivalent of white tie and tails, but she settled for a range of brightly coloured velvet skirts with brocade blouses. She was invited round the small debating societies in the men's colleges where she became an exhibit or an object to tease amidst great and often childish ribaldry on motions such as 'the women's colleges are impregnable'. She gained a strong impression that many of the male debaters had scarcely encountered girls before and did not know what to make of them.

It was a sign of how much national attention was still being paid to the Union that Janet Morgan heard about her defeat for the Presidency while she was appearing on the *Frost Programme* on television. Another flurry of media interest erupted when Geraldine Jones was elected President on her second attempt at the end of 1967. She believes that by that stage it was no more difficult for a woman than for a man to become President. 'People positively wanted the thrill (in 1966 I would have said frisson) of electing the first woman President. I had established myself as a competent speaker and I certainly had the best of the presidential debate, but the fact that nearly 700 people voted for me in an unprecedentedly high poll indicates surely that they were not voting on merit alone. I would probably have won even if I'd been a man, but not by such a margin.

'Once elected, nothing was further from my thoughts than putting feminine touches to the place. For me, Oxford was exhilarating because it was the only place where I could compete with men on completely equal terms. It is true that I cared about clothes but I don't think a desire to dress appropriately peculiarly feminine.'

Like Janet Morgan, Geraldine Jones was not a strident feminist. She chose 'Vive la Différence' as her farewell debate, where the television cameras were on her once again. There was little to hold women back in most walks of life, she said, but she felt distaste for the view that men and women were interchangeable. She joked that it had been the first term when men speakers had been chosen for their good looks and the women for their plainness.

The week that Geraldine Jones was elected, Robin Day came to the Union as a guest speaker. He used the occasion to recall the battle for the admission of women in his era. 'It was even suggested that the President was liable to become so insufferably vain in the execution of his power and patronage that he might easily succumb to and be corrupted by the wiles of ruthless young women who would become members of the Society. Even worse, it was also suggested – and I remember this distinctly – that Presidents would use their position to debauch innocent creatures who had thrown themselves at their feet.'

He went on to say how impressed he was by Geraldine Jones; she had made the nearest thing he had ever heard to an intellectual remark on the *Eamonn Andrews Show*. 'She has achieved a first more glittering than that which any examiner can ever award her. But she must face up to it that she is inescapably labelled for life. Whatever she does – her successes, her failures, her marriages, her divorces, all will be inevitably coupled with her achievement here. No news editor will ever forget her. She will have an eternal identity tag in the files of Fleet Street. But whatever her future, she will surely rank now amongst the immortals of this Society. Must we wait fifty years now for her to have a place of her own along these sombre walls? I am delighted, therefore, Mr President, to hear that you are setting up an expert committee of ex-Presidents to arrange for the unveiling of her bust.'

Even being sent up by well-known people was a flattering experience. Geraldine Jones, briefly, made national news, even though Cambridge had elected a woman President, Ann Mallalieu, first. Visitors to the Union all had tributes to make to her, some elegant, some less so. Speaking in her Presidential debate on 'this House has no confidence in politicians', Geraldine Jones had said that politicians were not interested in providing pleasanter recreational facilities for people. 'In my day,' remarked Brian Walden facetiously as the guest speaker on the other side, 'she would have been a pleasanter recreational facility.'

In the event, Geraldine Jones fulfilled none of Sir Robin's prophecies. She married a German diplomat and disappeared completely from the public eye in Britain. The celebrity aspect had been, she remembers, enormous fun but, even if it had been possible to prolong it, it would not have been compatible with growing up.

Other women, however, have found the Union a useful stepping stone to a career in much the same way as the men. Edwina Currie, an ex-Librarian, is the Union's first woman MP, nine years after the first Cambridge woman President to sit in the House, Helene Hayman, took her seat. Libby Purves, another ex-Librarian, has made a name as a writer and presenter of radio programmes. Benazir Bhutto, even under house arrest, is a major political figure in Pakistan.

In general, women in the Union have not behaved or been treated very differently from the men. There have been left-wing women and right-wing women; funny women and earnest women; women who have dressed to kill at the dispatch box or the rostrum and women who have gone from one oratorical triumph to another in the same skirt. The most recent woman to become President, Sandy Jones, once took off the cloak she was wearing to reveal a satin playsuit; Mrs Mary Whitehouse was there at the time to take part in a debate on pornography. Women have not, however, even monopolized Union dishabille. A few years before, a Viscount from Balliol had removed his trousers to make a point in a debate about tights.

Now that all but one of the men's colleges at Oxford are mixed, the proportion of women at the University has increased greatly. The proportion of women active in the Union has not risen by the same extent. It may be that fewer women than men possess the self-regard that is necessary for climbing the Union ladder, that, despite all the changes, the gentlemen's club atmosphere has not been completely dispelled, or that, like Shirley Williams thirty-five years before, they simply find the Union boring.

CHAPTER SEVEN

TO THE BARRICADES AND BACK 1960–1983

In the folk memory, student life in the 1960s consisted of one long demonstration, stretching from Aldermaston to the Clarendon Building in Oxford, on through Grosvenor Square, then three times round the London School of Economics and off towards the University of Essex. In fact, even at the height of the storm of protest the proportion of students mobilized in the cause of the revolution was very small. Oxford, seldom in the eye of the storm, preserved its rituals and its way of life with only minor modifications. Undergraduates still read Homer, fell into the river from punts, performed plays in rainswept college gardens, disgraced themselves at boat club celebrations and fell asleep in libraries.

The Oxford Union carried on in much the same manner as before. The officers went on wearing their white ties and tails, and entertaining their dinner-jacketed guests to meals before the debates. The scramble for office still depended largely on personalities; the periodic scandals and election tribunals turned for the most part on allegations of canvassing and manipulating college block votes, not on deep ideological splits. The Eights Week debates and their like continued, some with a period quality on motions like 'fings ain't wot they used to be' and 'the miniskirt does not go far enough', others more timeless like 'this Union should be consummated' and 'God is an Englishman'. It was a decade dominated at least as much by the revival of the Marx Brothers as by the revival of Karl Marx.

In 1968, the year in which French students manned the barricades, members of the Union packed into the debating hall to welcome the Queen on the first visit to the Society of a reigning monarch. She came in to loud cheers, and sat on the crossbenches to listen to a debate on the motion that 'personal liberty in Britain is being dangerously eroded.'

Nevertheless, the general level of undergraduate political awareness stood higher than in the 1950s. The far left, more numerous and more vociferous than before, had a presence in the Union, although as the decade progressed many of them abandoned it; and the issues which they featured on their placards certainly formed the subject matter of many Union debates, the Bomb in the early sixties, then later Vietnam, Rhodesia, race relations and student participation.

CND had a considerable following at the beginning of the decade in the university, although the Union only once carried a motion containing unilateralist sentiments. Peter Jay, President in 1960, was one of the leaders of the anti-CND Gaitskellites, fighting a battle at Oxford which mirrored the one in which his father Douglas Jay was active at Westminster. 'Underneath Mr Jay's music hall caperings,' wrote *Isis* of one of Peter Jay's anti-CND speeches, 'was revealed the callisthenics of the liberal-humanist conscience.' Another admirer wrote that he combined 'a tremendous logical depth with a Union manner that always commands the attention of the House.'

Nonetheless, Peter Jay needed three goes before he captured the Presidency. On the eve of his successful election against Alan Haselhurst, he was described as 'a thinker of tremendous depth capable of splitting the finest hair. To many in the Union, his logic is too specious and his distinctions too far fetched. His enemies are quick to brand him as too much of an intellectual to be a good President. Some even, looking no further than his bow-tie, have called him a fop. Yet on the whole his Union performances are impressive.'

During Peter Jay's term of office a small house narrowly carried the motion that neither country nor anything else were worth the use of nuclear weapons. More memorable, however, was a battle between Oswald Mosley and Jeremy Thorpe. Thorpe, normally so much in his element in the Union, admits that Mosley had the better of him. The debate was about South Africa's membership of the Commonwealth. Mosley was trying to make out a case that South Africa had been much more peaceful since Sharpeville, to which end he quoted a statement justifying the killing of civilians where necessary in the interests of law and order.

Jeremy Thorpe intervened: 'It worked in Budapest too.'

'I was quoting Asquith,' replied Mosley.

Thorpe intervened again: 'Speaking about the shooting of armed Boers?'

'No,' replied Mosley, 'In fact, the shooting of seven unarmed miners in 1893.'

The sons and daughters of famous fathers were everywhere in Oxford. A year after Peter Jay's term of office, Paul Foot held the President's chair. A liberal in the family tradition, but in that same tradition moving leftwards, he defended Fidel Castro in his Presidential debate, and asserted his commitment to unilateral disarmament by wearing a CND badge in his pink hunting jacket for Eights Week. His speeches were enlivened by material supplied by his friend Richard Ingrams. 'Paul Foot,' wrote an undergraduate political commentator called Hugo Young, 'has some witty journalistic friends full of gags to spice his speeches. But even irregular patrons can hardly fail to have noticed a certain shallowness in the few serious speeches he has been called upon to make. Until he is interrupted, he delights them with a hard-learned panache. But pure memory is an unreliable standby.'

The mood was turning against the Conservative Government. In 1960, the Union decided that it had no confidence in the Tory Party. Two future Prime Ministers were the guests at that debate. James Callaghan attacked the candyfloss civilization which he said the Government was offering, and criticized its lack of policy for solving Britain's industrial problems. Edward Heath claimed credit for the Government's progressive policies in Africa, its efforts to help the colonies achieve self-determination and its aid to the Third World. In 1961, the Union passed the traditional autumn motion of no confidence in the Government for the first time for ten years. Michael Stewart came down to attack the 'never had it so good' ethos. The claim could have been made, he said, in the reign of every English sovereign save, perhaps, William Rufus and Stephen.

The Union latched onto the satire boom with gusto, and everyone tried to impersonate Peter Cook impersonating Harold Macmillan. When a Labour Government was elected it was not long before undergraduates started subjecting that to both ridicule and straightforward hostility. In 1965 the Union passed a motion of no confidence in the Wilson Government by 411 to 305 votes. This was by no means, however, a sign that the Union had moved back to the right. Two socialist undergraduates, Tariq Ali and Stephen Marks, spoke in favour of the motion on the grounds that the Government had betrayed its supporters.

The jokes about Harold Wilson reappeared endlessly. He was called the man who could be relied upon to find the shortest breach between two promises, a man who could hold a debate with himself and come to a unanimous conclusion, a man who when he talked about forging the future in the white heat of the technological revolution knew what he meant by forging. A great deal of animosity against Harold Wilson and other individual members of the Government failed to disguise the lack of coherent thinking about how to improve on the Government's policies. It was not until 1969, when many of the revolutionaries had deserted the Union altogether, that a motion of no confidence in the Labour Government, defended on this occasion by Shirley Williams, was defeated.

The heroes of many politically-minded undergraduates in the 1960s tended to be black or from the Third World. In 1961 the Indian Prime Minister Nehru got a tremendous reception when he came to the Union during a break in the Commonwealth Prime Ministers' Conference. The speech which he made was largely a justification of India's policy of neutrality, which seemed an attractive stance to many undergraduates at the time.

In 1964 the American Black Muslim leader Malcolm X – by no means neutral – came down to speak on the motion that 'extremism in the defence of liberty is no vice, moderation in the pursuit of justice is no virtue'. 'When a man is moderate in defence of liberty for human beings, I say he is a sinner. The day the black man takes uncompromising steps and realizes that he is within his rights when his own freedom is being jeopardized to use any means necessary to bring about his freedom, I don't think he will be by himself. I believe that the day they do move, many whites will have more respect for them. There will be more whites than there are now on their side with this wishy-washy 'Love thy enemy' approach they have been using up to now.'

The Union was rather equivocal about Senator Robert Kennedy, who was invited in 1967 to give a talk rather than to take part in a debate. Seventy protestors outside the hall formed an archway of anti-Vietnam placards in front of the entrance. Inside, too, there were some hostile questions. Asked whether he renounced any intention of running for the Democratic nomination in 1968, he said 'I do.' 'What about the credibility gap?' shouted an undergraduate. There was no doubt, though, that the Kennedy charm worked on most of his large audience. He defused some of the anti-war feeling by hinting that secret peace talks were taking place and declaring his serious reservations about the bombing of North Vietnam. He appealed too to the idealism which students of the 1960s at least pretended they had. 'When leaving university are we going to say that we will get an economic advantage over our neighbour, a better house, or will we say that we will make ourselves part of something we aren't naturally part of? We have a piece of paper which enables us not to starve to death and our choice is whether we are going to be associated with those who are starving, those who can't get a job, those who are illiterate. You can change the world.'

Three standing ovations for Senator Kennedy followed after that, and he went out into Cornmarket to be mobbed by a huge crowd.

By the time Kennedy came to speak in the Union, the Vietnam issue had for some time been the focus of student protest. The Union made a notable contribution to the public debate about the rights and wrongs of the war in 1965, when it played host to a marathon Teach-in on Vietnam. The Conservative MP Eldon Griffiths who took part said that it was a disgrace that the debate was taking place at Oxford and not at Westminster. The event, which imitated similar ones in the United States, proved an interesting variation on set-piece debates. 'Part forum, part theatre, part seminar, part lecture,' wrote one of the organizers describing the concept afterwards, 'neither speakers nor audience are quite sure what balance should be achieved between ideas and emotion, between impartiality and polemics, between assertion and refutation.' The *Listener*'s critic wrote afterwards, 'It reminded me of a wrestling match: each side fouled with relative impunity, the crowd jeered and cheered in easy excitement.'

The organizers, Steven Lukes, Tariq Ali and David Caute, all left-wing critics of the Americans in Vietnam, proved extremely successful as impresarios. They secured the services of the Foreign

Secretary Michael Stewart, who had been criticized by left-wing Labour MPs for not meeting the Parliamentary Party to discuss his policy. He decided that he would attend the Union event rather than let the Government's case go by default. As he wrote in his autobiography: 'My advisers at the Foreign Office doubted whether it would be wise to accept: the anti-American feelings of the organizers were well-known, and those who disagreed with them were likely to get a rough ride. I decided, however, that I had a good case and knew enough about Oxford student audiences to put it over.'

Once they had acquired the valuable property of a contribution from the Foreign Secretary, the organizers managed to attract a leading American spokesman, Henry Cabot Lodge, former ambassador to South Vietnam. The BBC came down to cover the event in force. Radio Three cancelled their evening's schedule to give it continuous coverage and a team from BBC Television were there to record highlights for the *Gallery* programme.

Only the Russians and the Vietnamese Communists failed to attend. Despite a decision by Michael Stewart to exempt him from a rule requiring forty-eight hours notice before a journey of more than thirty-five miles outside London, the British correspondent of *Izvestia* refused an invitation to speak. Two North Vietnamese journalists sat in the gallery, but would not participate either. Left-wing English opinion was, however, well represented.

Anti-American protestors massed to make their views known. Professor Max Beloff was hissed when he opened the proceedings by saying the war might be over if there were teach-ins and the same publicity for them in Moscow and Peking. Beloff was accused of taking sides as chairman; he in turn felt that speakers who were supposed to be giving an objective account of the background were descending into polemic.

Ho Chi Minh's message to the American people was distributed round the hall and, during an early contribution from an air chief marshal, the shout went up: 'The Vietcong are a democratic movement and should have our support.' The audience cheered a critique of the American stance from Ralph Miliband of the London School of Economics.

Cabot Lodge misjudged the mood. He thought that he would arouse feelings of patriotism and Anglo-American solidarity amongst his audience by referring to Churchill, Dunkirk and the wonderful British bobbies; instead, he was greeted with groans, moans and hisses, amid general scepticism about his declaration that America was prepared to negotiate but now was not the time. He was clearly taken aback by his reception. 'Why do you laugh?' he asked. 'Why don't you listen to me? Give me a chance. I flew from Boston today specially to talk to you.' None of that helped his cause, nor did his appeal to the Master-elect of Balliol, Christopher Hill, who was in the chair at the time: 'Will you keep order, Mr Chairman? That's your job.' The age of deference was well and truly dead.

Michael Stewart was also heckled when he spoke, and accused of immorally supporting America. He claimed that a ceasefire could take place in Vietnam immediately, followed by a conference. It was not Britain or the United States who refused to negotiate, but North Vietnam, China and Russia. Who could defend the Communist refusal to come to the conference table? He pleaded too that the conflict could not be stopped by casual denunciation of the United States, nor by yielding unconditionally to the Communist demands.

Asked about Cabot Lodge's statement about the time not being ripe for negotiations, Michael Stewart turned round to Cabot Lodge and invited him to comment, but he did not. Another questioner wanted an explanation of an official American document which had suggested that only two and a half per cent of the Vietcong's arms came from the Soviet bloc. Stewart replied that he had deliberately avoided using American sources, and the audience laughed.

The Foreign Secretary had, by common consent, survived remarkably well and his speech was greeted with cheers – the feeling against the war was not yet at its height. *The Times* suggested that he had added considerably to his reputation, while the BBC said that the left had been given a drubbing, although afterwards the organizers accused the Corporation of presenting a one-sided version of events.

In Union debates proper, the left tended to be more restrained. Until the last year or so of the decade, many of their leading figures were keen to come and speak. Flamboyant left-wingers like Eric Abrahams and Tariq Ali appealed, because of their style, to others less committed than themselves. People sometimes wondered how committed Tariq Ali really was to the causes which he was championing. In fact, he has since moved even farther to the left, but at the time he was considered slightly dilettante. He came from a rich and aristocratic background, and the Union's staff liked him because they felt that he knew how to treat them. His justification for taking part in the Union's affairs was that they provided the left with the best forum available; when they found other means of presenting their case, they abandoned the Union. Ali went through the full *cursus honorum*, emerging as President after a fiercely fought election against Lord Hailsham's son, now Douglas Hogg MP.

In their Presidential debate, Douglas Hogg inveighed against 'the Saturday sandwich-board men of the left. Socialism is only practicable in two places,' he said, 'in heaven where they no longer need it and in hell where they already have it.' The left were eager to trip him up, and laughed uproariously after he said 'Conservatives reject out of hand all ideas,' and before he managed to complete the sentence with 'of a dogmatic kind.' Hogg, it was said by contemporaries, sounded much like his father. He had great fluency and an ability to roll high-flown sentiments off his tongue which gave him an air of precocious maturity. Nowadays, one former Union officer from an older generation in the Commons picks him out as the most obvious example of the Union manner in the House, although Douglas Hogg himself believes the Bar provided much better training for Parliament.

Tariq Ali on the other side of the motion launched into a great tirade against the right. All down human history, he said, citing Lloyd George's words, 'nine-tenths of mankind has been grinding the corn for the remaining tenth and has been paid with the husks and bidden to thank God they have the husks . . . Why is it that whenever there is a rotten cause to defend, whether it is fascism in Spain or racial intolerance or capital punishment, there is always a Conservative in some part of the country to defend it?'

Ali won the election by eleven votes after three recounts, with angry cries of 'foul' over the result. A tribunal, set up to investigate, fined Hogg for the endemically common and somewhat arbitrarily defined offence of infringing the canvassing rules. Ali boasted afterwards that he too had broken the rules, but had not been caught. He also claimed that half the Shadow Cabinet had come down to vote for Hogg, although there is no evidence that any of them except Lord Hailsham took part in the ballot. After the election, some votes for Hogg were found concealed in a book in the library where the count had taken place, but not enough to affect the result. More than most elections of the time, this contest had been treated as a battle between left and right as much as between rival debaters.

The Vietnam Teach-in came at the end of Ali's term. He also organized a rerun of the King and Country debate which caused almost as much of a storm as the original one. Two Union trustees resigned, and other senior figures connected with the Union protested strongly. In the event, with Reginald Maudling and Norman St John Stevas down to oppose the motion, it was just lost, amongst many allegations and counter-allegations about the way in which the votes were counted.

Tariq Ali continued to be teased as an upper-class revolutionary. He would admit freely that his family were well-to-do, but claimed that he wanted to go back to Pakistan and see that wealth was spread more evenly there. However he was not so purist in his revolutionary zeal that he was not prepared to wear a scarlet hunting jacket for Eights Week or to dance the night away at a Union Ball. 'Some people say that Tariq is too irresponsible to succeed politically,' said his *Isis Idol*, 'but I think that Tariq Ali, sedate barrister-at-law in the Punjab, will be a vastly different proposition from Tariq Ali, flamboyant undergraduate.'

Douglas Hogg had his chance to become President the next term. The *Oxford Mail* reported that he had established himself as a fiery but reasoned debater. 'Another and more energetic spare-time hobby is acting as the quarry for the huntsmen and hounds of the Oxford University Drag Hunt over a seven mile course.' *Isis* claimed that he was a curiously divided character; alongside his enthusiasm for drag hounds, he took work more seriously than most of the Union. 'It is difficult to discuss Douglas' political views,' said his *Idol*, 'for fundamentally he is not a politician; his speeches for instance are broad with little factual content, but much oratory, which normally comes off well . . . His skill at informal meetings is considerable; on one occasion, he managed to discuss PAYE and its relation to a more successful use of unemployment benefit for twenty minutes at an OUCA study group without actually being aware of what the initials represented . . . Broad historical sweeps, rather than detailed knowledge, are his forte.' Hogg could make the claim that his family were responsible for Ali's rise to power in the Union, since a relation of his had given land to one of Ali's forebears in recognition of his fine military service during the Indian Mutiny.

Some of the flavour of the early 1960s in the Union is preserved in a book by two Union officers about their debating tour of America, called *A Short Walk on the Campus*. Remarking on how right-wing most American students seemed to them, Michael Beloff and Jonathan Aitken say, 'In England, the student politicos are inevitably to the left of their parties (How many university Tories believe in an independent deterrent, capital punishment or the public schools? How many university Socialists believe in the American alliance, an incomes policy or check on immigration).' They talk of an Oxford full of its own self-importance as always, where 'at any Christ Church cocktail party the rooms will be full of self-appointed future Prime Ministers, and every prominent undergraduate believes that he carries a scrambler telephone in his attaché case.'

Michael Beloff cracked insults in the mainstream tradition of Union wits. He and Aitken developed an elaborate routine of exchanging slurs. 'Jonathan Aitken was born under Virgo,' Beloff might begin, 'the biggest single blow the science of astrology has ever received. He spends his evenings sowing his wild oats and wakes up praying for crop failure. He is, too, well known for his *chevalerie* – a French word meaning "horseplay".' Aitken would reply, 'Michael Beloff is a self-made man, thereby absolving God of a great responsibility.'

As the Vietnam issue intensified, the revolutionaries became noisier. Socialist undergraduates once again divided into two camps. In 1967, while Richard Crossman went to speak to the Democratic Labour Club in the Union, the Marxist-oriented Labour Club felt free to demonstrate outside. Crossman was due to have dinner first in the Union with his hosts. With demonstrators blocking the staircase, he was taken in through the kitchen. He records that he was somewhat surprised by the conversation at dinner. He asked the Chairman whether he did not feel a bit isolated making a gallant stand in favour of the Government at such a time. 'We're not supporting the Government,' came the reply. 'Our demonstration is tomorrow night. We wanted you to come and speak first so we could demonstrate afterwards.'

After addressing what turned out to be a small meeting since those attending had been carefully screened, Crossman emerged to make his way through the demonstration to Balliol College. 'Quite safely I moved along with these young men round me,' he noted in his diary, 'black beards, strange atmosphere and suddenly I remembered that this was the atmosphere of a Weimar Republic meeting when you had to be shepherded by the police, when your own supporters inside the hall were frightened and when, outside, there was the threatening force of the popular will. It shook me mainly because it all happened at Oxford. In the 1960s the mass of the student left is behaving in the way in which we used to say the fascists behaved in the 1930s.'

For the slogan-mongers of the left, there were endless causes in which to demonstrate their faith, and enemies on whom to pronounce anathemas. One old Etonian Marxist who had abandoned the Union in favour of the streets once tangled with some dockers demonstrating their support for Enoch Powell. 'Class traitors,' he shouted at them in cut-glass tones. His training on the playing fields of Eton gave him sufficient speed to run away in time, leaving a companion from a less privileged background to face the dockers' retaliation.

All Labour Cabinet Ministers who came down to Oxford during this period had brushes with the left, although some of them came out of the experience better than others. One of the leaders of the revolutionary students, Christopher Hitchens, made up for his participation in a bourgeois activity like Union debates by being as rude as possible to Establishment guests. In 1969, when Denis Healey was in the Chamber, he accused him of being on the end of a very elegant piece of string pulled by the State Department. He welcomed him to the debate on the grounds that Healey would learn something from what he as undergraduate proposer of the motion was going to say. Healey replied that Hitchens was clearly a very nice chap and nice chaps did not make competent revolutionaries. He went on to articulate a familiar theme in the age of protest: the real danger that people like Hitchens would get the people of this country to reject the idea that university education was a good thing.

The following year, within days of the American invasion of Cambodia, Michael Stewart, now Foreign Secretary for the second time, came to the Union to take part in a debate on the Government's foreign policy. The event saw the left's noisiest performance in the age of protest. As the Union Minute Book puts it, 'For the first time in the 147 years of the Society's existence, the House voted to stand adjourned *sine die* on account of riot.'

The uproar began as soon as the Foreign Secretary entered the hall with a barrage of hisses, boos and chants of 'Ho Ho Ho Chi Minh'. Christopher Hitchens, the left's voice on the order paper, made one of his elegant introductions. 'Mr Stewart is paid to say exactly what the American Government want him to say. He doesn't deserve a welcome and I'm not going to extend him one.' After remonstrations, Hitchens agreed to withdraw the last part of his remarks and substituted, 'I'm very pleased he's here because I'm pleased that for once a member of the Government is going to be exposed to a barrage of hostile criticism.'

In the event, the protestors shouted so loudly and for so long that Michael Stewart was prevented from speaking. A small group surged round him chanting 'Ho Ho Ho Chi Minh,' 'Victory to the NLF,' 'Resign you bum,' and 'Stewart, we want you dead.' A noose was let down from the gallery to hang just behind the Foreign Secretary's head. Eventually, the debate was abandoned.

'The extreme student left is at its worst one of the nastiest political phenomena that Britain has experienced in this country,' said a *Times* leader commenting on the incident. A correspondent wrote to the *Daily Telegraph* suggesting that less money should be spent on students and more on primary schools. Students of all political persuasions from Oxford wrote to the papers dissociating themselves from the small minority who had silenced Michael Stewart; many were critics of the Government's stance on Vietnam who felt that their cause had been harmed by the incident.

The protestors put their case too, with arguments typical of revolutionary left-wing attitudes at the time. 'If there was nothing more to democracy and free speech than the point-scoring, artificial debating that goes on in the Union then we were not concerned to preserve it,' wrote one. 'Indeed the numerous charges of undemocratic action that have been levelled against those who prevented Mr Stewart from speaking all presuppose that democracy can flourish, or at least survive, when complicated and diverse issues are dealt with in ten-minute speeches by people who do not necessarily believe what they are saying and who are concerned as much to score points off their opponents as to put forward serious points of view.'

The demonstrators argued ingeniously that everybody knew what Michael Stewart was going to say so that it was not a denial of free speech to stop him saying it again. Instead, they had used the Union to demonstrate their intensity of feeling about the Foreign Secretary's refusal to condemn the American invasion of Cambodia. 'We also wished,' wrote another of the protestors, 'to prevent Mr Stewart from airing his views in a place which gives a certain sanction and respectability to whatever he chooses to say. Far from being a forum for serious and concerned political discussion, or the free exchange of opinion in fair debate, the Oxford Union provides an undemanding and sycophantic audience for budding careerist politicians, before which they can demonstrate their technique in the art of debate and quibble.'

While few undergraduates approved of the treatment that the revolutionaries gave Michael Stewart, feeling against the war, particularly after the invasion of Cambodia, ran high. Leaders of the anti-war movement from the United States became great heroes. Professor Noam Chomsky had a huge overflow for his lecture about Vietnam. Many of his listeners were so impressed that they came back to hear a series of lectures which he gave on linguistics, which many found incomprehensible. At the Union, Dr Benjamin Spock was lionized when he said, 'I do not think this war is just slightly immoral. I think it is one of the dirtiest wars that have ever been fought.'

Protests and demonstrations abounded about other issues as well, race, Rhodesia and the Greek dictatorship among them, all of which were debated with some passion and commitment in the Union. The Liberals flourished, particularly after the emergence of the Red Guards at the Edinburgh Assembly in 1966; the Liberal Party formed a natural refuge for radical undergraduates who considered the Labour Government discredited. Many who were not supporters of the Liberal Party would have labelled themselves liberals with a small 'l'. Interest focused almost entirely on foreign affairs and social issues; there was much less concern about the economy, industry and wealth creation – few of those active on the political scene considered industry as a career. The establishment-minded tended to head for the city or the law, while for the more radical jobs in the media or with an element of social concern beckoned irresistibly. At the same time it was regarded as bad form to aim too obviously for success in the world. 'Careerist" was a frequent form of abuse. In an era when reasonable jobs could be more or less guaranteed to most Oxbridge graduates, people luxuriated in not worrying about the future, in being able to shoulder the cares of the world, in having time to hawk petitions and placards around instead of job application forms.

While the occasional outrageous right-winger would try and play it for laughs, the Conservatives in the Oxford Union remained, for the most part, progressives. Lord James Douglas Hamilton, President in 1964, returned to Oxford after he had gone down to propose a motion censuring the University proctors for punishing undergraduates who had taken part in a demonstration against the South African Ambassador. The 1960s President with the greatest panache, Robert Jackson, now also a Tory MP, eschewed the Conservatives altogether at Oxford. Following Harold Macmillon's advice not to become set too early into fixed party views, he laid himself open to Robin Day's jibe at his farewell debate that he was 'skilfully poised for a political career in any direction that may become acceptable".

Jackson's rococo speaking style went well with his waistcoats. 'His rather owlish mannerisms and protruding jawbone added to the overall effect of cynicism and donnish condescension. A brilliant performance,' said *Cherwell* of one effort. Jackson's forte was making funny speeches. On 'the mini-skirt does not go far enough', he confessed that he was preaching to the perverted and went on to explain history in terms of a neo-Marxist sexual dialectic. He began with Gandhi, who he claimed was the founder of the mini-skirt, and, according to *Cherwell*, 'delighted the house with a stirring plea for "the bosom which is like the forbidden city, Peking, and not a Paris full of tourists".' When he spoke in a serious debate about the Common Market, *Cherwell* said that he was not up to his usual standard. 'The jokes as usual were brilliant, but there was too much theory and no facts. The serious stuff fell flat.' Later, however, Jackson managed to bone up sufficiently on the EEC to become a Member of the European Parliament on his way to Westminster.

William Waldegrave, another President of the late 1960s, is now on the Tory benches in the Commons and in the Government as well. Unlike Jackson he was a Conservative at Oxford, but he found himself proposing in his Presidential debate 'that this House would abolish the armed forces'. The armed forces, he claimed, were militarily pointless, socially pernicious and financially incompatible with maintaining desirable living standards in this country. 'If he was not the son of an Earl," commented *Cherwell*, 'William Waldegrave would have jeopardized his chances of Bournemouth, South Kensington or Kinross with the speech he made, fifteen minutes very amusing demolition, whose high spot was the revelation of OTC contingency plans to evacuate Oxford in the event of Chinese invasion. The forces debased and constipated the economy. A laxative was needed.'

There is, of course, some tradition of debaters being prepared to take any side of any argument in the Union, but William Waldegrave was certainly well-placed with his speech to take left-wing votes in the election against his opponent, who was another Conservative. He was one of only three Tories to win the Presidency of the eighteen who served between 1965 and 1970. Even in this radical age, however, aristocratic birth still seemed to count for something. When William Waldegrave wrote the *Cherwell* column on the Union, his by-line included the prefix 'the Hon.'

As became an age when nothing, except possibly a correspondent's title, was considered sacred, *Cherwell* revived the tradition of scathing commentaries on the Union. Waldegrave himself once came in for a mauling by Robert Jackson, after he had spoken in a debate about the Commonwealth. 'Hon. William Waldegrave was but rarely overheard; and when he was, he seemed always to be talking about links – those binding the Commonwealth together. Among these, it seemed, were cultural links, legal links, cuff links, golf links and other links of many kinds. By a nightmare process, these links became bridges. Lucidity and intelligence are all that Mr Waldegrave requires – and some measure of audibility.'

Towards the end of the 1960s the left in Oxford were swept up in the demands flowing from the United States, France and newer British universities for student participation. 'Student militancy is a rejection of the whole orientation of universities and colleges as battery farms for broiler technicians,' said one of the advocates of participation in a Union debate in 1967. Students, the left believed, had to link up with trade unions and tenants' organizations to fight for radical change, although evidence of trade unionists and tenants welcoming them into their ranks was slight. Another speaker claimed that it was the duty of students, who had fewer vested interests than other people, to act as the conscience of society. He too appeared to place the sufferings of students of English forced to read the fourteenth century *Sir Gawain and the Green Knight* on a level with those of blacks and other oppressed minorities. The demands of student militants were ripe for caricature. In that same 1967 debate, Peregrine Worsthorne suggested that the militants displayed all the unforgivable rowdiness of a boat race night without any of its redeeming high spirits, and all the earnestness of a Fabian seminar without a shade of its intellectual rigour.

At the end of the day the revolutionary influence spread most successfully to the way that Oxford looked and dressed, not the way it was run. Denim outfits, gold-rimmed glasses, beards and long hair became *de rigueur* even for library-bound workoholics and rugby players and rowers. Oxford men all seemed to one of the more Conservative woman speakers in one Union debate to be in strict training for the Oberammergau Passion Play. Union photographs reveal Tories, Liberals and Socialists all looking equally hirsute. Giving tangible, and sometimes even odiferous, expression to the generation gap, saved on haircutting costs too, but sympathy for the oppressed did not extend to the barbers of Oxford, who must have been having a lean time.

The argument about officers' dress of course came up again in the Union, but several motions to abolish white tie and tails for the officers all failed. Colin Youlden, then a Communist, put the case in 1969. It was a time when the old ties which bound us to the nineteenth century were snapping, he claimed. The Union should get rid of a symbol of the nineteenth century; the officers had no need to look like Max Jaffa and the Palm Court Orchestra, or gigolos on the run from the 1920s. Caroline Harvey, who replied, made a plea for sartorial elegance, and for a harmless and delightful tradition thoroughly in keeping with the Victorian Zeppelin shelter which housed Union debates. The traditionalists won easily, as they had on the issue in the Union's earlier radical phase in the 1930s.

The Union politicians, although a more serious group than their fifties forbears, still went in on the whole for the Union manner, and were as obsessed with personalities as ever, chiefly each other's, but also those of leading politicians. Tony Benn delivered a powerful attack on the ethos in a speech in the Union in 1967. 'Debates have got to be about real problems. It is easy to devote a debate to comments and jokes about the people involved. If anybody really thinks the problems facing this country can be attributed to twenty people – this is the sort of preoccupation maybe fostered in the University of Oxford – he is off-beam.' He went on to criticize Oxford for its lack of interest in industry, and its nineteenth-century contempt for technology.

Other sixties' themes spilled over into Union debates. With R. D. Laing speaking on the winning side, the Society voted for legalizing cannabis. In 1961 they rejected a motion 'that the Western ideal of chastity is outmoded' despite a declaration by A. S. Neill, headmaster of the progressive Summerhill school and another cult figure of the decade, that most of the misery in the world came from sex repression. By 1966 they were declaring that sex was too interesting to be left to married people.

In 1962 the Union decided by a narrow margin that it did not believe in God. The most notable religious clash, however, came five years later when Ian Paisley, then a comparatively new phenomenon to people on the British side of the Irish Sea, made a televized speech in favour of the motion 'that the Roman Catholic Church has no place in the twentieth century'. The Union had heard plenty of tubthumpers, but they were taken aback by the violence of the delivery and language used by Paisley. 'The confessional is the spyhole of the priest,' he thundered, 'right into the hearts and homes of the people. I do not believe that any priest of Rome or another man should force himself into the marriage bed.' The members laughed at him for that; but when Paisley produced a communion wafer and held it up to denounce it as a biscuit used in idolatry, he caused uproar. He had succeeded in shocking a generation which considered itself unshockable. Still three years away from taking his seat in the House of Commons, Paisley demonstrated his idiosyncratic view of the parliamentary procedures adopted there. When an undergraduate tried to intervene during his speech, he said, 'If it's a point of order, I'll give way. If it's a point of information, I'll give the information myself.'

Speaking on the other side of the motion, Norman St John Stevas pronounced Paisley to be in a state of what the theologians call invincible ignorance. He was able to talk about assassination threats against him from Northern Ireland in a light-hearted tone which did not seem out of place in 1967, but which would have grated rather more after 1969. 'I do not encourage those who want to shoot our guest. I do not say to them shoot him. And again I do not say don't shoot him. I do say this: if you must shoot, for heaven's sake shoot straight.' Stevas said that Paisley had outraged everybody by holding up the wafer. There was great applause for that, and he had what, but for Paisley, might have been a highly sceptical audience listening sympathetically to his claims about the good which the Catholic Church had done in the world.

The climate of the times still left room for speakers who, like Kenneth Tynan, would make a speech in the Union more of a cabaret turn. Noel Picarda, Treasurer in 1962, once sat on a dispatch box and pretended to drive it like a bus up a steep mountain road. Gyles Brandreth, President in 1969, stood on his head in the debating hall. Chris Tookey, President in 1972, was much given to singing and playing instruments in debates. Sometimes, the cabaret artists could be even more serious about themselves than the politicians. In an interview for *Isis* with Anthony Holden, Gyles Brandreth was invited to answer the charge that he was a name dropper. 'One usually mentions those one has taken meals with,' he replied. 'For instance, the other day I had a pleasant day – lunch with the Head of New Scotland Yard, dinner with David Frost, and tea next day with Gerald Nabarro. Can't I say so? Humility. Well, I am not a humble person. I'm quite conceited; I certainly have in my own mind a high opinion of myself. Of course I am a conceited person, and conceit isn't an attractive quality in someone my age. My only saving grace is that, although I may be arrogant, sometimes I may be arrogant with just a midgeon of justification.'

After 1969 Northern Ireland again became a regular subject for debate in the Union. As the Society had heard from Carson and Redmond before the First World War, so now they listened to Jack Lynch, John Hume, Brian Faulkner, Liam Cosgrave and Merlyn Rees. One of the Irish debates, in 1971, coincided with a visit to Oxford for a separate meeting about internment by the Nationalist MP Bernadette Devlin. Roy Bradford, the Minister for Development at Stormont, was speaking in the Union, and Bernadette Devlin led a group of around three hundred protestors to the Union to demonstrate against him. Inside the debating hall Union members heard chanting, then banging on the doors; a brick hurtled through a window narrowly missing the Deputy Prime Minister of the Irish Republic Erskine Childers. The debate ended abruptly without a vote, and the audience ventured out of the hall in some trepidation to find luckily that the police had matters under control.

At the next Irish debate in 1972, when the Taoiseach Jack Lynch was the guest, no chances were taken. Large numbers of security men were brought into the debating hall, supposedly disguised as students, to which end they had donned floral shirts and floral ties which made them stand out a mile. Jack Lynch's speech was made on the eve of talks with the British Prime Minister Edward Heath, and received considerable newspaper coverage. He attacked the Border referendum which the British Government was planning at the time, but he argued against premature withdrawal of British troops from the North and said that the Republic was willing to do everything possible to work towards a settlement in Ulster. The Union voted overwhelmingly for Irish unity, as Harold Macmillan had urged his contemporaries to do in very different circumstances in 1912.

The Irish issue was one in which politically minded undergraduates, at least those who were not Irish themselves, took an intelligent interest without feeling enormous commitment and excitement. They approached most issues in the 1970s in the same mood; the passions of the sixties were subsiding. The far left, less numerous in Oxford now anyway, stayed away from the Union. Towards the end of the decade some of the moderate left started to boycott it as well, leaving the Conservatives decidedly dominant.

By 1972 the Union was prepared to reject a motion that it was the role of the student to change the world, though there were still advocates of the sixties ethos. Students, without a settled social position, said the proposers, had more time and enthusiasm to change the world; they had formed the nucleus of CND, the protests against apartheid and the fight against pollution. Speakers against the motion pointed out that students had had little success in arousing the workers, except against themselves. Their fervour against the Vietnam war had diminished because the danger of their being drawn into the war themselves had abated. Some, they suggested, had been bought off by drug pedlars, food-faddists and ecologists. The student, at all events, was now firmly entrenched on the bourgeois side of the barricades.

A further sign of the change in mood came in 1973, when the Union rejected a motion of no confidence in the Heath Government. In part the new atmosphere was undoubtedly due to unemployment. Undergraduates became considerably more alert to the competition for good jobs, which was becoming tougher as the seventies went on. Oxford undergraduates worked harder, and at the same time became more introspective, paying less attention to the state of the world, being swept up by fewer causes, joining fewer organizations.

The Union members who celebrated the Society's hundred and fiftieth anniversary in 1973 were more traditionally minded than most of the generations of the previous dozen years or so. The guest speakers indulged them with some appropriately hyperbolic remarks about the Union's role. 'What is the university?' asked Harold Macmillan, 'only the background against which the Union is cast.' Michael Stewart compared the Union with the House of Commons. 'Both have a reading-room, a writing-room, a bar and a restaurant, together with a debating room for the more politically minded members.' Jeremy Thorpe preferred to describe the Union as 'the nursery in which we were trained in the minor arts of doing down our opponents in debate.'

As more socialists abandoned the Union, the active members who remained split into factions loosely representing the left and right of the Conservative Party. Attendance was still often quite good, but it depended even more than ever on the presence of good guest speakers. At the end of the seventies, the Labour Club took to writing to sympathizers who had been invited to speak at the Union advising them to turn their invitations down. Nevertheless, prominent Labour figures continued to accept; the Union still provided the largest audiences of Oxford undergraduates, and most on the left were not prepared to let their case go by default, even in front of a hostile house. Arthur Scargill, Neil Kinnock and Michael Foot were all still prepared to accept invitations to speak.

As their counterparts had been in the 1950s, undergraduates tended to be uninspired by politics. A vogue for Evelyn Waugh's *Brideshead Revisited* moved a handful of Union members to sport wing collars and white silk scarves. Homosexuals drew attention to themselves and were noticed more; there was talk of a gay faction in the Union. Whereas in the sixties many who had been to public schools adopted working-class accents, now it was the other way round.

In 1975 the Union staged a debate which, perhaps for the first time since 1933, gave it some influence on national affairs. The debate took place a few days before the Referendum on the EEC, and was televised. Its considerable impact may well have swayed votes when the country went to the polls.

'This House would say "Yes" to Europe' was carried by 493 votes to 92, a result which led Mrs Barbara Castle, one of the speakers against the motion, to attack the Union's establishment-mindedness. 'They're voting for Europe because it seems to them assurance of the top people's jobs,' *Cherwell* quoted her as saying. 'And mark my words, they'll get fat jobs in Europe, these boys.' In her diaries Mrs Castle admits that she was paralyzed with terror at the occasion. She describes herself on the way over to the debating hall holding her head as high as Anne Boleyn's on the way to the scaffold.

The pro-market mood of the Union was evident from the beginning, with cheers for the two guest speakers in favour of the motion, Jeremy Thorpe and Edward Heath, and some boos and catcalls for Mrs Castle and her fellow opposer Peter Shore. Peter Shore was the first of the guests to speak. He made his presentation of the anti-market case with characteristic sincerity and vigour, and got a good reception, despite the hostility of his audience. The Treaty of Brussels, he said, had been signed without the authority of the British people. Their rights were being overridden by the superior laws and the rules of the Treaty of Rome itself. Jeremy Thorpe followed with a witty speech in the classic Union manner. He said that the dissenting Ministers had made clear their contempt and disgust for the terms which their Government colleagues had renegotiated with Britain's EEC partners. Would they be leaving the Government after a 'Yes' vote, he asked, or would they stay on half-heartedly but on full pay, like five maggots in the European apple?

When Barbara Castle was speaking, Thorpe intervened to repeat his question. 'If Britain votes to stay in the Common Market,' she replied, 'my country will need me more than ever.' There were howls of derision. She had gained a cheer earlier by asking whether it was internationalism to give priority to an Italian over a Malaysian, an Englishman over an Indian or a German over an Australian. But, on her own admission, her speech had been a flop.

Edward Heath's triumphant speech, on the other hand was seen as evidence of the strength of the political comeback which he seemed to be making after being ousted as Conservative leader by Mrs Thatcher a few months before. 'The only reason for the Referendum,' he said, 'is that neither Mrs Castle nor Mr Shore are prepared to accept the decision of Parliament. Those who oppose the motion want to remain with the past organization of the nation state which has brought about two world wars and mass genocide in Europe.'

The referendum debate came as a welcome relief for the officers of the time from their preoccupations with the Union's internal problems. For much of the decade, the Society had a fight for survival on its hands. The Union's financial position, after a dramatic recovery in the wake of Michael Heseltine's entrepreneurial Presidency, began to deteriorate rapidly. The cost of maintaining the buildings and paying the staff increased considerably. Membership began to fall off. After a series of annual deficits, the Union was in debt by the late sixties; by the early seventies the debt was growing at an alarming rate.

In 1970 the Union voted to turn its facilities over to a Central Students' Union; the idea, however, was rejected by the University, mainly on the grounds that the funds would have to be diverted from college junior common rooms, which found the suggestion unacceptable. Then, in 1972, the Union put up a scheme to raise money by developing its gardens for offices, shops and flats, only to have the plans turned down by Oxford City Council. There then followed a long battle to acquire charitable status for the Union, coupled with preparations for an appeal. Charitable status meant that the Union had nominally to hand over its premises and property to a charity to be known as the Oxford Literary and Debating Union; the idea had its opponents among purists who wanted things to stay exactly as they were and also among left-wingers who still saw the possibility of a central students' union. Nonetheless, the scheme was comfortably approved in a poll. Harold Macmillan, Lord Hailsham, Lord Redcliffe-Maud, Roy Jenkins and Robin Day became the trustees of the new charity, and they set about raising three-quarters of a million pounds.

The Union, said Harold Macmillan, launching the appeal, was a unique institution which had played a vital part in British political life for over a hundred and fifty years. The Society, a *Times* leader commending the appeal chimed in, should be supported 'for the sake of the ordinary undergraduate who will learn there the inestimable advantage of being able to speak in public with a reasonable degree of confidence, with sufficient lucidity and with some power to persuade.' The appeal inspired several Union critics to give vent. One of them called it 'an outmoded and unnecessary relic of a dying social élite', another 'the crumbling ruin of a decaying order'. Its undergraduate defenders pointed out in turn that membership of the Union was still high and that debates were thriving.

The appeal, boosted considerably by a visit to the United States by Harold Macmillan and Lord Goodman, wiped out the Union's debt by 1980. The Union is not free of financial problems yet, but there have been further energetic efforts, particularly by the senior officers and permanent staff, to put the Society on a sound long-term financial footing. The buildings, which were beginning to crumble in an alarming manner, are being restored with the help of grants from a charity called the Landmark Trust and the Historic Buildings Council. Membership has gone up significantly over the past three or four years.

Nevertheless, financial problems have forced themselves upon the attentions of successive undergraduate Union officers. Minds which in the past might have been preoccupied with devising provocative motions like King and Country or with finding out the most reliable way of concealing musicians in the gallery, have had to concentrate on the relative appeal and rates of return on jam served in individual plastic containers or in dishes, or on stratagems to stop speakers and their guests drinking too much deficit-swelling free Union booze. It undoubtedly did the officers no harm to come to grips with such mundane problems; they probably have found the experience useful. It can hardly, however, have been in the best interests of the Union or of its long-suffering and dedicated permanent staff that its problems were being tackled by undergraduates of varying degrees of experience and competence, who seldom spent more than a term in the same position in the hierarchy, and who were unlikely to be intimately concerned with the Society's affairs for more than a year or so altogether.

Meanwhile, the role of President of the Union had developed into that of a large-scale impresario. The numbers of guest speakers expected at debates swelled from two to four or more. Ideally the Union should be able to attract large numbers of people because of the intrinsic interest and excitement in the art of debate; undergraduates should come to speak themselves or to listen to their contemporaries speaking rather than to form a passive audience for assorted politicians and celebrities. Nevertheless, successive Presidents have firmly believed that the only way to attract large audiences is to pull in big names from London. Regrettably they are right. Supposedly sophisticated undergraduates are star-struck; they like to see and hear famous people in the flesh, particularly when that flesh is being illuminated by television lights. The more enterprising Presidents have staged events and meetings in addition to normal debates, perhaps in tacit acknowledgement of the fact that formal parliamentary debating is not to everyone's taste.

By the mid-1970s, the President's chair was being occupied by a series of Conservatives. Most, however, wore their politics lightly. Colin Moynihan, for instance, was very ambitions, successfully so since he became an MP at the age of twenty-seven in 1983 and qualifies as an obvious high-flyer from the Union of the 1970s. Yet he felt it a disadvantage to his chances in the Union to be linked too closely to the Conservative Association, not because the Union members disliked Conservatives but because they disliked people who were too obsessed with politics.

Moynihan's aim was to become President in his second year so that he could cox the Oxford boat in his third year. He managed to pick up a boxing blue as well. As a result, he attracted a substantial hearty vote in his election for President, a vote that was probably greater than any political faction at the time. On the night of his election, he took part in a boxing match against Cambridge. When he arrived at the Union to wait for the results, cuts and bruises had made his victorious face unrecognizable.

Serious debates during this period concentrated on social issues like abortion and divorce rather than politics. Humour was, of course, at a premium. Moynihan is very small, and he was the butt of endless puerile jokes about his size. Among the taunts, it was suggested that he had worked as a test pilot for Airfix; that as a footballer he had attracted a record transfer fee for joining Subbuteo; that he was the only officer who did not have to pay VAT on his evening dress because he could take a child's size. To show that he was not offended by all this, Moynihan had as his farewell debate, 'This House would rather be a dwarf than Snow White'. He rode into the Chamber on an 850cc motor-cycle to preside over the occasion, removing his leather jacket to reveal his white tie and tails underneath.

Colin Moynihan's opponent in his Presidential election was Benazir Bhutto, daughter of the then Prime Minister of Pakistan. She had at one point been the favourite to win, but she probably did herself a disservice by hinting in the Presidential debate that her father would contribute substantially to the Union's Appeal Fund if she were elected.

Another problem which Benazir Bhutto faced was the feud over whether or not a girl called Vivien Dinham should have been debarred from taking office as President. Vivien Dinham's offence was that she had held a party on the banks of the river for several hundred people on the eve of her election at which a green-coloured cocktail was served, together with Smarties. It was alleged that she had in this way been bribing the electorate. Benazir Bhutto belonged to the anti-Dinham faction, whose rivalry with the pro-Dinham faction made the Montagues and the Capulets look like old friends.

However, Benazir Bhutto did eventually become President in 1977. According to her friends, she was not greatly concerned about climbing the Union ladder at first, but when the office of President came within her grasp and she realized how much her father wanted her to achieve it, it became very important to her to win. In office, she was accused of being high-handed and despotic by her opponents. Her friends say that she was merely dynamic.

She insisted that speeches should last no longer than eight minutes and conducted a poll to find out who read which periodicals, so that money could be saved by cutting out the ones which were never opened. She decided to paint the President's office herself; the colour she chose was blue, and one or two of the books gained blue-edged bindings in the process. She mounted debates which included 'The West can no longer live at the expense of the Third World', 'Capitalism will triumph', 'Hanging is necessary for the self-defence of society' and 'this House likes dominating women'.

When Benazir Bhutto left Oxford, she found herself within weeks addressing massive audiences in Pakistan as she campaigned for her detained father. It was not a milieu in which elaborately constructed jokes and acquaintance with parliamentary ritual counted for a great deal, nor one where she needed to keep to eight minutes either. Nonetheless, she appears to have considered her Union experience useful.

In 1978, the Union invited ex-President Richard Nixon to Oxford to give a lecture. In some ways, the event echoed the 1960s. Nixon made his way down St Michael's Street through a demonstration of the kind that controversial figures have often faced outside the Union. An organization was formed called the Campaign to Resist the Efforts of the Ex-President, a mouthful which gave it the same acronym as the notorious CREEP, the Campaign to Reelect the President. Several hundred demonstrators chanted 'Arrest Nixon' and waved placards which bore slogans like 'If you can't just die just fade away' and similar messages of welcome.

Most of these demonstrators, however, were Americans. Inside the Union, the huge audience clapped Nixon solidly for two minutes as he entered, gave him a prolonged cheer when he stood up to speak and asked him questions in a remarkably polite manner, even if there was a tendency to concentrate on Watergate. When the President, Daniel Moylan, stood up to leave with the Nixon party, the audience interpreted this as a cue for a standing ovation. Not only had the Union swung to the right; the age of deference seemed to have returned as well.

Nixon warmed to the role of a distinguished elder statesman, ranging over East-West relations, Communism and the fate of South East Asia. 'I like Russians and Chinese as people,' he said, 'I just don't like Communism.' Brezhnev, he suggested, was a realist. 'He wants the world, but does not want war.' As for his own achievements, he claimed that the new relationship which he had established with China had been the most important. On Watergate, the ex-President admitted, 'I screwed it up and I paid the price.' He also disclosed for the first time that he had authorized illegal wiretaps and break-ins to uncover an Al Fatah group in the United States shortly after the attack on the Israeli atheletes at the 1972 Olympic Games.

Daniel Moylan, who chaired the Nixon meeting, was another high-flying Conservative in the 1970s mode. The son of a Birmingham bus driver, he spoke in the Union with a plummy accent, well-tailored to his right-wing views. He joked once that he had been born with a silver spanner in his mouth. Moylan was known as a Union wit. 'I saw the honourable opposer talking to a corpse in the gutter. I knew it was the honourable opposer because the corpse yawned' was one of his efforts. When he was being serious, his views about rolling back the powers of the state went down well in a Union where the views of the radical right were coming into fashion. His friends say that his normal light-heartedness belied a depth of political conviction and an ambition which is likely to see him in a position of prominence before too long. Like other contemporary Presidents, he acknowledges that 'President of the Oxford Union' is a useful qualification to brandish before a Conservative selection conference. He fought but lost a marginal seat in 1983.

Another figure picked out by his contemporaries as a household name in the next century is William Hague, President in 1981. Hague is a state schoolboy whose opinions would not have sounded out of place at Arnold's Rugby. He burst onto the national political scene at the age of sixteen at a Conservative Party Conference where he attacked the Shadow Cabinet's leadership from the right in a supremely confident sub-Churchillian style which won him instant media attention. He featured prominently in the next day's *Daily Mail* and appeared on television, thus ensuring that he arrived at Oxford with a reputation which the Union wanted to puncture.

There were strenuous efforts to have Hague's nomination papers declared invalid when he first stood for office in the Union. Hague was a polished and confident performer; his detractors said he did not actually know a great deal and seldom came up with any material not to be found in a Conservative pamphlet. Yet they could not deny that he had the Union manner. In 1981 he spoke in a debate about the newly formed SDP against Mrs Shirley Williams. An opponent had likened Mrs Thatcher to the punk rock star Sid Vicious. 'If Mrs Thatcher's the Sid Vicious of the political world, then the SDP must be Abba,' pronounced Hague. He readily adapted too to another Union tradition, the nineteen-year-old trying to sound like the sixty-nine-year-old. 'I am not convinced,' he said of the SDP, 'that they will always have the resolution or the courage to stand up against what they believe to be wrong and put forward what they know in their hearts to be right. In politics, Mrs Williams, it isn't enough to be nice.'

The deferential, apolitical-cum-conservative, fun-loving atmosphere has persisted into the 1980s. It is perhaps the normal atmosphere of the Union from which the moods of the 1930s and the 1960s were aberrations. Motions like 'this House would hope to revisit Coronation Street rather than Brideshead', 'this House would prefer to be middle-aged', 'this House would rather be witty than pretty' and 'that innocence is bliss' have all been debated recently. More serious debates have centred round issues like sexual morality, religion, education and broadcasting. Politics no longer predominate, though there was a brief flurry of enthusiasm when the SDP was formed and the Union passed a motion 'that this House would support the Social Democrats'. But detachment from political events was such that there was no mention of, let alone a motion about, the Falklands War while it was taking place.

Only the defence issue has stirred real passions recently, but the Union has not really reflected the full heat or balance of opinion in the argument. Presidents have twice in the eighties revived the King and Country motion, each time to see it defeated. The revival in 1983 coincided with the fiftieth anniversary of the original debate, and showed the Union's continuing ability to attract publicity. Lord Beloff made the most memorable speech against the motion, fifty years after he had acted as a teller for the ayes in 1933. 'I wish to apologize to the memory of those who died in the war,' he said, 'and to warn against the kind of foolish arrogance that led us to make statements that were factually and morally untrue.' Malcolm Bull, who later became one of the few contemporary Presidents who are Labour supporters, proposed the motion with a statement of pacifist principles. He had the support of Helen John of the Greenham Peace Women, Lord Soper and Tariq Ali. Lord Home added ex-Prime Ministerial weight to the opposition along with Douglas Hogg. The motion was defeated by 416 votes to 187, amidst extravagant expressions of patriotic fervour.

The Union was subjected once again to the argument that it does not represent undergraduate opinion at Oxford. This is, of course, and always has been, perfectly true; it has suffered considerably as a debating forum in the last ten years from the fact that relatively few socialists have been active there. At the same time, the mood of the whole university has been Conservative for some time, as has that of the whole country, so that the Union may not be as far out of line as all that. OUSU, the students' union which has emerged in the last decade, has also had a great many Conservative Presidents.

The Union continues to attract large houses for big debates, and its membership has started rising again. Many still consider the style of debating mannered; they find the spectacle of nineteen and twenty-year-olds behaving with the pomposity of people double their age unedifying. But although the guests are more prominent, and the undergraduates are sometimes more prone to put on an act, or to clown, the forms of parliamentary debate are still observed, and prowess at mastering those forms is still admired. Speaking in the Union remains at least a test of nerve; it is as difficult as it ever was to impress what has always been a hypercritical audience.

Rightly or wrongly, presiding over the Union remains a qualification which is respected. Seventies Presidents are climbing much the same ladders at much the same speed as their predecessors.

The Union of 1983 makes a time capsule superfluous for anyone who wants to recapture the mood of past eras. Old members going back in search of eternal youth will find the same sort of youths engaged in the search for premature middle age as there always have been. A debate night follows a pattern which has changed very little in 160 years.

The readers who have been frowning over their work in the New Library have gathered up their ring-binders and bicycled back to college. The room has been taken over by the pre-debate sherry party. The officers, all male, are immaculate in their white ties and tails; they appear to have added ten years to their ages by changing out of their jeans. As they circulate amongst their guests, they are unmistakably the grandees of the court. The lesser undergraduate luminaries, paper speakers, committee members and hangers on, cluster round in their dinner jackets. They try to be polite to the guests, but they appear more animated when they turn to discussing amongst themselves the prospects of the various runners in the elections a week hence. They speak in home counties' accents, almost without exception, although their school backgrounds are, for Oxford, quite mixed.

Dinner is by candlelight, in the style and of the standard of a good Oxford high table. The Senior Librarian says grace beforehand. After the dessert, the President invites the guests to raise their glasses; the toast is the Queen, Visitor of Christ Church. The formalities are conducted with great relish.

Women seem more in the minority than usual amongst the Union activists round the table, especially considering that they now account for around forty per cent of the University's undergraduates. A girl at dinner explains her theory that as the Union became more conservative, the tide of female emancipation started to be reversed. The men liked to assign women to suitably feminine roles. They saw them as hostesses for Union functions, and little else. A public-school group which had been dominant recently had tried to perpetuate a male dining club ethos at the Union; they had been rather gauche and ill at ease with women, and did not seem to like them around. Prospects for women were now, she said, becoming brighter again.

There is a Liberal undergraduate at the table; two of the officers belong to the SDP and the President-elect is a socialist. The dinner is, nonetheless, a mainly Conservative gathering. The rank and file who come to listen to debates, say the undergraduates, represent a better cross-section of opinion. The disapproval of the Union in the Labour and Liberal Clubs prevents some from seeking office there, but few from attending.

The Education Secretary Sir Keith Joseph, who is the star guest speaker of the evening, makes a late entrance at dinner and is greeted with great warmth and politeness. The previous day, the Government has announced cuts in real terms in the education budget and a rise in student grants below the rate of inflation, but there is no demonstration outside the Union, and the subject is hardly raised at all during the ensuing debate.

Over in the debating hall, a crowd of four hundred has gathered. This is the second big Union debate in three days, so the turnout is very respectable. The undergraduates in the audience would not look out of place in the 1950s. Most of them are wearing jackets, quite a large proportion ties. The girls have more of Selfridges than of Greenham Common about them. Only up in the gallery is there any deviation from the sartorial norm, a handful of young men and women with their hair dyed green. They do not interrupt the proceedings, nor do any speakers make any reference to them. They are almost the only visible evidence that the hall is filled with students and not young farmers from Suffolk.

Once the debate begins, we are in an Oxford Union in which F. E. Smith or Ronald Knox would feel quite at home. The minutes are read with great bombast. The Secretary assigns each speaker his due rank and station in the Society (Joe Bloggs, ex-returning officer, spoke next). The hierarchy is as always taken very seriously. The President reproves the Secretary for digressing to try to raise a laugh from his minutes, so the Librarian and the Treasurer make more succinct attempts at humour during their announcements.

Then the House is onto the motion. It is a variant on a well-worn theme, but one given new topicality by the Prime Minister, that 'Victorian values have their place in shaping twenty-first century society'. The proposer is languidly fluent, but fails to break through the autumn chill to inspire his audience. Still, they show none of the sceptical hostility with which a 1960s house would have greeted a contemporary who asked what the real and admirable Victorian values were and answered his own rhetorical question by listing hard work, patriotism, religious observance and belief in the family.

The opposer is another Tory, but a more left-wing one. Just as sixties Oxford saw much of the most interesting debate as taking place within the left rather than between left and right, so now the Union of the 1980s is interested in debate within the right. This speaker has fun with Samuel Smiles, quoting him in a passable Yorkshire accent which overlooks the fact that Smiles was a Scot. 'Nothing sharpens a man's wit like poverty,' quotes the opposer, 'that is a lesson that Alderman Roberts of Grantham had obviously dunned into his daughter Margaret Hilda.' He goes on to speak grandiloquently of the true nature of equality, liberty and fraternity in a manner which former Prime Ministers and Oxford undergraduates, but few in between them, can sustain with conviction.

'We have just heard a speech from the honourable opposer which was very well read,' counters the next speaker. He takes an even more Victorian view than the proposer, praising Sir Keith Joseph as an enemy of moral neutralism; values should be decided upon, conducted and taught, he says. Even Victorian hypocrisy had its merits; by keeping quiet about adultery, the Victorians kept marriages together and saved children from the hardships of a broken home.

Then there is something of a *tour de force* from the Librarian. His assets are his timing and his complete command of his audience. Where others are thrown off their stride by interventions, he parries them skilfully or brushes them away with a flick of the wrist. There is nothing very special about either his phrasing or the content of his speech, but he has the gift of making the audience listen to him. 'With its infant mortality rate,' he says, '1883 would have been a good year for the Thatcher Government. At last the Government would be undertaking its duties; indeed undertaking would be its principal duty.' It is excruciatingly forced, but somehow he manages to make the line work, and he leads on up to a purple peroration. 'Mrs Thatcher may have deceived herself, her Cabinet and the whole nation twice, but don't in God's name let her deceive you. Throw out this motion.'

A short and lively floor debate follows before the guests speak. This is an innovation designed to make the Union more of a genuine debating club for undergraduates and less of a place to come and hear famous people speak. After this, the guests are heard politely. Sir Alfred Sherman says undergraduates, like the Victorians, should be moved by a feeling of responsibility to those less privileged than themselves. Sir Keith pays the undergraduates the compliment of dissecting their speeches rather than launching into a prepared text. He puts the Librarian in his place: 'I would not have believed that so much anachronism and so much snobbery could be packed with so much style into so cheap a package.' He goes on to praise the age of self-improvement and to claim that Western society is beginning to recover confidence in its attitudes towards the individual and society. On the other side, Dame Mary Warnock reminds the Union of the Victorians' regrettable attitude towards women, and suggests that people's assumptions and values, particularly about work, are going to have to be totally different in the twenty-first century.

The motion is lost by 150 to 222. The voting system is as unreliable as ever. Some of those leaving through the Noes door are against going back to the Victorian Age; others just want to find the fastest route to the bar. Yet on the whole it appears that, traditionalist though the Society may have become again, the majority of members do not regard themselves as neo-Victorians.

As always, the main talking point afterwards is the performance of the speakers. X, it is said, has improved his chances in the elections; Y was good, but he always makes the same speech; A's intervention was unfair to B, whom A is known to dislike intensely. The critics of the Union would recognize in this generation all the shortcomings which they have noted down the years, the youthful self-love, the posturing, the insularity of the Oxonocentric view of the world.

The defenders would find many admirable aspects of the evening. The parliamentary forms are observed more punctiliously than ever. The speeches have a real polish, reflecting the amount of care which has been lavished on them. They are almost all well-delivered, and there is some genuine cut and thrust in the interventions and the replies to them. Sharp words are used, but couched in courteous language. Formal debate may not count for as much as it once did in the outside world, but here in the Oxford Union it is alive and well.

CHAPTER EIGHT

THE OXFORD UNION AND THE ART OF PUBLIC SPEAKING

When people comment that a politican has the Oxford Union style, it is sometimes meant disparagingly. The suggestion is that the speaker in question is good at playing with words, but short on ideas and substance. Such an accusation has been levelled on occasions at Michael Foot, Michael Heseltine, Jeremy Thorpe and other illustrious ex-Presidents. Equally, many have passed through the Union to achieve a reputation based far more on their grasp of detail than on their capacity for oratorical fireworks. Neither Edward Heath, for instance, nor Michael Stewart would ever be accused of belonging to the Brock school of oratory.

What the Society's products do have in common is an interest in public speaking as an art. Almost all of them regard the Union as the whetstone on which they sharpened skills essential to any form of public life. There is less agreement about precisely what those skills are.

Harold Macmillan believes that in the Union one learnt by listening as well as by speaking what it was that would begin to interest and hold an audience. 'Some of the things that I remember vaguely being impressed by, though not quite knowing the reason, were afterwards explained to me as I learnt later in the House of Commons. The first rule, perhaps, of any speech of that kind is that it should be light and shade; one should vary the pitch and vary the pace. If a man speaks just on one note like a gramophone record or some sermonizer, you can't listen to it. The second is the temptation of young men, at seventeen or eighteen, to make it like an essay and cover the whole subject. The speech becomes a historical or economical or political essay. Even if it has been good, it would be more suitable to the *Economic Journal* than to a speech. In a speech, you have to say one or two things, one at the most really. Supposing you were speaking now, say on the economic issues; you're against monetarism or for monetarism; you're a deflationist or an inflationist. You must stick to your point. You can go round it, and say amusing things about it and serious things, decorate it, but it must be quite clear what you have said. If you produce an essay, especially in ten or fifteen minutes, you have not said enough about any point for it to stick in anybody's mind. Therefore it has no effect. That we learnt. But of course far the best thing it did was to teach us to treat each other properly, to behave like the House of Commons, to treat each other perhaps even more solemnly than the House of Commons, to speak like gentlemen and not like hooligans, to try and get some shape and system into a speech, and to behave.'

Mr Macmillan admits that he was always nervous before making a speech, 'Terribly nervous all my life. It's still so. Now I can't speak from notes. I never spoke much from notes, but now that I am blind I cannot use notes at all. One is very nervous, yes, but one comforts oneself with this; the kind of man at a city dinner who has to speak and who puts his hands in his pockets and says "I'm not at all nervous" makes an awfully bad speech. It's an art like any other art. You might ask, "Is the actor nervous when he goes on the stage on the first night?" Of course he is.'

'The art of oratory to all young people now is almost dead, because it's disappeared from the House of Commons. We no longer have great public meetings. Even political meetings in the ordinary elections are very few. Elections are fought on the television, and the television has taken the place of oratory. Theirs is a completely new technique which took me quite a time to learn, and it's roughly this. In a great meeting, five hundred, a thousand people, the Albert Hall, the meeting makes the speech. Somebody interrupts. You pick it up, take up a point and so on. A lot comes back to you from the audience. There are emotions, there are interruptions.

'When you first go on television, it is as if you stood one side of the net and hit the ball over the tennis net and nobody ever hit it back. Nothing comes back. In the old days, we did not even have interviewers. You were put in front of a camera and expected to speak into it. Well, people began by making speeches, or they had something written down. They're awful. Nobody can listen to them. The art of television is entirely different, and I always remember how it first occurred to me. The night before I became Prime Minister, I had to make a television, and I had only done about two or three in my life. My very nice director, of propaganda or something, said "there'll be twelve million people listening". I said suddenly to myself, "No there won't; there'll be two or three."

'When you do a television, you must remember that the audience is two or three. It is Father and Mother. Perhaps the daughter has just come in. Two or three, four perhaps at the most. So nothing comes back. It's entirely different. You speak as we talk. You don't finish the sentence. You don't make great Ciceronian speeches. You don't try to speak like Burke. It is a conversation. Once you have learnt that, it is an entirely different technique. Then of course it becomes easier.

'In the Oxford Union, we were long before that, and we spoke or tried to speak in the traditional, well-established English tradition of speaking, that had lasted through the nineteenth century and was still going on in the beginning of the twentieth century.'

When Harold Macmillan first stood for Parliament, he soon discovered that speeches which went down well with the undergraduates in the Union were received rather differently in Stockton on Tees. 'It didn't take more than a few days to find out that they didn't go down at all. I was very lucky in having a more or less Labour constituency, purely working class, and one soon discovered that that wouldn't do. When there was supposed to be an ordinary schoolroom meeting, very often there was no meeting at all, and everyone booed the whole time. I soon discovered the way to get over that. You stood on the table and said, "We won't have a speech. We'll have questions." Then, if you answered questions for an hour, you'd made your speech, without them knowing it, because in the answers to your questions you'd made your points.'

Harold Macmillan is half American, but his admiration for the United States does not extend to the way people speak in public there. 'In Congress, I don't think anybody listens to the speeches. They print them and circulate them. The Senate, I think, has good debates. I do not think that the House of Representatives has very good debates. Of course the real harm that my poor America has done is to invent a thing called a speechwriter. That has really destroyed the whole point of speaking. I have never delivered a speech that I hadn't composed in my life. But people like Ike and Kennedy used to explain to me how they had a speechwriter, and they could not have composed all those speeches. The other day, I listened to President Reagan. It was a very interesting speech, but quite obviously some group of people had written this speech. It quite destroys the art. It destroys the reality. This mechanization of it all is to me a very great pity.'

Even Kennedy, whom Mr Macmillan admired greatly, does not rank very high in his view as a speaker. 'You felt the phrases were produced by the whizz-kids, you know, not by him.' Churchill, Britain's other great Anglo-American Prime Minister, he puts in a separate category. 'He invented a style for himself. Every word and fact was written. He wrote every word. There would be a little pile of manuscript, a hundred pages, arranged in a particular kind of way, like the Psalms, so he could see it. He never referred to them. Once he had written them, he knew them by heart. But he could if he had to. It was because he was not a natural speaker. In his first speech, when he was first in the House of Commons, he broke down. His method had disadvantages. It was very good for a public meeting. It had disadvantages in the House of Commons, where he was undoubtedly nothing like as good as Lloyd George or even as Balfour. If you have got it all written down, it makes you very fixed. Balfour said of him that his batteries were very powerful but not at all mobile. That is true. Whereas if it is not written and somebody makes a point, gets up and so on, you can switch and change the argument. He was very good because he was a great politician, but he was not a natural orator. He was a literary orator.'

I asked Mr Macmillan for his definition of a natural orator. 'He needs some Celtic blood. You must be Highland, Welsh or Irish, somewhere! You must be an artist. Churchill was a literary artist. His speeches were beautifully written and they were very powerful. Of course, when he was a great man, people did not interrupt him; but I do remember one or two occasions, even in his last Government, when he was put off his stride. He could not quickly change. He had to make the rest of the speech.'

A different era, a different milieu, a different style. Beverley Nichols was not a politician, but he cared passionately about standards in public speaking. His own speeches might seem rather mannered today, but he did take the trouble to write down in some detail the principles of his style. The approach which he adopted represents a significant strand in the Oxford Union tradition.

He writes of his first speech in the Union, 'I learned it by heart. Not only did I learn it by heart, but I learned it musically, making full use of the art of alliteration. I can still see it in my memory, with the consonants in capitals. For example: "Such Conduct, on such an oCCasion, is not only beneath Contempt, it is beyond Comprehension." If oratory is an art, and a musical art, as I believed in those days and still do, one must understand the orchestration of the words, and one must also appreciate that certain words, in any speech, have the same colour and quality as certain instruments in an orchestra. Conduct, Occasion, Contempt, Comprehension . . . these are words of percussion, and they were used in a percussive context.'

The sort of speech which Nichols made depended greatly on the speaker's presence. Others attempting such a stylized manner could easily make themselves look ridiculous. Nonetheless, there is something to be said for taking as much care over preparing a speech as Beverley Nichols did, a practice which he contrasted with the habits of later and lesser generations. 'On the infrequent occasions when I have revisited Oxford in recent years to speak at the Union, I have been unimpressed. Most of the speeches sounded as if they had been compiled by computers and they were badly delivered, in a dreary monotone. None of the speakers knew what to do with his arms or his legs. I soon discovered what to do with mine. Nothing at all. Very few Englishmen can make oratorical gestures without looking ridiculous. Worst of all, many of the speeches were actually *read*, and even if they were not read in their entirety, there was a constant reference to notes. This surely was inexcusable. I have never used a note in my life. A speaker should walk out onto the platform with empty hands and nothing up his sleeve. To speak with notes is as deplorable as to play the piano with a score, turning the page in the middle of a melodic line.'

Nichols had more to say about bad speaking. 'The worst speaker of recent times, and I suspect of several centuries, was a man whom I greatly admire – Sir Anthony Eden. If he had been even reasonably articulate, the whole lamentable concatenation of events which led to the disaster of Suez need never have occurred. But he was not articulate. After hearing one of his speeches Winston Churchill, who was a loyal friend and colleague, observed, 'Dear Anthony delivered himself of every commonplace in the English language, with one exception.' When asked to name the exception, Winston replied, 'You will find it written up in all places of public convenience. It is "Kindly adjust your dress before leaving." These are hardly the words to inspire a great nation in times of mortal danger.' Of Churchill on the other hand, Beverley Nichols once wrote, 'He mobilized the English language.'

Lord Hailsham, President of the Union ten years after Beverley Nichols, believes that oratory is to some extent self-taught. 'But it's taught by practice, and the Union was the place where I practised. You start by having to learn a certain nuts and bolts. You've got to be able to frame a sentence. You've got to be able to compose a speech within a given time, and bring it to an end. You've got to be able to throw your voice so as to fill the room, but not excessively. The business of speaking is very largely a craft, as well as an art-form.

'You can of course learn to think quickly, and if you do that is a very valuable acquisition throughout your life.'

Lord Hailsham recognizes that styles in oratory do change. 'One doesn't notice it, of course, because the fish does not notice the flow of the stream, but quite undoubtedly in the nineteenth century they spoke in a different way. I remember old G. M. Young telling me that if you had heard a nineteenth-century Liberal public speaker, he would have said, "I believe in the good old cause, the good old cause for me . . .", and that would have been his way of speaking. But there are certain things which never get out of date, the telling phrase, the short sentence. It may be that the pronunciation of English is changing. I think it is. But there are certain things which you learn which are part of the craft.'

Lord Hailsham does not approve much of gestures. 'If you see someone waving his arms about, you know he is a bad speaker. If you are going to use a gesture, use something expansive. On the whole, I am a believer in not scratching your head, and keeping your arms fairly quiet.

'You speak much better extempore. But of course, in practice in the modern world, you have got to have delivered a speech to the press in advance or the editors do not print it. So you have got to learn the art of either speaking from notes or speaking from memory. If you want to make a good speech, then I think the short occasional speech, the kind of speech of which Harold Macmillan is such a master, although carefully prepared, is better without notes.'

The greatest speaker whom Lord Hailsham remembers was Lloyd George. 'He had a simplicity of style and a gift of phrase. The Whitechapel speech, which was very offensive and caused deep offence at the time, was a very clever piece of oratory. He was very effective when he was laying into the House of Lords. "The aristocracy is like cheese. The older it gets, the higher it becomes."

Hailsham's contemporary Sir John Hackett is another practised speaker who believes in preparation. 'I remember the Duke of Edinburgh saying "here is this swan gliding over the surface of the pond. You admire its suppleness and ease, and the skill and grace with which it moves. What you do not realize is that it is paddling like hell underneath." Most speeches which come off really well are rather like that. You have to do some preparatory thought, and the more you do, the more easily they run.'

Sir John, unlike Harold Macmillan, is not nervous when he speaks. 'I dislike it very much. I dislike the intrusion into a reflective private life which being obliged to get up and deliver oneself in public involves. It does seem to be an intrusion. But nervous? No, I don't think so. I mean it is their fault if they ask you to do this. As they have only themselves to thank, you can get on with it. What you have to do is to see that you do not go on for too long, which is a very great danger.'

Sir John sees Harold Macmillan's parallel with acting. 'You do not listen to yourself, but you want to be aware of yourself. You have to be aware of the relationship between yourself and an audience. In things like these television chat shows, if you have someone in opposition to yourself, if you can make him lose his temper, he's all yours. You can feel the studio audience dropping away from the man who is a little rude.'

Edward Heath, like Beverley Nichols, sees the parallels between public speaking and music. There has to be structure in a speech, he believes, just as there has to be structure in a piece of music. Like Nichols too, he has a strong dislike of speaking with copious notes. 'Looking back to the first guest speaker I can recall in the Union, it was Sir John Simon, who of course had a most distinguished parliamentary career, ending up as Lord Chancellor. He wound up the debate, and did it without a single note. I was absolutely full of admiration for somebody who could answer the points which had been raised at the box and by other speakers, and put the whole thing together in perfect shape, and carry the House with him. So that made me make up my mind that one day I must be able to produce a speech without using a note. I do it today in the House of Commons because I realized then how much more effective you can be in influencing people, which after all is the main purpose of the Union's debates, by being able to master the points which are being made by other people as you go along, and having the answers to them ready in your mind, to get the structure in your mind and then produce a whole speech.'

Edward Heath believes that there is a recognizable Union tradition. 'It does give people a fluency, and this is very noticeable when you compare them with other speakers. It was really Churchill who produced the other form of parliamentary speaking. As he was not able to speak fluently, strangely enough, he always had his speech in his hand. Of course, one of his famous remarks is "If you have notes, don't try to hide them. Brandish them." He always had a fistful of his speech and he brandished it. This meant that when he was at the dispatch box, every single word was there. Before he made a speech in the House, you could see him altering them as he went along; every so often I would be sitting next to him. This turned House of Commons speeches very much into written documents; and as most Ministers have not got people who can write speeches like Churchill, of course they are infinitely worse. As Ministers became more and more pressed for time, so the speeches with which they were presented by their civil servants stayed unaltered by the Ministers themselves, and this made things still worse.

'So the process of having everything word for word down in writing really has led to the present style of Ministerial speaking from the despatch box. I always remember that Baldwin made the abdication speech when Edward VIII abdicated from a couple of notes on the back of an envelope. That was all he had. It was said that Bonar Law as Chancellor of the Exchequer made his budget speeches without having any notes. So the parliamentary style has changed a great deal in the last eighty years or so. I think it is regrettable. I think it is a great pity. But of course, with the advent of radio and television, every word that a Minister utters has become so important that he is terrified – or certainly his officials are terrified – that he might put in the wrong sentence or the wrong word, then there is a great international incident. I am sure that the Union encourages the right style of speaking.'

Roy Jenkins does not consider it essential to be able to speak without notes. There is an art, he points out, of reading without seeming to read, if a speech has been semi-learnt. He looks back on Richard Crossman as a model for debating speeches. Crossman's technique, he suggests, was rather like that of a man riding a bicycle along the edge of a cliff. He would go to great lengths to establish the other person's case; any minute you felt that he would fall over the cliff and concede the argument, but in the end he would produce a dazzling refutation.

Jeremy Thorpe is another Union hand who admits to nerves, at least when he began public speaking – he was physically sick before he made his first speech in Oxford at Campion Hall. He believes it is a great help to have a heckler to put down decisively early on in a speech. It is all, he suggests, a matter of confidence. He cites Churchill; it matters first who you are, secondly how you deliver your speech, thirdly what you say. Jeremy Thorpe is conscious, all the same, that the Union and Parliament are two different styles. Parliament likes facts and dislikes elaborate playing on words. 'You're not in the Oxford Union now,' is an intervention which has been heard more than once in the House of Commons.

Brian Walden, on the other hand, argues that the standard is actually higher in the Oxford Union than in the House of Commons. 'You can make good speeches in the House of Commons, but you can't debate as you can in the Oxford Union.' For sheer technique, he remembers being impressed above all by Aneurin Bevan, although he disagreed with his views. He heard him speak on German rearmament at the Labour Club in Oxford. 'You could hear a pin drop. It was so quiet you could hear him breathing.' Bevan built up a catalogue of the world's tensions and problems which he brought to a climax with a rhetorical question: 'What is the miraculous cure for all that? – 55,000 German bayonets.' The silence was broken by roars of applause. Walden does believe firmly in speaking without notes. 'That way you can look people straight in the eye. The thing to do is to keep as still as you possibly can.'

Michael Heseltine is at his best as a speaker at the Conservative Party Conference. When he addresses the representatives, the disarray of his hairstyle invariably contrasts with the careful structure of a speech which combines jokes at the Labour Party's expense with a stirring appeal to Conservative values calculated to rouse the most stuporous of his audience to their feet. He has had far more difficulty assuming the same command over the House of Commons. Nevertheless, he believes that his Oxford Union training should have equipped him better for the Commons than for party platforms. 'It is a more intimate style. It is a much more defined style than you get on a party platform. You are dealing with a different audience. The undergraduate audience has a degree of political sophistication which is probably unequalled anywhere else outside Parliament. Whereas the big political audiences represent a very wide spectrum of political sophistication, of interest and awareness and are not usually as receptive to the rather discursive and highly polished stylized style of the Oxford Union or to some extent of Parliament.'

Unlike some other former Presidents in politics, Michael Heseltine admits that he used to speak from notes in the Union. 'They were immensely detailed notes. It was probably a pity, probably a mistake, but I was not all that confident. I never did get confidence in the Oxford Union. It was not until some time later that I felt properly at ease on a platform. You never feel at ease on a great occasion until you start speaking. Then you can feel totally at ease. But in the moments up to getting to your feet, the more important the occasion, the more nerve-racking it is. At the Oxford Union, I never remember feeling in command of an audience.'

Had the young Michael Heseltine dropped his notes, he would have been worried. 'I remember one of my friends here, who died sadly as a young man, a chap called Andrew Cuninghame, who was President a few terms before me. I have never seen it on a platform before or since, but he literally said, "I am sorry, Mr President, I shall have to sit down." He had forgotten absolutely what he was going to say and where he was in the speech. I vowed that would never happen to me. It is very rare nowadays that I get up without some sort of notes. I often do not refer to them, but they are there. I shall never forget that experience.'

Heseltine admits that this style has changed a great deal since he left Oxford. 'I think my speaking has changed almost out of all recognition. I was never regarded as a particularly good speaker when I was here. I was not a bad speaker, but if anyone looking back had asked who at the time of their Presidency would figure among the great public speakers, my name would not figure on that list. I would think that would be a fair judgement from my own recollection of my performances there.

'To make great speeches, you have to be in command of an

audience. You have to feel rapport with that audience. I never felt it with the Oxford Union. I have felt it since coming back, but never when I was President or in the earlier stages before that.'

Michael Heseltine does not admit to any models for his speaking style now. 'I come from South Wales. I have a certain amount of Welsh blood. I do not think you can leave that out of the equation. It is there, and it comes through. The more committed one is, the more involved in the speech, the more it tends to come through. I would not have ever said, however, "That's what I want to be like." If you think of the people who are distinguished public speakers, they are not modelled on anybody. They are their own thing. They are characters. They are orators in their own style. Indeed, they become associated with their own style. There is no comparison between MacLeod or Quintin Hailsham or Macmillan or Michael Foot or Aneurin Bevan, people I remember who were very distinguished. They were all in their own way doing their own thing.'

Heseltine has a particular admiration for Harold Macmillan as a commentator on speeches as well as a speaker. 'I remember I was going to speak in the Cambridge Union and I was very late. So often in my profession people are rushed onto the train not having prepared anything. I got to Cambridge having prepared all except the last five minutes of the speech, which of course is the critical part really. I thought I would bluff my way through that. And I did it. Macmillan happened to be there. He was being presented, I think, with honorary membership of the Cambridge Union. Afterwards, there was a little touch on my arm, and I looked and there was Harold Macmillan. He said to me, "That was a very good speech. A very good speech. But take my advice. Always prepare the end first." He had spotted exactly what I had done.'

Although his own technique has changed, Michael Heseltine accepts that there is a definable Oxford Union style. 'People do identify it, and I think it is there. I think the mannerisms, the polish, the timing, the play with words, the sense of occasion, all of those things come from this place. It is a very precocious situation. In early life, you are pretending to be the elder statesman, and why not? Other people pretend they are all sorts of things. You do learn the tricks which are characteristic of the style of the place. There is a kind of house style, I think, in the Oxford Union.'

One enduring impression remains with everyone who has made a success of the Union. That is the capacity of the place to terrify all who attempt to speak there. A peer who was a dazzling success in the Union remembers always being frightened there, as well as always cold. Another equally eminent former officer recalls sheer panic hitting him in the gentlemen's lavatory before a big debate. A recent President confirms that the audience can still be very cruel and very frightening. As a forum for testing nerves to the limit, if nothing else, the Union merits its place as a training ground for public speaking.

APPENDIX A

THE WIT OF THE OXFORD UNION

The Union prides itself on its wit, its epigrams and its funny stories. Many of the best lines depend on the person delivering them or on knowledge of the personalities involved. Much that seems brilliant when spoken looks decidedly flat in print. Most of the best Oxford Unionisms are recycled down the generations, maturing with age as they are retold. Some of them appear in the narrative of this book. Here are some others.

BEFORE THE FIRST WORLD WAR

An undergraduate was accused of illegally keeping a barrel of beer in his rooms. He claimed that he had been prescribed it by his doctor to make him strong. Asked whether the prescription had been effective, he said, 'When the barrel came I could scarcely lift it; now I find it quite easy.'

'British statesmen are eternally seeking publicity instead of giving thought to the questions of the time. They are like the American politican of whom it was said that when he went to a wedding he was vexed because he could not be the bride, and when he went to a funeral he was continually filled with envy that he could not be the corpse.'

BETWEEN THE WARS

'Mr Lloyd George's policies are all a piece of mysticism; they begin in mist and end in schism.'

'The Liberal Party is one of the fast disappearing features of rural England.'

'The Liberal Party has been called a flock of sheep without a shepherd. It might rather be called a flock of quarrelsome shepherds without a sheep.'

'The difference between American and English politicians is that in the States they will do anything for money whereas in Britain they just take the money and won't do a darn thing for it.'

'The Liberal Party is like a lobster, by nature blue, except when it gets into hot water, when it turns red.'

'The new President, Mr Arthur Irvine, is a symbol of unity because he is a Liberal who advocates Socialist policies for Conservative reasons.'

'The honourable opposer is like one of those people who go out to the colonies to take up the white man's burden and lay it down with great accuracy and precision on the black man's shoulders.'

'British public men are at their wits' end – not a long journey.'

'The theatre should hold up a mirror to nature, not a magnifying glass to mediocrity.'

'The difference between a silent film and a talkie is that the half-witted dialogue is now supplied by the company instead of the audience.'

On a slow news day, the editor of a Fleet Street newspaper asked his foreign editor what was happening in Bulgaria. He was told that there was nothing going on there at all. The next day a story appeared in the paper under the headline 'Ominous Silence in Bulgaria.'

'As for the Ten Commandments, even Solomon in all his glory was not troubled by some of these.'

1950s and 1960s

'In Oxford, I had hoped to find the dons informed, distinguished and God-like. Instead, I have found them deformed, extinguished and cod-like.'

There was an Arab oil sheik who was so rich that he oiled his bicycle with Benedictine.

'If honourable members are going to laugh every time they hear something they don't understand, they're going to have a hilarious evening.'

'Do I hear hissing? There is always hissing when the waters of heaven fall upon the fires of hell.'

'A progressive Conservative is someone who becomes progressively more Conservative as he grows older.'

'The speakers opposite are like the death watch beetle, and not only in appearance.'

'Warden Spooner might well have described the honourable gentleman as a shining wit.'

Post-1970

'The honourable opposer's speech was very similar to Noah's Ark; it drifted endlessly on the waters, found no solid ground and was filled with all manner of strange things – with all of them in tedious duplicate.'

'You, Sir, asked us to vote for you and for good administration of the Society's affairs, but unfortunately we are not allowed to vote twice.'

'Your position, Sir, is a brilliant compromise on the part of the Union: a compromise between leaving the Chair empty and putting in a President.'

'I am told, Sir, that the City Council wanted to name a street after you, but they couldn't find one narrow and twisting enough.'

'I remember, Sir, that you once said you had half a mind to be President, and, as I told you, that would be all that was necessary. Which is just as well, because it's all you've got.'

'When I arrived here, the President shook me warmly by the neck and offered me a drink. When I asked him for something tall, cool and full of gin, he said: "You'd better meet my girlfriend."'

'His suit always fits him like a glove; it sticks out in five places.'

'He is a masterpiece of the taxidermist's art.'

'The honourable member aspires to be a barrister. I looked up barristers in the encyclopedia the other day. You'll be interested to know that they are listed between bankrupts and bastards.'

'The honourable member once made a lot of money on the greyhounds, as a jockey.'

Disraeli was once asked to define the difference between a calamity and a catastrophe. He said, 'If Mr Gladstone were to fall into the Thames, that would be a calamity. If someone were to fish him out again, that would be a catastrophe.'

'If the honourable gentleman did not have a moustache, he would be a bareface liar.'

'A debate without the honourable member would be rather like *Hamlet* without the third gravedigger.'

'The honourable opposer's previously expressed opinions led me to believe that he was tottering on the edge of a precipice. From what he has said tonight, I am pleased to say that he has taken a giant step forward.'

'I would remind honourable gentlemen that the bar is open during the honourable opposer's speech.'

'The last speaker has a special regard for honesty; he saves it for special occasions.'

'When one thinks of the next speaker, the words 'pompous', 'boring' and 'windbag' do not immediately spring to mind; one has to wait for his speech for that.'

'He is an able historian. He has described the discovery of Rhodesia by Cecil Rhodes as the coincidence of the century.'

'The honourable member is a man of balance; he has a chip on both shoulders. He is a man of discrimination; he can tell the difference between right and wrong if given two guesses. He is a man of many parts; and it is a misfortune that they were assembled by British Leyland on a Friday.'

'The list of successes in his career has not been such as to require the Recording Angel to take up shorthand.'

'There was some applause during the honourable member's speech, even if it was only from one man at the back slapping his face to try to keep himself awake.'

'Back in the valleys, he was known as Dai Bungalow – nothing upstairs.'

'Statistics show that in the London area there's a man being knocked down every five minutes, and I can tell you he's getting pretty fed up with it.'

'The only way this Government can shorten the dole queues is to get people to stand closer together in them.'

'A member of Parliament is invited to stand, wants to sit, and is expected to lie.'

APPENDIX B

PRESIDENTS OF THE UNION SINCE 1900

Year	*Name*	*Died*	*College*	*Career*
1900	R. C. K. Ensor	1958	Balliol	Academic at Corpus Christi and Nuffield Colleges
	Raymond Asquith	1916	Balliol	Killed in action in First World War
	Rt Hon Harold Baker	1960	New College	Liberal MP for Accrington 1910–1918
1901	Algernon Cecil		New College	Author 'British Foreign Secretaries' etc
	T. Cuthbertson		Corpus Christi	
	Sir George Tomlinson	1963	University	Colonial Service
1902	Lord Lindsay of Birker	1952	University	Master of Balliol College
	Sir Eric Macfadyen	1966	Wadham	Liberal MP for Devizes 1923–24; pioneer of rubber industry
	Lord du Parcq	1949	Exeter	Judge of the Appeal Court
1903	Herbert Asquith	1947	Balliol	Author 'The Volunteer' etc
	F. W. Curran		Lincoln	
	Sir John Brooke	1937	Corpus Christi	Public Servant; Ministry of Transport and Electricity Commision

Presidents of the Union Since 1900

Year	*Name*	*Died*	*College*	*Career*
1904	Most Rev. William Temple	1944	Balliol	Archbishop of Canterbury
	W. A. Moore		St John's	Editor, *The Calcutta Statesman*
	E. S. Jose		Hertford	
1905	J. St G. C. Heath		Corpus Christi	
	Lord Craigmyle (A. Shaw)	1944	Trinity	Liberal MP for Kilmarnock 1915–23; Director, the Bank of England
	M. H. Woods	1929	Trinity	Journalist, *The Times*
1906	H. M. Paul		New College	
	Hon H. Lygon		Magdalen	London County Councillor
	Sir Gervais Rentoul	1946	Christ Church	Conservative MP for Lowestoft 1922–34; Chairman 1922 Committee
1907	Rt Rev N. S. Talbot	1943	Christ Church	Bishop of Pretoria
	William Gladstone	1915	New	MP for Kilmarnock Boroughs 1911–15; killed in First World War
	W. S. Armour		Jesus	Editor, *Northern Whig*, Belfast
1908	C. T. le Quesne QC		Exeter	Barrister, Recorder of Plymouth
	Sir Hugh Hallett	1967	Christ Church	High Court Judge
	Rev M. H. Richmond		New	Hon Canon of Norwich
1909	Rt Revd Monsignor Ronald Knox	1957	Balliol	Translator of the Bible
	Rt Rev Edgar Swain	1949	St John's	Bishop of Burnley
	R. G. D. Laffan	1972	Balliol	Bursar of Queen's College, Cambridge
1910	Hon R. S. A. Palmer	1916	University	Killed in First World War
	L. J. Stein	1973	Balliol	President of the Anglo-Jewish Association
	A. W. Cockburn Q.C.	1969	New	Chairman of the County of London Sessions

Year	*Name*	*Died*	*College*	*Career*
1911	Rev Nathaniel Micklem	1976	New College	Principal of Mansfield College; President of the Liberal Party
	R. Bevir	1916	Hertford	Killed in First World War
	Philip Guedalla	1944	Balliol	Historian and biographer
1912	Frank Griffith	1962	Balliol	County Court Judge and Liberal MP for Middlesbrough W 1928–40
	Robert Barrington-Ward	1948	Balliol	Editor of *The Times*
	G. S. Woodhouse	1916	Lincoln	Killed in First World War
1913	Lord Monckton of Brenchley	1965	Balliol	Minister of Labour and Defence
	W. J. Bland	1918	Lincoln	Killed in First World War
	Godfrey Talbot	1916	Christ Church	Killed in First World War
1914	Sir Ernest Roberts	1969	Trinity	Conservative MP for Flintshire 1924–29; Chief Justice in Rangoon
1914	A. H. M. Wedderburn KC	1968	Balliol	Barrister, LCC Member
	A. F. H. Wiggin	1935	Oriel	Diplomatic Service
1919	Lord Hore-Belisha	1957	St John's	Liberal Nationalist, then Independent MP; Minister of Transport; Secretary for War
	Thomas Earp	1958	Exeter	Literary and artistic critic
1920	Constantine Gallop QC	1967	Balliol	Master of the Bench, Middle Temple
	Sir John Russell	1978	New	Barrister, Chairman of the London Conservative Union 1953–55
	Beverley Nichols	1983	Balliol	Journalist, author and composer
1921	Alec Beechman QC	1965	Balliol	Liberal Nationalist MP and Chief Whip
	Captain Cecil Ramage		Pembroke	Barrister, Liberal MP 1923–24

Presidents of the Union Since 1900

Year	*Name*	*Died*	*College*	*Career*
(1921 cont)	Kenneth Lindsay		Worcester	Independent MP, Parliamentary Secretary, Board of Education
1922	J. Victor Evans		St John's	Barrister, Independent Nationalist MP
	Ralph Carson	1977	Oriel	Lawyer on Wall Street
	Edward Marjoribanks	1932	Christ Church	MP, biographer and poet
1923	J. Douglas Woodruff	1978	New	Journalist, Editor of *The Tablet*
	Gordon Bagnall		St John's	Journalist
	Christopher Hollis	1977	Balliol	Author, Journalist and Conservative MP for Devizes
1924	Professor Christopher Scaife		St John's	Academic, Professor of English in Cairo and Beirut
	Lord Gardiner		Magdalen	Lord Chancellor, 1964–70
	The Earl of Dundee (Scrymgeour Wedderburn)	1983	Balliol	Conservative MP, Foreign Office Minister, Deputy Leader, House of Lords
1925	Robert Bernays	1945	Worcester	Liberal MP, Health and Transport Minister
	Sir Vincent Lloyd-Jones		Jesus	High Court Judge
	Lord Molson		New	Conservative MP, Minister of Works 1957–59
1926	Sir Gyles Isham	1976	Magdalen	Actor and farmer
	Prof Lindley Fraser	1963	Balliol	Professor of Political Economy, Aberdeen University; Head of BBC German and Austrian Services
	Lord Boyd of Merton (Alan Lennox-Boyd)	1983	Christ Church	Colonial Secretary 1954–59
1927	Sir Roger Fulford	1983	Worcester	Writer, historian, President of the Liberal Party

Year	*Name*	*Died*	*College*	*Career*
(1927 cont)	John Playfair Price		New	Foreign office – series of diplomatic and consular posts
	Malcolm Brereton	1942	Balliol	Killed in Second World War; law, BBC
1928	Sir Dingle Foot QC	1978	Balliol	Liberal and Labour MP; Solicitor-General 1964–67
	Aubrey Herbert	1981	University	Broadcaster and Liberal politician
	S. Stopford Brooke	1976	Balliol	Stockbroker and Liberal candidate
1929	Prof. Roger Wilson		Queens	Professor of Education, University of Bristol
	Lord Hailsham (Quintin Hogg)		Christ Church	Lord Chancellor 1970–74, 79–
	Lord Stewart of Fulham		St John's	Labour Cabinet Minister 1964–70
1930	Edgar Lustgarten	1978	St John's	Barrister, journalist and broadcaster
	J. P. W. Mallalieu	1980	Trinity	Labour MP for Huddersfield 1945–79 and junior minister
	Lord Boyd-Carpenter		Balliol	Chief Secretary to the Treasury 1962–64; Chairman of the Civil Aviation Authority
1931	Lord Foot (John Foot)		Balliol	Solicitor and Liberal peer; Chairman of the UK Immigrants Advisory Service
	Sir Geoffrey Wilson		Oriel	Civil Servant, Chairman of the Race Relations Board, Chairman of Oxfam
	Toby O'Brien	1979	Exeter	Director of Information for the Conservative Party
1932	Sir Arthur Irvine	1978	Oriel	Liberal and Labour MP; Solicitor-General 1967–70
	Brian Davidson		New	Businessman, Director of Bristol Siddeley

Presidents of the Union Since 1900

Year	*Name*	*Died*	*College*	*Career*
(1932 cont)	Lt-Col J. C. Smuts	1979	University	Army
1933	Frank Hardie		Christ Church	Author and academic
1933	Lord Greenwood	1982	Balliol	Labour MP 1946–70; Cabinet Minister 1964–70
	Michael Foot		Wadham	Leader of the Labour Party 1980–83
1934	Dosoo Karaka	1974	Lincoln	Journalist; editor of *The Current* of Bombay
	Sir Keith Steel-Maitland	1965	Balliol	Businessman; chairman of an estates company
	W. G. Murray	1938	Balliol	Journalist and broadcaster
1935	David Lewis	1981	Lincoln	Leader of the Canadian New Democratic Party
	Rev James Hickerton		St Catherine's	Baptist Minister
	Brian Farrell		Balliol	Reader in Mental Philosophy, Oxford University
1936	Ian Harvey		Christ Church	Conservative MP for Harrow E 1950–58; President of the Conservative Group for Homosexual Equality
	Bill Shebbeare	1944	Christ Church	Killed in the Second World War
	James Brown		Balliol	Judge, Recorder of Belfast 1978–82
1937	Lord Mayhew		Christ Church	Navy Minister 1964–66; Labour and Liberal MP; Liberal peer
	Patrick Anderson	1979	Worcester	Writer
	Alan Fyfe	1944	Balliol	Killed in Second World War
1938	Sir Raymond Walton		Balliol	Judge
	Philip Toynbee	1982	Christ Church	Author and critic
	Alan Wood	1957	Balliol	Writer

The Oxford Union

Year	*Name*	*Died*	*College*	*Career*
1939	Edward Heath		Balliol	Prime Minister 1970–74
	Sir Hugh Fraser	1984	Balliol	Conservative MP since 1945; Air Secretary 1962–64
	Sandy Giles*		Balliol	Colonial Service
	Sir Nicholas Henderson		Hertford	Diplomat; Ambassador to Bonn Paris and Washington
1940	Madron Seligman MEP		Balliol	Businessman and Member of the European Parliament
	Sir Robert Edmonds		Brasenose	Diplomat, High Commissioner for Cyprus
	Sir James Comyn		New	Judge
1941	Indar Bahadoorsingh		St Catherine's	
	Rev Kenneth Riddle		St Catherine's	Anglican Priest
	Michael Kinchin-Smith		Christ Church	BBC; Secretary, Crown Appointments Commission
1942	Gershon Hirsch (now Aveny)		Brasenose	Israeli diplomat
	F. P. R. Hinchcliffe		New	Judge
	Cameron Tudor		Keble	High Commissioner for Barbados in London
1943	Rev Herbert Clarke		Jesus	Anglican Priest
	Courtney Blackmore		Keble	Lloyds
	Sir Godfrey le Quesne		Exeter	Judge in Jersey
1944	Hon Kenneth Lamb		Trinity	Broadcasting; Director of Public Affairs of the BBC
	Prof Fernando Henriques	1976	Brasenose	Director, Centre for Multi-Racial Studies, Exeter University
	Tony Pickford		Oriel	

* Elected but did not hold office because of war service

Presidents of the Union Since 1900

Year	*Name*	*Died*	*College*	*Career*
1945	Alan Gibson*		Queen's	Broadcaster, BBC radio commentator
	Rudi Weisweiller		New	International financial consultant
	Anthony Walton QC		Hertford	Barrister
	Dr John Long		Queen's	Chemist, Director of ICI
1946	Lord Wigoder QC		Oriel	Liberal Chief Whip, House of Lords
	Anthony Crosland	1977	Trinity	Labour Cabinet Minister 1965–70, 1974–77
	Group Captain Ronald Brown		Brasenose	Surgeon, RAF Medical Branch
1947	Roger Gray QC		Queen's	Recorder of the Crown Court
	Tony Benn		New	Labour Minister 1964–70, 1974–79
	Peter Kroyer		Christ Church	
1948	Clive Wigram	1956	Oriel	Barrister
	Lord Boyle	1981	Christ Church	Cabinet Minister; Vice-Chancellor of Leeds University
	Seymour Hills	1964	St Catherine's	Printer, Industrial Consultant
1949	Sir Peter Kirk	1977	Trinity	Conservative Minister and Leader of European Parliament delegation
	Rodney Donald		Christ Church	Financier
	Sir Richard Faber		Christ Church	Diplomat, Ambassador to Algeria 1977–81

Year	*Name*	*College*	*Career*
1950	Uwe Kitzinger	New	Director of Oxford Centre for Management Studies
	Sir Robin Day	St Edmund Hall	Broadcaster
	Godfrey Smith	Worcester	Author, *Sunday Times* columnist
1951	Jeremy Thorpe	Trinity	Leader of the Liberal Party 1967–76

* Elected but did not hold office because of war service

Year	*Name*	*College*	*Career*
1951 (*cont*)	Sir William Rees-Mogg	Balliol	Editor of *The Times*; Chairman of the Arts Council
	Ivan Yates (d.1975)	Pembroke	Journalist on *The Observer*
1952	Sir Peter Blaker	New	MP for Blackpool S, since 1964; Foreign Office and Defence Minister
	Howard Shuman	New	Administrative Assistant to American Senators
	Sir Patrick Mayhew	Balliol	MP for Royal Tunbridge Wells since 1974; Solicitor-General
1953	Bryan Magee	Keble	Writer; Labour and SDP MP for Leyton 1974–1983
	John Peters	Balliol	Civil Servant; Assistant Undersecretary, MoD
	Sir Andrew Cuninghame (d. 1959)	Worcester	Foreign Office
1954	Tyrell Burgess	Keble	Director of Institutional Studies, NE London Poly
	Raghavan Iyer	Magdalen	Academic in California
	Michael Heseltine	Pembroke	Cabinet Minister 1979–
1955	Jeremy Isaacs	Merton	Chief Executive, Channel Four Television
	Anthony Howard	Christ Church	Deputy Editor of *The Observer*
	Desmond Watkins	Keble	Industrialist, with Shell
1956	Alec Grant	Merton	Barrister, former Labour member of the GLC
	Roy Dickson	Exeter	Jamaican civil service
	Edmund Ions	Merton	Academic; Reader in Politics, York University
1957	Jeremy Lever QC	University	Lawyer and Fellow of All Souls College
	Hon Peter Brooke	Balliol	MP for City of London since 1977; Education Minister
	Brian Walden	Queen's	MP for Birmingham All Saints 1964–77; television presenter

Presidents of the Union Since 1900

Year	*Name*	*College*	*Career*
1958	Lalithe Athulathmudali	Jesus	Minister of Trade and Shipping in Sri Lanka
	Stuart Griffiths	Magdalen	Script editor, Plays, BBC TV
	Ron Owen	Christ Church	Personnel Officer in industry
1959	Lashman Kadirgamer	Balliol	Lawyer in Sri Lanka
	Anthony Newton	Trinity	MP for Braintree since 1974; Health Minister
	Joe Trattner	St Catherine's	American lawyer
1960	Ian Lyon	Oriel	Journalist; editor *International Tax Free Trader*
	Peter Jay	Christ Church	Television presenter; journalist; Ambassador to USA 1977–79
	Robert Rowland	Keble	BBC, Open University
1961	Phillip Whitehead	Exeter	Labour MP for Derby N 1970–83; television producer
	Paul Foot	University	Journalist on the *Daily Mirror*
	Howard Preece	Merton	Journalist
1962	Hugh Stephenson	New	Editor, *The New Statesman*
	John McDonnell	Balliol	Barrister
	Michael Beloff QC	Magdalen	Academic and barrister
1963	G. R. Karnad	Magdalen	Actor
	Jeffrey Jowell	Hertford	Barrister
	Anthony Hart	New	Civil Servant
1964	Garth Pratt	Christ Church	Liberal political activist
	Lord James Douglas-Hamilton	Balliol	Conservative MP for Edinburgh W since 1974
	Eric Abrahams	St Peter's	Minister of Tourism in Jamaica
1965	Professor Neil MacCormick	Balliol	Regius Professor of Public Law, Edinburgh University
	Tariq Ali	Exeter	Journalist and Marxist politician
	Douglas Hogg	Christ Church	Conservative MP for Grantham since 1979; Whip
1966	Joshua Bamfield	Pembroke	
	Jeremy Beloff	St Catherine's	Businessman; Procter and Gamble
	Montek Singh	Magdalen	World Bank

The Oxford Union

Year	*Name*	*College*	*Career*
1967	Ronald Cohen	Exeter	Investment banker
	Stephen Marks	New	Journalist, *International Socialism*
	Robert Jackson	St Edmund Hall	MP for Wantage since 1983; MEP since 1979
1968	Geraldine Greineder (nee Jones)	St Hugh's	Housewife
	Hon William Waldegrave	Corpus Christ	Conservative MP for Bristol W since 1979; Environment Minister
	Ian Glick	Balliol	Barrister
1969	David Walter	Trinity	Political Correspondent, ITN
	Colin Youlden	Merton	Academic
	Gyles Brandreth	New	Writer and broadcaster
1970	Guy Harkin	Hertford	Polytechnic lecturer and Labour councillor
	Stephen Milligan	Magdalen	Foreign Editor of *The Sunday Times*
	Eric Parsloe	Ruskin and Corpus Christi	Businessman
1971	Michael House	Exeter	Barrister
	Susan Kramer (Nee Richards)	St Hilda's	Housewife in USA
	Christopher Tookey	Exeter	Television producer, TV-AM
1972	Julian Priestley*	Balliol	EEC administrator and Labour candidate
	Pradeep Mitra	Balliol	Academic
	Patric Dickinson	Exeter	Rouge Dragon Poursuivant, College of Arms
	Philip McDonagh	Balliol	Irish Foreign Office
1973	Michael Austerberry	Trinity	Civil service
	Colin Maltby	Christ Church	Business
	David Warren	Exeter	Foreign Office
1974	Simon Walker	Balliol	Journalist, USA
	Michael Soole	University	Barrister
	Robert McDonagh	Balliol	Irish Foreign Office
1975	Robert Scoble	Nuffield	Australian Foreign Office

* Resigned

Presidents of the Union Since 1900

Year	*Name*	*College*	*Career*
(1975 cont)	Victor van Amerongen	Magdalen	BBC Producer
	David Soskin	Magdalen	Business consultant
1976	Andrew Bell	University	Shell-UK
	Hon. Colin Moynihan	University	Conservative MP for Lewisham E since 1983
	Hon. Richard Norton	New	Merchant banker
1977	Benazir Bhutto	LMH	Leader, Pakistan People's Party
	Victoria Schofield	LMH	BBC Radio producer
	Damian Green	Balliol	News Editor, Times Business News
1978	Nicholas O'Shaughnessy	Keble	Academic; Lecturer at the University of Wales
	John Harrison	Merton	Schoolmaster at Rugby School
	Daniel Moylan	Queen's	Banking
1979	Alan Duncan	St John's	Oil trader
	Philip May	Lincoln	Stockbroker
	Michael Crick	New	Journalist, ITN
1980	Warwick Lightfoot	Exeter	Bond trader
	Nicholas Prettejohn	Balliol	Management consultant
	Rupert Soames	Worcester	In industry (Marconi)
1981	Andrew Sutcliffe	Worcester	Barrister
	Alexandra Jones	New	Graduate student in USA
	William Hague	Magdalen	Shell-UK; aide to Sir Geoffrey Howe during 1983 election
1982	Kevin Brennan	Pembroke	Journalist on a community newspaper
	Paul Thompson	Corpus Christi	Stockbroker
	Christopher Wortley	New	Jardine Matheson
1983	Hilali Nordeen	Balliol	
	Andrew Sullivan	Magdalen	
	Neale Stevenson	Christ Church	
1984	Malcolm Bull	Balliol	
	Melvyn Stride	St Edmund Hall	

BIBLIOGRAPHY

CHAPTER ONE

The Oxford Union 1823–1923 Herbert Morrah *Cassell 1923*
The Oxford Union Christopher Hollis *Evans 1965*
A History of Oxford University V. H. H. Green *Batsford 1974*
Gladstone Philip Magnus *John Murray 1954*
The Later Cecils Kenneth Rose *Weidenfeld 1975*
John Buchan Janet Adam Smith *Thames and Hudson 1979*
Superior Person Kenneth Rose *Weidenfeld 1969*
Curzon Leonard Mosley *Longman 1960*
F. E., the life of F. E. Smith, 1st Earl of Birkenhead 2nd Earl of Birkenhead *Eyre and Spottiswoode 1959*
F. E. Smith, First Earl of Birkenhead John Campbell *Jonathan Cape 1983*

CHAPTER TWO

A Spiritual Aeneid Ronald Knox *Burns Oates 1950*
Life of Ronald Knox Evelyn Waugh *Chapman and Hall 1959*
The Knox Brothers Penelope Fitzgerald *Macmillan 1977*
Winds of Change Harold Macmillan *Macmillan 1966*
Harold Macmillan Nigel Fisher *Weidenfeld 1982*
My Dear Timothy Victor Gollancz *Gollancz 1952*
Life in Edwardian England Robert Cecil *Batsford 1969*
A. P. H., His Life and Times A. P. Herbert *Heinemann 1970*
A. P. Herbert Reginald Pound *Michael Joseph 1970*
Harold Laski Kingsley Martin *Gollancz 1953*
Life of G. D. H. Cole Dame Margaret Cole *Macmillan 1971*
Acquaintances Arnold Toynbee *O.U.P. 1967*

Walter Monckton: the Life of Viscount Monckton of Brenchley Lord Birkenhead *Weidenfeld 1969*

CHAPTER THREE

English History 1914–1945 A. J. P. Taylor *O.U.P. 1965*
Children of the Sun Martin Green *Constable 1977*
The Unforgiving Minute Beverley Nichols *W. H. Allen 1978*
Speeches and Writings S. W. R. D. Bandaranaike *Privately published*
Evelyn Waugh Christopher Sykes *Collins 1975*
Evenlyn Waugh's Diaries ed. Michael Davie *Weidenfeld 1976*
Letters of Evelyn Waugh ed. Mark Amory *Weidenfeld 1980*
Decline and Fall Evelyn Waugh *Chapman and Hall 1928*
The Right Honourable Gentleman Roger Fulford *John Murray 1945*
A Chapter of Accidents Goronwy Rees *Chatto 1972*
My Oxford ed Ann Thwaite *Robson 1977*
Father of the House John Parker *Routledge 1982*
Life and Labour Michael Stewart *Sidgwick 1980*
On Larkhill J. P. W. Mallalieu *Alison and Busby 1893*
Way of Life John Boyd-Carpenter *Sidgwick 1980*
A Start in Freedom Hugh Foot *Hodder 1964*

CHAPTER FOUR

Party Games Christopher Mayhew *Hutchinson 1969*
The King and Country Debate 1933: Student politics, Pacifism and the Dicatators Martin Ceadel *Historical Journal 1979*
Michael Foot: A Portrait Simon Hoggart and David Leigh *Hodder 1981*
Edward Heath George Hutchinson *Longman 1970*
Roy Jenkins John Campbell *Weidenfeld 1983*
Tony Crosland Susan Crosland *Jonathan Cape 1982*
Mussolini Denis Mack Smith *Weidenfeld 1981*

CHAPTER FIVE

Travelling Tongues Kenneth Harris *John Murray 1949*
Tony Benn: A Political Biography Robert Jenkins *Writers and Readers Publishing 1980*
Day by Day Robin Day *William Kimber 1975*

Jeremy Thorpe: A Secret Life Lewis Chester, Magnus Linklater and David May *Fontana 1979*
Beyond the Tingle Quotient Godfrey Smith *Weidenfeld 1982*
Backbench Diaries Richard Crossman *Hamilton 1981*
The Nigel Barton Plays Dennis Potter *Penguin 1968*

CHAPTER SIX

A Short Walk on the Campus Jonathen Aitken and Michael Beloff *Secker and Warburg 1966*
Collisions David Cante *Quartet 1974*

CHAPTER SEVEN

Diaries of a Cabinet Minister vol 2 Richard Crossman *Hamilton 1976*
The Castle Diaries Barbara Castle *Weidenfeld 1980*
Camford Observed Jasper Rose and John Ziman *Gollancz 1964*

INDEX

Index

Index

Index